THIS SPORTING LIFE
1878~1991

This Sporting Life, 1878-1991 was organized by the High Museum of Art.

This exhibition is supported by a grant from the National Endowment for the Arts, a federal agency; the Dorothy Smith Hopkins Exhibition Endowment; the Members Guild of the High Museum of Art; UPS Truck Leasing; Primerica Financial Services; and *Sports Illustrated.* The catalogue is made possible, in part, by funds from the Fay and George Owen Sheffield Memorial Endowment and THE LUBO FUND.

Cover Illustration

DAVID GRAHAM
*The Post Bulletins Practicing
at Graham Park, Rochester,
Minnesota, 1988*
Courtesy Laurence Miller
Gallery, New York
(cat. 184)

This Sporting Life, 1878-1991 was presented at the following venues:

High Museum of Art
Atlanta, Georgia
16 May - 13 September 1992

Sarah Campbell Blaffer Gallery
University of Houston, Texas
1 November - 16 December 1992

de Saisset Museum
Santa Clara University
Santa Clara, California
12 January - 21 March 1993

Delaware Art Museum
Wilmington, Delaware
16 April - 13 June 1993

Albright-Knox Art Gallery
Buffalo, New York
25 June - 29 August 1993

THIS SPORTING LIFE

1878~1991

EDITED BY

ELLEN DUGAN

WITH ESSAYS BY

HARVEY GREEN

JOHN M. HOBERMAN

PETER SCHJELDAHL

HIGH MUSEUM OF ART
ATLANTA, GEORGIA

RICHARD AVEDON
Lew Alcindor, 61st Street and Amsterdam Avenue,
New York City, May 2, 1963
Collection of the Center for Creative Photography,
The University of Arizona, Tucson (cat. 103)

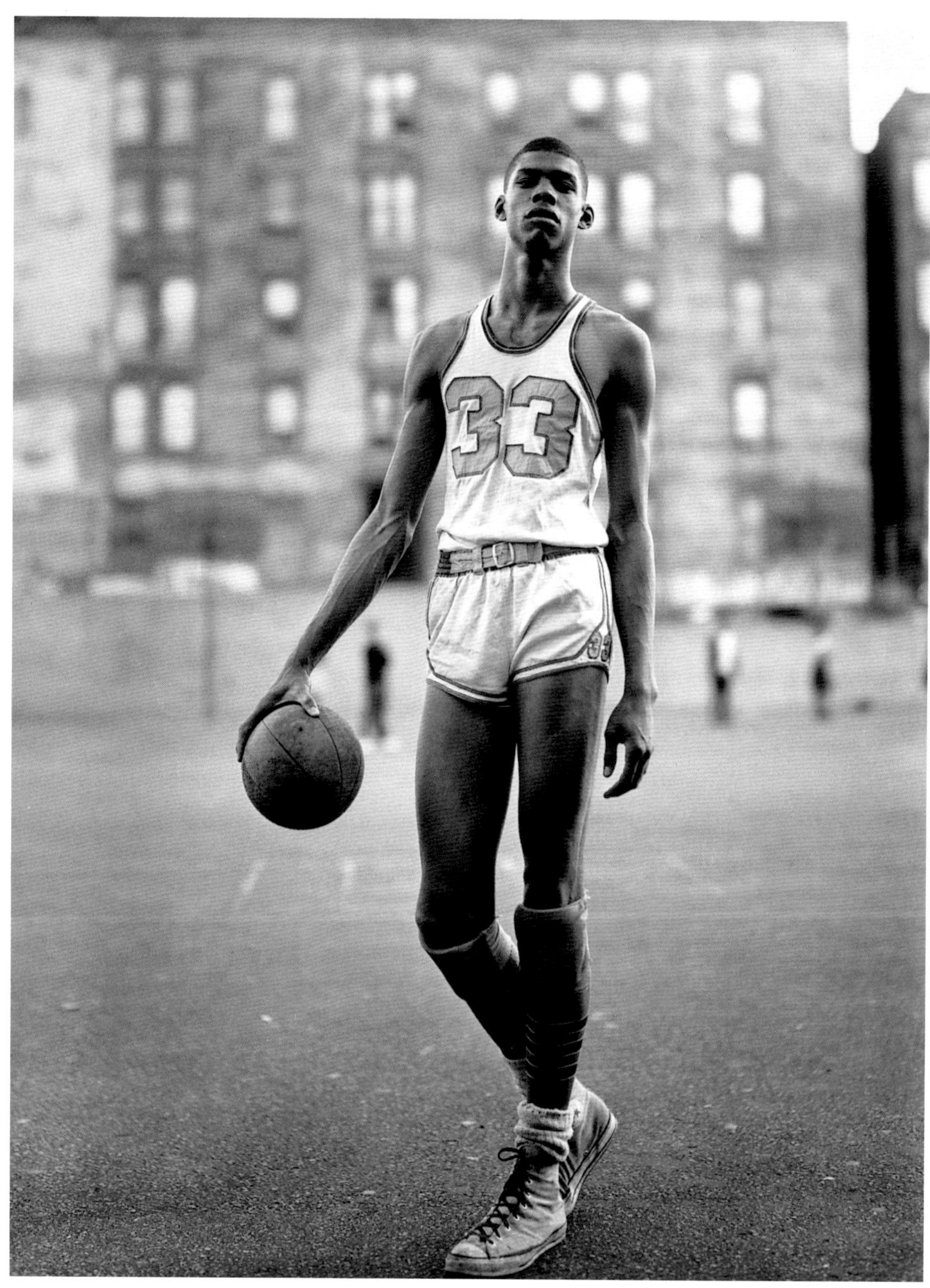

Table of Contents

LENDERS TO THE EXHIBITION

Dr. and Mrs. Michael Adams
Mauro Altamuro
Amateur Athletic Foundation of Los Angeles
Archiv Baumeister, Stuttgart, Germany
Archiv Rolf Jeck, Basel, Switzerland
The Arkansas Arts Center Foundation Collection, Little Rock
Association des Amis de Maurice Tabard, Paris, France
Atlanta Historical Society, Georgia
August Sander Archive, Cologne, Germany
Bill Bamberger
Anthony Barboza
Martine Barrat
Barry Whistler Gallery, Dallas, Texas
Robert Beck
Wm. B. Becker
Paul Berger
Blockson Afro-American Collection, Temple University, Philadelphia, Pennsylvania
Bonni Benrubi Fine Art Photographs, New York
Brent Sikkema Fine Art, New York
Lucinda Bunnen
Butler Institute of American Art, Youngstown, Ohio
Jack Carnell
Henri Cartier-Bresson
Center for Creative Photography, The University of Arizona, Tucson
Colorado Historical Society, Denver
Dawes Memorial Library, Marietta College, Marietta, Ohio
Joe Deal
Mitch Epstein
The Estate of Robert Capa/International Center of Photography, New York
Etherton/Stern Gallery, Tucson, Arizona
Fay Gold Gallery, Atlanta, Georgia
Felicia Murray, New York
Larry Fink

Fondation Asher Edelman, Musée d'Art Contemporain, Pully/Lausanne, Switzerland
Fraenkel Gallery, San Francisco, California
Stephen Frailey
Ron Geibert
George Arents Research Library for Special Collections, Syracuse University, Syracuse, New York
Monah L. Gettner/Hyperion Press Ltd., New York
The J. Paul Getty Museum, Malibu, California
Jay Greenstein and Family
Cathryn Griffin
Michael W. Griffith
Chris Hamilton
Hargrett Rare Book and Manuscript Library, University of Georgia, Athens
William Heick
High Museum of Art, Atlanta, Georgia
Hirshhorn Museum and Sculpture Garden, Smithsonian Institution, Washington, D.C.
David Hockney
Houk Friedman, New York
Howard Greenberg Gallery, New York
Walter Iooss, Jr.
International Center of Photography, New York
International Museum of Photography at George Eastman House, Rochester, New York
James Danzinger Gallery, New York
Janet Borden, Inc., New York
John Weber Gallery, New York
Keith de Lellis, New York
John Kennard
Paul Kwilecki
Laurence Miller Gallery, New York
Baldwin Lee
Neil Leifer
Wayne Levin
Lewis Lehr, New York
Division of Prints and Photographs, Library of Congress, Washington, D.C.
Lieberman & Saul Gallery, New York
LIFE/Time Warner Inc., New York
Patricia Stevens Lowinsky
Skeet McAuley
Mike Mandel

The Metropolitan Museum of Art, New York
Ministère de la Culture, Association française pour la diffusion du patrimoine photographique, Paris, France
The Minneapolis Institute of Arts, Minnesota
The Museum of Contemporary Art, Los Angeles, California
The Museum of Fine Arts, Houston, Texas
The Museum of Modern Art, New York
Museum of the City of New York
National Baseball Hall of Fame & Museum, Inc., Cooperstown, New York
New Orleans Museum of Art, Louisiana
The New-York Historical Society
Lorie Novak
Pace/MacGill Gallery, New York
Gordon Parks
Howardena Pindell
Robert Miller Gallery, New York
Chuck Rogers
San Francisco Museum of Modern Art, California
Francesco Scavullo
Jill and Richard Schloss, New York
Schomburg Center for Research in Black Culture, The New York Public Library
W. Michael Sheehe, New York
Holly Solomon Gallery, New York
Sonnabend Gallery, New York
Sports Illustrated
Staley-Wise Gallery, New York
Jan Staller
Staten Island Historical Society, New York
Mark Steinmetz
Texas Gallery, Houston
Walker, Ursitti & McGinniss, New York
Geoff Winningham
The Witkin Gallery, Inc., New York
Yancey Richardson/Lumina Fine Photography & Art, New York
Zabriskie Gallery, New York
John G. Zimmerman

PREFACE

Our love and enjoyment of sports has increased exponentially thanks, in part, to the refinement and expansion of the role the camera (and its relatives) has played in capturing and disseminating the moments of great drama, curious asides, and intricate skills. One can hardly think of sports now without relying on an indelibly etched image of a great sporting feat that has been photographically generated. The development of sophisticated photographic technology has not only shaped our perception of sports, but, more importantly, our view – and interpretation – of the world as well.

This Sporting Life, 1878-1991 takes as its subject the evolution of modern sports as recorded by the camera and considers the relationship of sport to social and cultural issues in the U. S., Europe, and Russia. The High Museum of Art is extremely grateful to those individuals, publications, and collections that are lending their prints to enable us to present this show to the public. We are indebted to those museums which have agreed to host *This Sporting Life* following our presentation in Atlanta. I wish to thank Marti Mayo, director of the Sara Campbell Blaffer Gallery at the University of Houston, Patricia A. Wilkinson, interim director of the de Saisset Museum at the Santa Clara (California) University, Stephen T. Bruni, executive director of the Delaware Art Museum in Wilmington, and Douglas G. Schultz, director of the Albright-Knox Art Gallery in Buffalo, New York, for their support and cooperation with the High's staff in planning and realizing this national tour.

In addition, we are grateful to the Museum Program of the National Endowment for the Arts for a grant which enabled Ellen Dugan, our chief curator of education, to conduct critical research in the preliminary phases of organizing this exhibition. The Dorothy Smith Hopkins Exhibition Endowment at the High Museum of Art and funds generated by the Members Guild of the Museum were also instrumental in supporting her efforts. The Primerica Foundation and *Sports Illustrated* provided additional monies and in-kind assistance, repectively, which are greatly appreciated. This publication has been made possible, in part, by funds from the Fay and George Owen Sheffield Memorial Endowment at the High Museum of Art, UPS Truck Leasing, and THE LUBO FUND. Finally, I would like to salute the exemplary curatorial work on this project by Ellen Dugan, both a fine colleague and a dedicated sports fan. Let us hope that the fusion of excellence found in the photographs included in this exhibition and the games and feats depicted therein will enable us all to see our human condition more clearly and with greater insight and compassion.

Ned Rifkin
Director
High Museum of Art

ACKNOWLEDGEMENTS

An exhibition and publication of this scope could not have been accomplished without the contributions of many individuals and the cooperation of many institutions. I am deeply grateful to the many lenders without whose generosity no undertaking like this exhibition would be possible and to the numerous collectors, galleries, private dealers, and other individuals who offered information, insights, and valuable assistance. They have my profoundest thanks for the many kindnesses they have extended to me throughout the course of this project.

In addition to their essays, the authors of this book, Harvey Green, John M. Hoberman, and Peter Schjeldahl, have provided valuable information, guidance, and assistance, and it has been a pleasure to work with them.

This project was truly a collaborative effort, and I am grateful to the entire staff of the High Museum of Art for their expert help and friendly counsel. The High Museum's program of both collecting and exhibiting vintage and contemporary photography grew significantly during the twenty-eight-year tenure of Gudmund Vigtel, director emeritus. I am indebted to him for his support of this exhibition and catalogue from the outset, and for granting me the time and resources apart from my usual work as Chief Curator of Education to undertake this project. Ned Rifkin, director, has enthusiastically carried forward with this project and his considered judgment has enriched its focus. My special gratitude goes to Kelly Morris, Margaret Miller, and Amanda Woods, who have edited the book and guided it through all phases of its production, and to Robert Evans for his skillful and sensitive design of the volume.

Warmest thanks go also to the entire Department of Education staff, docents, and interns, particularly Celia Cola, Linda Dubler, Ruth Hablutzel, Jennifer Jacobs, Joy Patty, and Christine Puttgen, Florence Anne Slingluff, and Gregory Waddell; Marjorie Harvey, manager of exhibitions, and the entire crew of art handlers led by Nancy Roberts; Sue Deer, director, marketing and communications, and her staff; Hilda Cyphers, Tracey Bridges, and Darlene Schultz of the Members Guild; Colleen Callahan, membership manager; Ellen Carr and Betty Sanders, development associates; Maureen Marks, merchandise manager; and Faith Russler, Clay Bullock, and Gene Ussery of the Robert W. Woodruff Arts Center.

Four of my colleagues deserve special recognition. Jody Cohen, associate registrar, has shown extraordinary care and consummate professionalism in her work on the exhibition, and I warmly thank her for her fine efforts. Leah Greenberg, development associate, grants, has, as with every project on which we have worked together, given fully of her time, talents, and friendship. Finally, Stacia Schmidt and Carolyn Cline, administrative assistants in the Department of Education, have made considerable contributions to the exhibition, catalogue, and accompanying programs. For their exemplary diligence and enviable equanimity, I owe them both a debt of gratitude.

Finally, I wish to acknowledge my parents for their constant and sustaining encouragement, and my husband, Dennis, to whom I dedicate this book, for his unstinting and affectionate support.

Ellen Dugan
Chief Curator of Education
High Museum of Art

INTRODUCTION

From 1860 to about 1910, as a result of revolutionary changes in transportation and communications networks, as well as the widespread availability of new materials and products (for example, the portable hand-held camera, roll film, mass-produced sporting goods, the safety cycle, the stopwatch), both photography and sports took on most of their modern characteristics.[1] The sudden surge of interest and participation in each sphere of activity was, as Harvey Green explains in his essay, as much a reaction to as a product of the new, industrialized order. Both were vigorously promoted to the burgeoning middle class as progressive, moral forces that could regenerate the body, elevate the mind, or serve as a "safeguard against materialism....a safety-valve of the community," whose inclinations might otherwise lead it into "channels less refining, and perhaps into dissipation and crime."[2] Out of this vortex of social, economic, and technological change and transformation, sports and photography emerged in the 1920s as agents of mass culture – separate but inextricably linked – which reflected and increasingly defined the imagery of our public and private life.

The cultural historian Alan Trachtenberg has written: "The camera offered what seemed a new relation to the physical world, especially to its transitory nature and the illusory character of its surfaces. The photograph's mirror-like ability to capture the moment and preserve its uniqueness made the camera seem (as it still does) a near-magical device for defeating time, for endowing the past with a presence it had previously had only in memory. The immediacy of lived experience frozen forever and forever recoverable: this came to seem the domain of the photograph."[3] As Trachtenberg suggests, the camera image engendered a new diachronic relation of subject and viewer that has particular relevance to the theme of sports. Most games are played out within a set time scheme – so many rounds or quarters – or determined by some other measure, like a mark or distance to bettered. Within these bounds, athletes and spectators alike share a heightened, often excrutiating awareness of being rooted in a very specific unrepeatable present, and yet of standing on a threshold of consciousness outside of it. The novelist Robert Coover described this feeling in his 1985 essay on watching World Cup soccer:

> The way time works, for example: not only is it, as in most games, a time outside of time, abstract and somehow absolute, it is also relentlessly non-stop. Except for the half-time interval (a modern corruption), there are no time-outs in soccer, no breaks, the flow of the game is ceaseless, the demands on spectator and player alike uncompromising. . . . Once the player has fallen into the game, there is no getting out; he must stay with the flow, maintain the rhythm, press for advantage, preserving all his skills, his mind locked

into the shifting patterns. And the spectator, though less arduously, shares this experience, of falling out of historical time and geographical space into a kind of ceremonial trance, timeless and centripetal.[4]

Timebound but atemporal, immediate yet distancing, sports, like photography, embodies the paradoxical qualities of time, as much as it refers to time. For the photographer, the traditional goal had been not only to stop time and motion, but to do so without destroying the very illusion of it. As a continuously interconnected series of gestures, actions, and formations unfolding in and blending over time, sports demanded that the artist formulate new working methods if the special challenges they posed as a subject were to be surmounted.

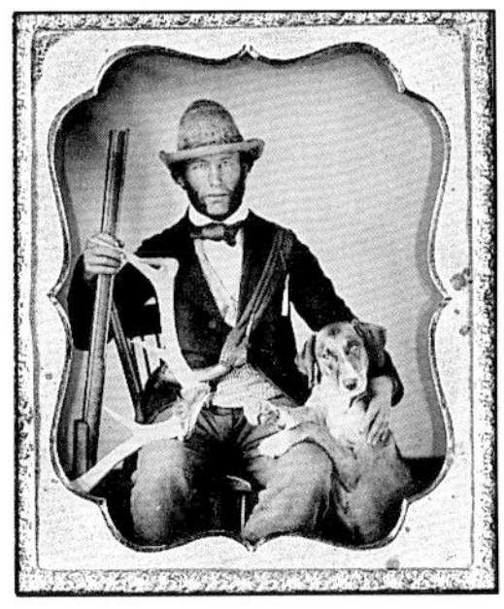

Fig. 1

ANONYMOUS
American, dates unknown
Portrait of a Male Hunter,
ca. 1855-60
Ambrotype
3 1/2 x 2 3/4 in.
(8.3 x 6.9 cm.)
Collection of the
International Museum
of Photography at
George Eastman House,
Rochester, New York

In the earliest days of the medium, photography required long exposures to compensate for primitive lenses and the slow speed of light-sensitive materials. Images of subjects that could not remain immobile were virtually impossible. Because of these technical limitations, it was the physical concreteness of the sportsman and not the temporal dynamics of sports that was first recorded. Both the 1850s studio portrait of a Midwestern hunter with his dog, musket, powder horn, and trophy (fig. 1) and William Henry Jackson's view, from 1883, of elegantly dressed tourists trout-fishing in the Rockies (cat. 2, page 75) derive their authority from stasis and descriptive clarity rather than from any transitory sweep of movement. In Walt Whitman's estimation, early photography was a "peopled world, though mute as the grave," and despite continued refinements in apparatus and materials in the mid-nineteenth century, human movement was rarely conveyed, except as a phantasmal blur.[5]

The first artist to arrest movement systematically was Eadweard Muybridge in the seminal work begun in 1872 under the patronage of Leland Stanford, ex-Governor of California, railroad magnate, and owner of a world-famous stock farm for the breeding and training of thoroughbreds and trotters. By this time, horse racing had emerged as the first successfully commercialized spectator sport on a national scale, with uniform rules and officially legitimated records and statistics. Turfmen and fans had always been preoccupied with time as a measure of a horse's performance and abilities. However, the huge profits now to be made from the sport turned large stables like Stanford's into "laboratories of speed," where rational, scientific methods were increasingly applied to the costly business of training the swiftest horses.[6]

With the seemingly objective proof of the camera, Stanford wished to settle once and for all the controversy about "unsupported transit" – that is, whether a horse had all four feet off the ground at any stage in its gallop. Muybridge's photographs (now lost but reproduced in other graphic media by his contemporaries) were crude silhouettes but clearly proved that indeed all four feet are off the ground at one point, but bunched under the belly, and not in the rocking-horse configuration always presumed by artists, anatomists, and horse fanciers. In 1877, Muybridge continued his motion research and invented a more sophisticated imaging system of twenty-four cameras with special double shutters tripped electronically by a thread or thin wire as the horse or sulky moved past. The serial format he devised allowed for unprecedented analysis of the successive movements of horses which if studied frame by frame gave an approximation of the continuity of action over time (cat. 1, page 73). Against Whitman's observation that photography evoked a stilled world, Muybridge could maintain that "into the surprising attitudes of the horse in the photographs is at last breathed the breath of life."[7]

From 1884 to 1887, under the auspices of the University of Pennsylvania, Muybridge extended his research to other animals (the more exotic models from the Philadelphia Zoo) and to men and women in action, including running, walking, throwing a baseball, hitting a tennis ball, or boxing. In speeds of up to 1/6000th of a second and from front, back, and foreshortened views, Muybridge captured even subtler movements such as the tightening of muscles or shifts of weight, as when a discus is about to be released from the athlete's grasp (cat. 6, page 74). Muybridge's work, along with the experiments of his contemporaries Etienne-Jules Marey and Thomas Eakins (cat. 3, page 73), revolutionized photography and our understanding of sports by making visible for the first time the forms underlying natural phenomena.

Further technological improvements like the single-lens reflex and 35mm cameras, standardized black-and-white and color roll film, the strobe and high-powered portable flashes, interchangeable lenses, and motorized drives soon permitted the dissection of time and movement in increments that Muybridge could only have imagined. The impact of a kicker's boot when it penetrates the football (cat. 52, page 90), the forward rush of a sportscar (cat. 24, page 80), the graceful arc of a diver (cat. 50, page 92), the ferocity of an uppercut to the chin (fig. 2), the chaotic struggle for control of the hockey puck in the crease (cat. 101, page 46), the explosive confrontation of twenty-two football players on a field (cat. 116, page 106), and the airborne suspension of a basketball player as he goes to the hoop (cat. 174, page 55) — all these images capture much of what is registered yet rarely perceived by the human eye.

While these photographers literally give form to the peak or decisive moment, the medium's technical latitude has also been exploited in more unorthodox ways to reflect highly subjective concerns or the emblematic meanings of sports within modern culture that are discussed in the essays by John M. Hoberman and Peter Schjeldahl. Among the richly-variegated techniques used (either for purely formal or polemical reasons) have been blurring and exaggeration (cats. 25, 42, 117, 184, pages 81, 83, 107, 56), audacious cropping (cats. 53, 76, pages 89, 98), unusual vantage points (cats. 33, 48, 168, pages 86, 96, 54), superimposition of negatives (cat. 32, page 87), multiple exposures (cat. 66, page 90), extreme close-ups (cats. 49, 99, 108, 130, pages 91, 104, 114, 109), near-abstraction (fig. 3 and cat. 100, page 110), the manipulation of the print's surface through drawing or painting (cats. 35, 127, pages 87, 111), and the combination of images (either original to the photographer or co-opted from some other source and often accompanied by text) that are reconstructed into a seamless whole (cats. 28, 39-41, 60, 165, 178, pages 86, 45, 94, 62, 47).

All of these works, from the exactingly transcriptive to the most fictive, depend upon our firm belief in photography as yielding objective, unmediated truth. Without this faith in the unadulterated purity of the photographic image (whether still or moving), sports as we know it today — global in perspective, attraction, and influence — would be inconceivable. Jack Carnell's photograph of the "spectators" at the 1984 Summer Olympic Games (cat. 158, page 72) and Larry Sultan's picture of his father watching a televised baseball game (cat. 162, page 61) show the extent to which the mass media not only records but can displace direct knowledge with a simulation more powerful than the real experience of sports.[8]

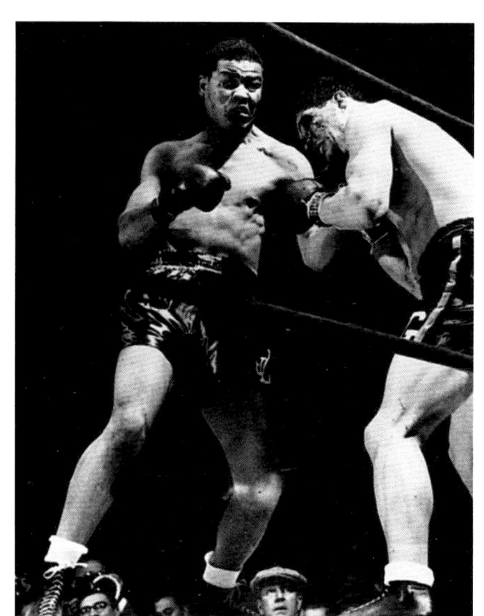

Fig. 2

JOSEPH COSTA
American, born 1904
HAROLD E. EDGERTON
American, 1903-1990
Joe Louis and Arturo Godoy,
1940
Gelatin silver print
13 3/4 x 11 in.
(34.8 x 27.9 cm.)
Collection of the
International Museum
of Photography at
George Eastman House,
Rochester, New York.

Some artists, like Nancy Holt (cats. 163, 164, page 118), Mauro Altamura (cat. 152, page 119), Howardena Pindell (cat. 118, page 53), and Paul Berger (cat. 135, page 119) have integrated the very form and content of modern sports information systems (television, video, computer, and digitalized electronic images) into their work, while other artists have appropriated the visual language of the media itself to comment upon the pervasiveness of sports as an ally of mass consumerism.

The link between the camera-made image, advertising, and sports is not new. It has a tradition that goes back to at least 1886 when tobacco companies used cards bearing the likenesses of baseball players, wrestlers, pugilists, billiards players, and other sportsmen as premiums with their products (cat. 9, page 76). Throughout the late twenties and thirties, the modernist vocabulary also found its way into advertising. For example, Edward Quigley's close-in, dramatically lit image of a tennis racket and ball (cat. 59, page 95) was used by the National Dairy Council in a print campaign to give milk a more glamorous appeal. Sports and fitness, divorced from their original connections with building individual character and social cohesion, now came to reflect and define more privately held desires and aspirations. Annie Leibovitz's witty celebrity portraits, created for American Express, are a famous and influential example of this genre within contemporary advertising. In her wistful, "field of dreams" shot of the great pitcher Tom Seaver (cat. 173, page 65), we see the retired star "standing in a sandlot, gripping a baseball and staring off into the distance as if he's still looking for the catcher's signal."[9] Through the photograph, we are invited to envy his "sheer ease of being, his offhand glamor, and casual, sexy familiarity" – star qualities we can emulate and possess but only if we buy into the exclusivity that the product purports to offer. Bruce Weber's fashion shots for Calvin Klein and Ralph Lauren, like his non-commercial work from which it is virtually indistinguishable (cat. 154, page 120), capitalize less on celebrity currency than on erotic fantasies objectified in the form of the beautiful, languorous, athletic male body. It is not the benefit of sports but their association with the world of fame, sex, wealth, and power that is now packaged for mass consumption.

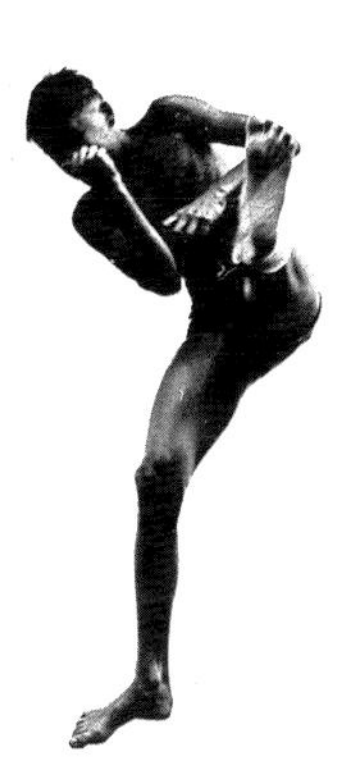

Fig. 3

AARON SISKIND
American, 1903-1991
Pleasures and Terrors of Levitation #25, 1956
Gelatin silver print
8 9/16 x 12 7/8 in.
(21.8 x 32.7 cm.)
Collection of the High Museum of Art;
Gift of Mr. and Mrs. Robert Menschel

Jeff Koons's *SILK* (cat. 165, page 62), contrived from a series of sneaker ads, and Frank Majore's large, highly stylized tableaux of golf equipment (cats. 171, 187, page 70) self-conciously highlight the artificiality of the photographic image by their direct or oblique references to the conventions of television, movies, and advertising. And in doing so, they force us to reflect upon the illusions constructed about and through sports by a media-infused culture.

The exhibition *This Sporting Life, 1878-1991,* together with this publication, present a wide range of images that show us the actual look of sports – the athletes, the action, the spectators, the equipment, the spectacle, and the landscapes in which these dramas are enacted. The often stunning visual beauty, emotional resonance, and technical bravura of these works are compelling in themselves and bear repeated viewing. Ultimately though, the aim of this project has been to suggest the deeper connections between sports and photography that have indelibly shaped, and in turn been shaped by, our modern culture. As the late baseball commissioner A. Bartlett Giamatti has written, "Sport is an instrument for vision, and it ever seeks to make the common – what we all see, if we look – uncommon. Not forever, not impossibly perfect, but uncommon enough to remain a bright spot in the memory, thus creating a reservoir of transformation to which we can return when we are free to do so."[10] Through these photographic works, sport is transformed again from a "bright spot in the memory" into a collective history through which we can discover the complex meanings of our past, the palpable quality of the present, and the emerging shape of that which is yet to come.

ENDNOTES

1. For further information, see John R. Betts, "The Technological Revolution and the Rise of Sports, 1850-1900," in *The Sporting Image: Readings in American Sport History*, ed. Paul J. Zingg (Lanham, Md., 1988), 171-94.

2. Quoted in Sarah Greenough's essay on American pictorial photography in *Photography in Nineteenth-Century America*, ed. Martha A. Sandweiss (Fort Worth and New York, 1991), 265. See also Harvey Green, *Fit for America: Health, Fitness, Sport and American Society* (New York, 1986; Baltimore, 1988).

3. Alan Trachtenberg, *Reading American Photographs: Images as History, Matthew Brady to Walker Evans* (New York, 1989), 288.

4. Robert Coover, "Soccer as an Existential Sacrament," *Close-Up* 15, no. 1 (Winter 1985): 85.

5. Quoted in Alan Trachtenberg, "Photography: The Emergence of a Keyword," in *Photography in Nineteenth-Century America*, 25. On the use of blurred and overlapping images caused by time exposures for aesthetic purposes, see Adam D. Weinberg, ed., *Vanishing Presence* (Minneapolis and New York, 1989).

6. Melvin L. Adelman, "The First Modern Sport in America: Harness Racing in New York City, 1825-1870," in *The Sporting Image*, 125.

7. Quoted in *Eadweard Muybridge: The Stanford Years, 1872-1882* (Stanford, Calif., 1972), 123.

8. For further commentary on the mass media and Olympic sport, see Peter Schjeldahl, "Anti-Olympus," in *10 Photographers: Olympic Visions* (Los Angeles, 1989), 10.

9. David Talbot, "A Celebrity Sell," *Interview* 19, no. 12 (December 1989): 108. Also, see the title essay by Andy Grundberg in *Images of Desire: Portrayals in Recent Advertising Photography* (Philadelphia, 1989), 3-16.

10. A. Bartlett Giamatti, *Take Time for Paradise: Americans and Their Games* (New York, 1989), 15.

RATIONAL MUSCLE CULTURE

**Religion, Sport, and Photography
in Turn-of-the-Century America**

*Rational muscle culture, . . . for its moral effects, often for the young
the very best possible means of resisting evil and establishing righteousness, is the gospel I preach to-day. . . . We are soldiers of Christ,
strengthening our muscles not against a foreign foe, but against sin
within and without us. We would bring in a higher kingdom of man,
regenerate in body; make it more stalwart, persistent, enduring, taller,
with better hearts, stomachs, nerves and more resistful to man's great
enemy — disease.*   G. STANLEY HALL (1902)

This passage by the eminent American psychologist G. Stanley Hall[1] demonstrates the inter-
mingling – and perhaps equation – of the aims of sport, religion, and science in turn-of-the-
century America. Hall's imagery is that of evangelical Christianity: the reference to "soldiers of
Christ" perhaps recalled the popular hymn "Onward Christian Soldiers"; Hall termed his position a "gospel"; he "preached" in order to fight "sin and establish righteousness"; and he wanted
people "regenerate in body" to resist "evil." Typical of many of his era's most important thinkers, Hall blended this ecclesiastical language with that of the secular world. He favored "rational" physical development and "muscle culture," using the latter term to connote management,
growth, and control, as in the words "agriculture" and "horticulture." In the last sentence he defined the "regenerate" body by identifying its physical characteristics rather than its moral qualities. By the end of the passage the voice is that of the secular scientific physician, not the minister. Equally important was Hall's indication that muscular development and religion were
necessary to properly raise children lest the country fall prey to the threats of anarchy and cultural decline that many turn-of-the-century Americans saw all about them.

The rise of sport and the advent of various crusades for fitness in the United States coincided
with, among other phenomena, the spread of photography in America, an increase in the re-
spect accorded physicians and scientists, a resurgence of evangelical and "liberal" Christianity,
a rapid expansion of industrial productivity and consumption, and a deepening pessimism
among some American elites about the vitality of Anglo-American culture. Coincidence does
not necessarily imply causality, but does perhaps suggest that there may be interrelationships
in the ways these developments fulfill Americans' intellectual, social, and cultural needs or desires. In this essay I will try to demonstrate that sport, religion, and photography in the United

States share some cultural roots and overlap in their relationships to Americans' everyday lives. I will examine the web of connections among religion, science, and cultural criticism in the late nineteenth and early twentieth centuries, demonstrating that sport and fitness were one important strategy for regenerating the populace. Then I will attempt to show that embedded in the aesthetic and cultural assumptions of sports photography in this era are elements of these intellectual and social forces.

Photography and organized sport, and to a lesser extent the religious enthusiasms of the late nineteenth century, were novel elements in American culture. None entirely embodied or reflected all of the complex aspects of American society, but each was a part of it. Independent of one another, yet linked, religion, sport, and photography illuminated the sometimes contradictory nature of American culture at the turn of the century. All were grounded in a belief in the importance of the seemingly neutral truth of the material world, of things, of the body, of the realism of the camera.

Anglo-American culture from its inception was a blend of hope for material or spiritual gain and fear of failure. John Winthrop promised the early settlers of Massachusetts Bay Colony that "the eyes of the world shall be upon us" as the Puritans sought to cleanse their church in the New World; Virginians saw prosperity in tobacco and other crops, but also found disease and financial failure; William Penn hoped for a Quaker haven in Pennsylvania, but his followers also found competition for land and civil strife with other settlers and with native populations; in Georgia, James Oglethorpe sought to create a useful and ameliorative place for debtors and others looking for a new start, yet the wilderness in that colony, as in others, offered as many chances for escape from the law as it did for the regenerative experience of work.

By the late nineteenth century, the legacy of the American experience was a divided one. Surely the rapid growth of the country and the obvious material accomplishments of science and technology – shown so clearly at the periodic international expositions that began with London's Crystal Palace in 1851 – signalled a bright and prosperous future. Optimistic Darwinians built upon the great biologist's theories published in 1859 in *On the Origin of Species* to conclude that, as D. H. Wheeler put it in *Popular Science Monthly* in 1873, "history shows us a struggle of races, and we who survive are ready enough to believe that the strongest survive because they are the best."[2]

But beneath the surface of Wheeler's and other brash and sunny analyses of the American scene was the implication that as surely as the nation had risen it, like other great republics and empires, could fall. The survival of the nation was dependent upon remaining pre-eminent in the struggle for existence that even Darwin's severest critics conceded was the norm.[3] Thus as they congratulated themselves for their achievements, Americans – and Europeans – fretted about the future, since at the foundation of Darwin's work was the assumption of constant change.

Worries about the effects of the pace of American urban business life in particular grew in number and intensity as the century proceeded. In 1867 an article in *Harper's Weekly* warned that "when the constitution is weak and the system depressed by the *wear and tear* of business life, which makes such tremendous drafts upon the body and mind, unless some healthful and strengthening tonic is resorted to, prostration will ensue and disease creep unawares upon the victim of negligence."[4] The passage identified a peril and a hope: it posited that weakness (and, by inference, death) could be forestalled, if not avoided, by responsible individuals. No longer was it simply God's will that disease would "creep unawares" upon men, women, and children.

Businessmen were not the only people threatened by the unseen forces of disease and debility. Vegetarian physician and breakfast food magnate John H. Kellogg was one of the many writers who attacked American women for their allegedly poor physical condition. "The declining strength and health of American women," he wrote in *The Household Manual* (1882), "has come to be a very common observation. . . . Physicians generally acknowledge that at least three-fourths of their practice is derived from diseases of women."[5] For most of these critics, whose litany of complaint grew longer as the nineteenth century wore on, the declining condition of Americans was a result of too much sedentary "brain work" or not enough housework. Both could lead to a condition of "nervous debility." "In these days when . . . probably more people are supported by brain work than ever before," wrote Edwin Temple in *The Household Magazine* in 1881, it was more common to find people with a "fine and delicate [mental] organization . . . [subject to] depression of the spirits." "The results," wrote Edward H. Clarke in *Sex in Education, or, A Fair Chance for Girls* (1873), "are monstrous brains and puny bodies; abnormally active cerebration, and abnormally weak digestion; flowing thought and constipated bowels; lofty aspirations and neuralgic sensations. . . ." Diocletian Lewis, one of the leaders in the drive for more physical education and exercise, characterized Americans in his often reprinted *New Gymnastics* (1862) as having" pale faces, distorted forms and painful nervousness."[6]

Much of the criticism and medical advice centered around the concept of a declining or potentially declining store of "nervous energy" or "vital fluid." Seizing upon the enthusiasm for and limited knowledge about the body and one of the era's new sources of power, electricity, all sorts of healers and con artists tried to profit from Americans' fears of losing their place or failing to gain in the struggle to survive and succeed. "Electric" oils and other bottled nostrums, galvanic batteries, and "electric" hair brushes that produced enough static electricity to provide a small jolt were hawked to the unsuspecting and often desperate public.

More legitimate, or at least more restrained in their promises and analyses of the problem, were some of the physicians who wrote about the problem of the alleged dissipation of nervous energy. Physician George Beard was probably the first to fully describe the condition, which he called "neurasthenia" in the *Boston Medical and Surgical Journal* in 1869. He expanded his discussion in his book *American Nervousness*, published in 1881.[7] Beard and others agreed that neurasthenia was found only in civilizations that had progressed far enough beyond the subsistence level of agriculture and manufacturing to produce a large number of people who no longer worked on the farms or with their hands. Beard figured that it was primarily an urban or suburban residents' ailment, simultaneously a sign of success or progress and an insidious internal threat to that class of people cultural critics assumed were responsible for the advanced state of society. Women, who were not allowed to work in the business or professional sectors, nonetheless were thought to suffer from the neurasthenia, in part, some critics maintained, because improvements in household technology had freed them from much of the physical work of housekeeping and because many had forsaken the farm for the city and suburbs.[8]

The idea that neurasthenia was an inevitable result of the otherwise positive scientific, economic, and technological progress of the United States built upon Darwin's ideas of evolution and dovetailed with the analyses of late-nineteenth-century sociologists and anthropologists. These social scientists constructed a theory of gradual development of the human race from animalistic brutality to civilization in which Americans found both reassurance and discomfiture. Congratulating themselves for their advanced position in the world, they also recognized that, given Darwin's emphasis on process, their current status was not guaranteed – evolution did not cease.

The social sciences focused attention on the visible, and like the natural sciences, concentrated on observation and classification to reveal relationships between groups that were hitherto unknown. By studying the physical characteristics of people, animals, and plants, natural and social scientists were certain that they could establish a hierarchy of beings, and ultimately discern the behavioral characteristics of their subjects. The lingering influence of phrenology in the nineteenth century is in part explained by this yearning for certainty and predictability. Phrenologists argued that by carefully observing and analyzing cranial shape they could reveal personality traits. In their heyday, which began in the 1850s and lasted until nearly the end of the century, "readings" seemed to be the only "scientific" way to probe the surface presentation of self in a society that appeared to be confusing and full of poseurs and con men.[9] Phrenologists and others figured that they could identify a "criminal type" by the shape (or weight) of his or her brow and skull, for the most part basing their conclusions on cranial measurements of the incarcerated. This concentration on the visible reinforced the dramatic cultural impact of photography, since it was a chemical and apparently neutral rendering of physical reality for examination without the evanescence or erosion of time. Landscape photographs such as those of William H. Jackson or Carleton E. Watkins, microphotographs, medical record photography, astronomical images captured with the aid of telescopes, anthropological photography such as the work of A.C. Vroman or Edward Curtis, the motion studies of Eadweard Muybridge (cats. 1, 6, 7, pages 73, 74) and others, and the multitudinous portraits made since the advent of the daguerreotype were all part of the attempt to examine, probe, and classify the material world.

In the late nineteenth century most American and European social and natural scientists were white males, and therefore comfortable placing Caucasians at the peak of the human pyramid. They further divided the white race into hierarchically arranged groups: by gender (men at the top), by nationality (Anglo-Saxons and other northern Europeans at the apex), and by class (the wealthy and educated in the first position). "The gulf that separates Shakespeare and Newton from the Papuan is wider than that which separates the Papuan from the gorilla and the chimpanzee," wrote George Beard in 1871.[10]

Eugenics, or selective breeding by humans, was one outgrowth of the classification of the human species. Popular in Europe and the United States, its advocates cited the successful development of hardier and more productive strains of grains, fruits, vegetables, and livestock as evidence of the need for control of childbearing. They argued that unless the "better sort" of people, whom they usually identified as white, academically successful, lawabiding, Christian, and of Anglo-Saxon or northern European descent, married each other and had large families, democracy and capitalism as they knew it would fail, victims of "race suicide." Critics with a eugenics bent frequently combined phrenology, anthropology, sociology, and ersatz evolutionary biology in their often alarmist tracts. Mary Wood-Allen, in her popular guidebook, *What a Young Woman Ought to Know* (first published in 1899), warned her readers that "through the law of inheritance have arisen the intellectual, the moral, or the criminal types of humanity, and the process is continuing; . . . all weakening of the individual, either in bodily strength or intellectual power or moral fiber, tends to produce a like weakness in posterity."[11] In *The Passing of the Great Race* (1916), Madison Grant lamented ethnic mixture and attributed the best of civilization to the "Nordic races." Grant found fault with the allegedly superior types for their smaller families, their liberal openness to immigration, their penchant for unhealthy cities, and an almost suicidal valor in battle. (Grant ignored the efforts of the Immigration Restriction League, which had been founded in the 1890s by American elites to halt the flow of "new" immigrants from southern and eastern Europe who had been arriving in large numbers since the 1880s.)[12]

Eugenics advocates drew a barrage of criticism from nearly all of the American secular and religious spectrum, but the idea of improving the human race by human action was in the mainstream of Americans' ideas about the human condition. Scientific and religious thinkers shared the assumption that the physical world displayed evidence of divine creation. By 1850 the core of Protestant theology had evolved to a position that concentrated on human history to mark the major events and advances of Christianity. The perfectionism of many mid-nineteenth-century reformers, which asserted that human society could and must be cleansed of sin to provoke the Second Coming of Christ, was fueled by this linkage of science and religion. "What . . . is to hinder an organism from becoming, in the process of time, comparatively perfect?" asked William Alcott in 1839.[13] Even those who believed that Christ would appear suddenly, before the millennium, such as the Millerites of the 1840s or the followers of late-nineteenth-century preachers such as Dwight Moody or Billy Sunday, agreed with the perfectionists that those to be saved would probably manifest their goodness with physical well-being as well as moral strength.[14]

Sport and fitness were identified by many critics as ways to reverse or hold fast against the forces of cultural and moral decline. One of the earliest and clearest statements of the linkage between Christian behavior and sport and fitness emerged from the public-school culture of Victorian England. The phrase "muscular Christianity" was coined by a reviewer of Charles Kingsley's *Two Years Ago* (1857), but the idea that morality was a function of muscularity is more commonly associated with the fictional accounts of the mythical Tom Brown, who was immortalized in Charles Hughes's *Tom Brown's Schooldays* (1857) and in numerous novels about the virtuous young man published thereafter.[15]

In the United States Tom Brown's adventures were less popular than they were in England, but the idea of muscular Christianity found a receptive environment. A review in *Godey's Lady's Book* of Guillaume Depping's *Wonders of Bodily Strength and Skill* (1871) noted, that "In these days, when 'muscular Christianity' is so popular with nearly all classes of people, a book which treats in systematic form [the subjects] of bodily strength and skill will find abundant favor."[16]

"Physical culture," as the activities ranging from calisthenics to contact sports were called in the latter part of the nineteenth century, and "muscular Christianity" were embraced by reformers intent upon bringing the millennium to the human race and by those with more secular goals that ranged from finding individual happiness to providing for the safety of their race or nationality. The idea of the body as instrument for the use of the soul focused Americans' attention on both the process of physical development and the physical fact of the body. Photography became a critical tool for analysis of the body and its potential perfection or decay, and was eagerly used by scientists, physical educators, athletic coaches, and cultural critics. All recognized that the physical development of the body took place in increments that were imperceptible from day to day, thus necessitating periodic documentation in a precise, scientific manner.

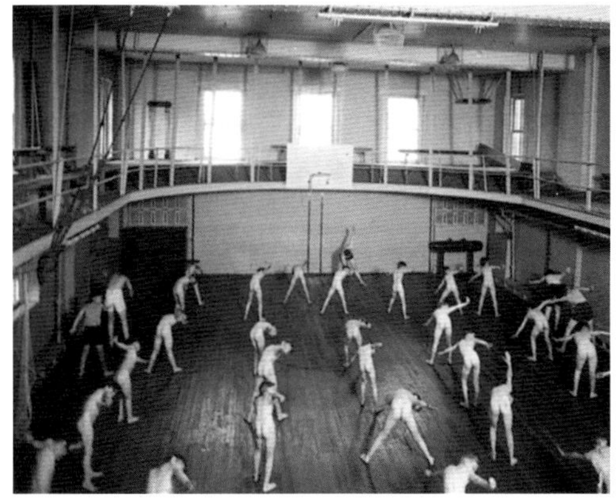

Cat. 19

HARRY P. FISCHER
YMCA, Marietta, Ohio,
ca. 1910, printed later
Harry P. Fischer Collection,
Dawes Memorial Library,
Marietta College, Ohio

This scientific measurement of levels of fitness and physical development (which were usually equated) was important because it could provide evidence and encouragement for exercise and sport as weapons in the struggle against neurasthenia and other diseases of the age. William Blaikie, who lectured throughout the United States and wrote several books on exercise and athletics, was convinced that "one who is trained in this way will safely pass the overwork of the brain and nerves which to-day breaks down so many useful, but physically untrained, men and women, while they should still be in their prime, until nervous exhaustion has become a disorder familiar to almost every physician in the land."[17] By the 1880s schools and seminaries regularly advertised their efforts at physical education for their charges, sometimes to the point of defensiveness about intellectual pursuits. Ingham University, a small school located in LeRoy, New York (between Buffalo and Rochester), assured parents in their 1885 catalog that "special attention is paid to health and physical culture. Regular habits of life are maintained; with daily recreation, fixed hours for retiring and rising, etc. Care is taken to prevent anything like overwork. Students who have entered in good health have uniformly preserved it."[18]

Between 1830 and 1885 most of the advocates of physical culture favored calisthenic or gymnastic exercises for both sexes, rather than training for and playing sports. Guidebooks for exercisers were abundant and ranged from the general, such as Diocletian Lewis's *New Gymnastics* (1862), to S. D. Kehoe's *The Indian Club Exercise* (1866), which detailed the various swings and exercises the physical culturist could try with the clubs.[19] Proponents of exercise commonly used a combination of arguments to convince Americans of their position, including scare tactics (avoiding disease and death), religious responsibility (caring for the soul's physical manifestation), and political and "racial" responsibility (preserving the American republic and Anglo-American institutions in the face of the "threats" of immigrants and the political upheaval with which they were associated). Critics and the general public could find ample visual evidence of the decline from the ancient Greek ideal of the well-muscled and well-proportioned body. Images of the ancients were exhibited in city art galleries, depicted in periodicals, displayed in parlors as inexpensive reproductions of sculpture and paintings, and demonstrated in the photographs of classical art works that were available in huge numbers to consumers of even modest means after the Civil War. The critics were merciless. "To those who have seen the wan cheeks, stooping shoulders and sunken chests of the school-children of to-day," wrote James Smart in *A Manual of Free Gymnastics* (1864), "no argument proving the necessity of physical culture, need be made."[20]

By the 1880s sports had joined gymnastics and calisthenics as a proper means for achieving the ends sought by secular and religious cultural critics. While games and athletic contests had been part of the American settlers' experience since the early seventeenth century, organized sport and training for it became an increasingly important part of everyday life as Americans began to see the world in terms of a Darwinian struggle to survive. For the most part the equation of field performance with preparation for life was directed toward men; women were denied access to most sports, especially contact sports. Tennis, golf, and croquet, for example, were acceptable activities for women, as Alice Austen's ca. 1884 image of the Staten Island Cricket and Tennis Club demonstrates (cat. 5, page 75). Evidently posed for the camera, the photograph reveals the limited nature of acceptable action for women – proper and restricted by petticoats and corsets.

But for many women, corsets and heavy petticoats were undone, as it were, by the bicycle (cat. 12, page 77). By the 1890s coaster brakes and pneumatic tires were common, and the "bicycle craze" had begun. Young women in particular loved the freedom their new mobility provided, both from confining clothes and over the ground. While relatively few women adopted the still-radical bloomer costume, many banished cinched waists and voluminous underclothing in the cause of exercise. Some critics worried about young couples escaping chaperones – just what the young wanted to do – and about bicycle seats harming a woman's reproductive organs, but their cries were to no avail. And at least as many critics and domestic advisors celebrated the exercise "the wheel" encouraged. The popularity of the bicycle had another effect more closely linked to photography in the United States. Amateur camera clubs were organized throughout the country, a result of both newly found mobility for the young and the marketing of the relatively simple camera such as the Kodak Number One.

Even less constricted than the bicyclists were the subjects of the multitude of physical education photographs produced at the turn of the century, such as this plate from Francis Benjamin Johnston's "Washington D.C. Public School Survey" of ca. 1900 (fig. 1). In this genre of images the young women were usually shown in stylized poses demonstrating some aspect of their regimen of calisthenics or gymnastics. Almost always the women depicted are adolescents dressed in the loosely fitting garments health and fitness reformers advocated; corsets and long petticoats were banished from the school gymnasium. Adult women were seldom recorded, for the most part because such activity by them in public was still considered improper. In the privacy of their homes, however, exercise with the multitude of apparatuses available was encour-

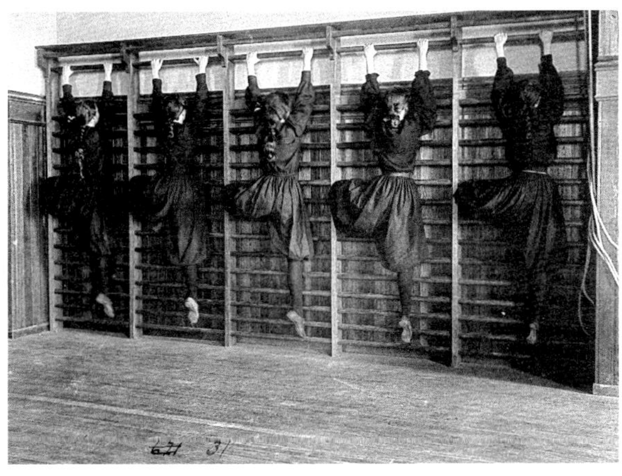

Fig. 1

FRANCIS BENJAMIN JOHNSTON
American, 1864-1952,
Western High School,
from "Washington, D.C.
Public School Survey,"
Plate 31, ca. 1900,
Cyanotype,
6 1/2 x 9 1/8 in.
(16.5 x 23.2 cm.)
Collection of the
Division of Prints
and Photographs,
Library of Congress,
Washington, D.C.

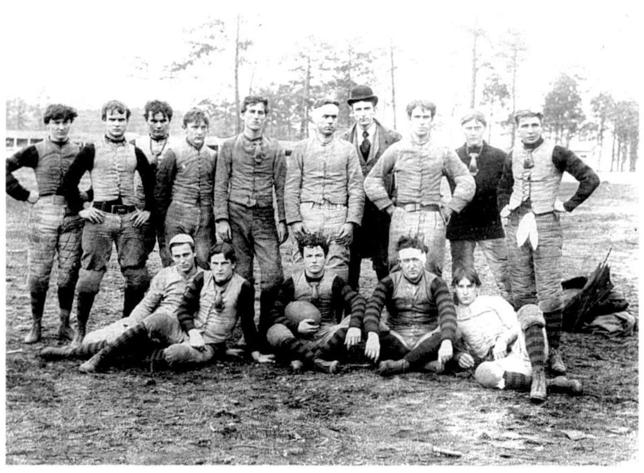

Fig. 2

ANONYMOUS
The University of Georgia Football Team, ca. 1898, Gelatin silver print, Collection of Adelaide B. Wolfe, Bainbridge, Georgia

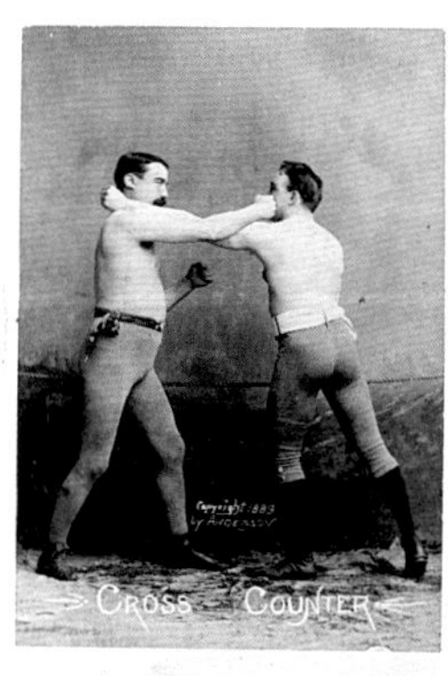

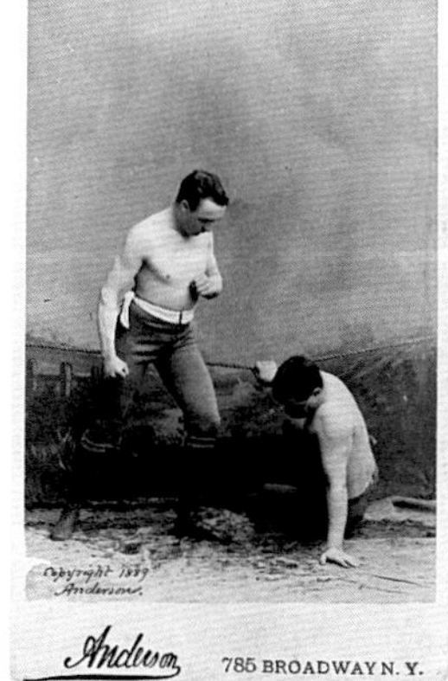

Cat. 10

ANDERSON COMPANY
Boxing Cards, 1889
a. *Cross Counter*
b. *Knockdown*
Collection of the Division of Prints and Photographs, Library of Congress, Washington, D.C.

aged. Physical training and conditioning were considered important – even critical – for women who wished to bear healthy children and avoid neurasthenia and hysteria, but sports and competition were generally to be avoided lest a woman injure her procreative possibilities or become too "manly."

For men competitive field sports increasingly took on the characteristics or at least the language of warfare. Football in particular attracted many of the physical culture advocates of the late nineteenth century, despite the growing violence of the sport. So brutal had the game become that there was serious consideration of outlawing it at the turn of the century. Stricter rules and somewhat better padding stifled that effort, as did the pervasive conviction that contact sports provided young men with a "safety valve" for emotions that could prove dangerous to society. In an article in the *Journal of Hygiene and Herald of Health* in 1895, B. W. Mitchell argued that "football has ended a career of debauchery for more than one youth."[21] If the historian Frederick Jackson Turner was correct in his essay of 1893, "The Significance of the Frontier in American History" – that the frontier had been a "safety valve" for Americans crowded in cities and that it had vanished – then the advocates of "manly sport" had a convincing argument for a culture fearful of its ability to survive in an age of what seemed to be dizzyingly rapid demographic and technological changes. The photograph of the University of Georgia football team (ca. 1898) shows both the "manly" visage and the violence – note the bandages – of the game (fig. 2).

Football, crew, baseball, and even boxing (which had begun to shed its back-room, outlaw, brawling image) appealed to Americans because they seemed to be scientific and complex. There was a mechanistic aspect to these sports, as the repetitive regimen of training for performance demonstrated. The 1889 sequence of Anderson Company cabinet photographs of boxers (cat. 10, this page) in part served to reveal elements of what was to be termed the "sweet science." Crew was a special favorite of physical culture proponents because it instilled teamwork and discipline without the violence of football or the working-class associations of boxing and baseball. Rowing was popular throughout the United States by the 1880s, and was the subject of works by both painters such as Thomas Eakins and photographers such as Charles Currier (fig. 3).

These and other sports were favorites of religious members of the elite such as Luther Gulick, who, as head of the Springfield Training School of the YMCA, is credited with articulating and promulgating much of that organization's philosophy that competitive sports were an essential element in the development of good Christians. In *The Efficient Life* (1909), Gulick identified both the pathway to the athletic millennium he sought and the dangers of not taking that route. "Bodily vigor is a moral agent, it enables us to live on higher levels, to keep up to the top of our achievement. We cannot afford to lose grip on ourselves."[22]

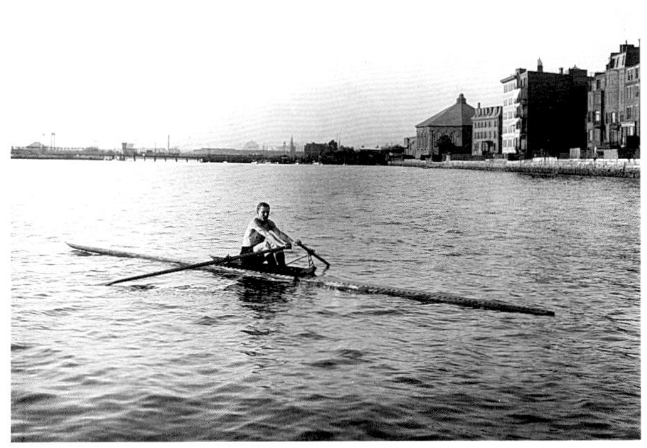

Fig. 3

CHARLES H. CURRIER
American, 1851-1938,
Single Sculler on the
Charles River, Cambridge,
Massachusetts, ca. 1890s,
Gelatin silver print
from vintage
glass plate negative,
8 x 10 in.
(20.3 x 25.4 cm.),
Collection of the
Division of Prints
and Photographs,
Library of Congress,
Washington, D.C.

In their acceptance of the fit and competitive human body as a measure of character, Gulick, the physical education pioneer Dudley Sargent, the football coaches Walter Camp, Amos Alonzo Stagg, and Loren Deland, James Naismith (whom Gulick commissioned to develop a non-contact winter sport, basketball), and other advocates of sport were akin to proponents of the "social gospel," a strong current of liberal thought in the Protestant churches of the turn of the century. Thinkers such as Washington Gladden, Walter Rauschenbusch, Lyman Abbott, and Simon Patten argued that improving the material environment bettered the chances for individual and societal regeneration. This theory, like the ideas that formed the core of "muscular Christianity," centered attention on material reality, and imbued the physical world with an importance that centuries of Judeo-Christian thought had ignored or denied.[23] Documentary photographs such as those by Jacob Riis and Lewis Hine were an important part of this effort, since they revealed with allegedly unbiased truth the reality of the living conditions of the poor. Hine's 1909 image of pin boys in a New York subway bowling alley (cat. 21, page 24) not only details the work of the young pin setters, it suggests the broad popularity of the sport, especially in winter. Turn-of-the-century newspapers in both large cities and small towns commonly carried news of local industrial and other leagues, and many elite private clubs installed alleys in their basements so members could partake of the sport but not of the working class.

The emphasis and celebration of the physical nature of life that in part characterized Protestant theology, scientific inquiry, and historical thinking (in particular that of Turner and other environmentalists) was also a critical element in the enormous popularity and cultural power of photography. Photography, as Allen Trachtenberg, Susan Sontag, and others have pointed out, seemed free of the interpretive freedom of the painter, sculptor, or engraver. Although framing, posing, and darkroom manipulation of images were common practices since 1839, Americans still considered photographs "true," "scientific," and "real."

The "faithful witness" also demonstrated the limitations of human perception.[24] The works of Eadweard Muybridge and Etienne-Jules Marey (fig. 4), for example, revealed a reality previously unseen. In thousands of images they analyzed the details of movement in humans, animals, and machines. They treated the body as a neutral reality to be studied and analyzed. Viewers tolerated nudity or near nudity in such photographs because of the empiricism of the image: horses, acrobats, and athletes were equal. Portraits of athletes drew upon the traditional visual vocabulary of painting and sculpture, as well as the conventions of scientific imagery of microphotographs and medical documentary photography. Bodybuilder and showman Eugene Sandow often posed in only a strategically placed leaf and sandals, yet his body was so close to the classical ideal that even the YMCA was a customer for the thousands of images of the great strongman and others of his ilk. Strongman, photographer, and fitness instructor Arthur Gay photographed men in both classical poses and in the act of lifting great weights. Unlike Sandow, who often replicated classical statuary in his publicity photographs, Gay and the subjects

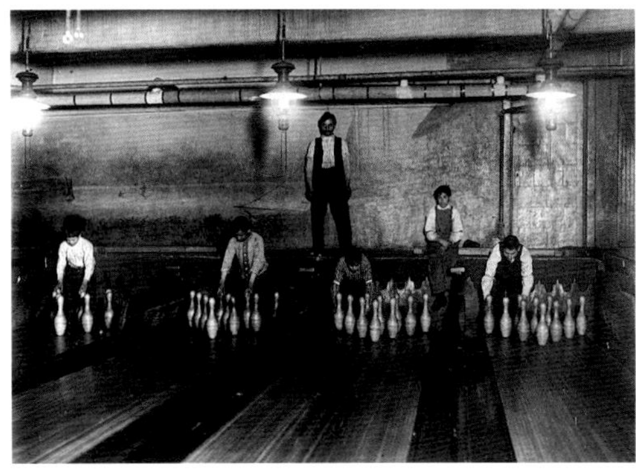

Cat. 21

LEWIS W. HINE
*Pin Boys in a Subway
Bowling Alley,
New York City,* 1910
Collection of the
International Museum
of Photography at
George Eastman House,
Rochester, New York

of his images adopted more straightforward poses that emphasized muscle mass and power. Gay's photographs (cat. 29, page 82) are of a later vintage than are Sandow's (roughly twenty-five years), and perhaps reflect Americas' greater ease with musclemen or, more obliquely, the desires and insecurities of American men – especially middle-class, white-collar men – in the 1920s and 1930s.

More common than the publicity photographs of Sandow, Gay, or wrestler George Hackenschmidt (who posed as a Roman gladiator) were baseball trading cards, which were usually given away with tobacco. These, like the famous "Old Judge" cards (cat. 9, page 76), also drew upon the aesthetic heritage of classical and Renaissance painting and sculpture, but were less closely linked to evolving cultural visions of the ideal body. The appeal of these cards traded on the enormous and ever-growing popularity of spectator sports such as baseball and boxing.

Like sport, science, and religion, photography provided at least a semblance of order and rationality, and seemed to promise greater access to the mysteries of the material world. The medium could also be a servant of the regenerative possibilities offered by these other activities. Photography's apparent neutrality eased the erotic nervousness engendered by visible nudity and affirmed the idea that the body was more than the mere shell of the soul, as in Harry P. Fischer's ca. 1910 photograph of the Marietta, Ohio, YMCA (cat. 19, page 20). Photography, moreover, was a critically important agent in the dissemination of the idea that the physical

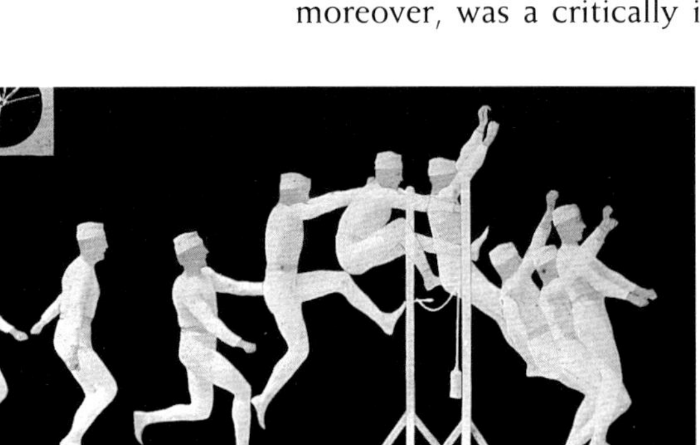

Fig. 4

ETIENNE-JULES MAREY
French, 1830-1904,
*Man performing a high
jump,* 1890-1891,
Chronophotograph
retouched with gouache,
6 x 11 1/3 in.
(15.3 x 28.7 cm.)
Collection of the Museé
Marey, Beaune, France

characteristics of the muscled and toned body were evidence of the discipline and vitality many Americans thought essential for a culture entangled in an inevitable struggle for survival.[25]

By 1900, photography was also a vital part in the calculus of national strength and sporting achievement that European and American cultures asserted and used for their imperial and other political ends. Sociologists and anthropologists commonly used photographs to support theories explaining racial and ethnic differences and superiority, and business and government exhibitors at world's fairs often included images of their citizens as well as those of products and processes in their displays. The New York State Commissioners' Report of the Paris Exposition of 1900 noted, "One of the interesting exhibits in Class three was that of J. C. Hemment's series of photographs illustrating typical games and sports in American colleges. The development and training of our college athletes and our gymnasium facilities were a revelation to the foreign world, and was of particular interest at this juncture owing to the overwhelming victory of our college athletes at the Olympic games held during the summer."[26] The revival of the ancient games had begun in Athens but four years previously; by 1900 they were perceived by many as a test of national strength. Categorizing and hierarchically arranging the races and nationalities of the world, often with the aid of photography, helped rationalize the goals of empire-building. The most familiar example of this justification is probably Rudyard Kipling's call to the British to bear the "white man's burden."

The popularity and power of photography were in part a result of its widespread accessibility as both an activity and a product. Faster shutter speeds and simplified processing technologies for developing negatives and making prints broadened Americans' involvement with the medium, but much of photography's power lay in its unprecedented possibilities for capturing and reproducing the visible world with apparent neutrality at a time when scientific inquiry and methods had become pre-eminent. Photography also dovetailed closely with religion – at least liberal Protestantism – because of the emphasis on material reality and ameliorating social evils, as well as the "muscular Christian's" equation of physical well-being with moral behavior. Finally, the medium also reinforced and heightened Americans' enthusiasm for sports because it both examined and publicized these activities. Because photography had both the capability to stop and portray action that had occurred but that had never been seen and the capacity to portray the body in the older aesthetic frameworks of painting and sculpture, it was, in the end, a medium that embraced the old and the new, the scientific and the religious, the real and the imaginative.

ENDNOTES

1.   G. Stanley Hall, "Christianity and Physical Culture," *Pedagogical Seminars* 9 (1902): 375, 377-78.
2.   D. H. Wheeler, "Natural Selection and Politics," *Popular Science Monthly* 3 (1873): 320-32.
3.   Darwinian theory was not, as is often suggested, rejected or criticized outright by the church or other critics. Natural selection, which was oversimplified to mean "survival of the fittest," was an easy fit in a country wedded to unrestricted economic competition. The idea of imperceptibly slow change in the species was a bit more controversial for those who believed that the universe was created in exactly the time outlined in the Old Testament (calculated by Archbishop Ussher of Armagh, Ireland, to have occurred in 4004 B.C.). The elements of Darwin's theories that rankled the most people were the theories of random variation, which seemed to leave no place for God, and the scientist's later emphasis on the linkage of the human race to simians.
4.   "Wear and Tear," *Harpers Weekly* 11, no. 561 (September 28, 1867): 623.
5.   John H. Kellogg, M.D., *Household Manual of Domestic Hygiene, Food, and Diet* (Battle Creek, Mich., 1882), 120.
6.   Edwin Temple, "Overstudy," *The Household Magazine* 14, no.6 (June 1881): 129; Edward H. Clarke, *Sex in Education, or, A Fair Chance for Girls* (Boston, 1973), 41; Diocletian Lewis, *The New Gymnastics for Men, Women, and Children* (Boston, 1862), 9.
7.   George Beard, "Neurasthenia, or Nervous Exhaustion," *Boston Medical and Surgical Journal*, no. 3 (1869): 217; *American Nervousness, Its Causes and Consequences* (New York, 1881).
8.   Americans were not the only neurasthenics. See, for example, Rudolph Arndt, *Die Neurasthenie . . .* (Vienna, 1899). On the subject of women and neurasthenia, see, for example, [Arabella Kenealy], "A Lady From the Girl of Today," *Medical Record*, 55 (1899): 719.
9.   See Karen Halttunen, *Confidence Men and Painted Women: A Study of Middle-Class Culture in America, 1840-1870* (New Haven, 1982); John Kasson, *Rudeness and Civility: Manners in Nineteenth-Century Urban America* (New York, 1990), 103-11.
10. George Beard, *Eating and Drinking: A Popular Manual of Food and Diet in Health and Disease* (New York, 1871), 91.
11. Mary Wood-Allen, *What a Young Woman Ought to Know* (Philadelphia, 1899, 1913), 219.
12. Madison Grant, *The Passion of the Great Race* (New York, 1916). See also Albert Wiggam, "Can We Make Motherhood Fashionable?" *Physical Culture* 45, no. 5 (May 1921): 22-23, 90-93; Irving Fisher, "Impending Problems in Eugenics," *Science* 13 (1921): 214-31.
13. William Alcott, *Library of Health* 3, no. 95 (1839), quoted in James C. Whorton, *Crusaders for Fitness* (Princeton, 1982), 117.
14. Howard Mumford Jones, *The Age of Energy: Varieties of the American Experience, 1865-1915* (New York, 1971), 28-29.

15. Bruce Haley, *The Healthy Body and Victorian Culture* (Cambridge, Mass., 1978), 107-9, 214, 221.

16. "Literary Notices," *Godey's Lady's Book* 82, no. 488 (February 1871): 193-94.

17. William Blaikie, *Sound Bodies for Our Boys and Girls* (New York, 1884), iii; see also Abba Gould Woolson, *Dress Reform* (Boston, 1874), 120.

18. *Fifty-First Annual Catalog of Ingham University* (LeRoy, N.Y., 1886), 29.

19. Diocletian Lewis, *The New Gymnastics for Men, Women, and Children* (Boston, 1873); S. D. Kehoe, *The Indian Club Exercise . . . Also Remarks on Physical Culture* (New York, 1866). See also William Alcott, *Lectures of Life and Health, or, the Laws and Means of Physical Calisthenics for Schools and Families* (New York, 1856); Russell Trall, *The Illustrated Family Gymnasium* (New York, 1857).

20. James H. Smart, *A Manual of Free Gymnastics and Dumb-Bell Exercises for the School-Room and Parlor* (Cincinnati, 1864), iii.

21. B. W. Mitchell, "A Defense of Football," *Journal of Hygiene and Herald of Health* 45 (1896): 93.

22. See Donald J. Mrozek, *Sport and American Mentality, 1880-1910* (Knoxville, 1983), 202-5; Luther Gulick, *The Efficient Life* (New York, 1909), 107.

23. See, for example, Washington Gladden, *Applied Christianity: Moral Aspects of Christianity* (Boston, 1886); Walter Rauschenbusch, *Christianity and the Social Crisis* (New York, 1907); Simon Patten, *The Social Basis of Religion* (New York, 1911).

24. Alan Trachtenberg, *Reading American Photographs: Images as History, Matthew Brady to Walker Evans* (New York, 1989): xiii-xvii; Susan Sontag, *On Photography* (New York, 1977); Miles Orvell, *The Real Thing: Imitation and Authenticity in American Culture, 1880-1940* (Chapel Hill, N.C.,1989).

25. See Jackson Lears, *No Place of Grace: Antimodernism and the Transformation of American Culture, 1880-1920* (New York, 1982).

26. *Report of the Commissioners Representing the State of New York at the Universal Exposition at Paris, France, 1900* (Brooklyn, 1990), 80-81.

CREATING THE 'NEW MAN'

German and Soviet Sports Photographs
Between the Wars

For just over a century now, the science of photography has made sportive motion visible and comprehensible in the same way that stroboscopic techniques have revealed the secrets of natural motion. Indeed, without high-speed photography, the celebrated heroes of the 100-meter dash – and many others – would be little more than blurred and fleeting images in the public eye. "I am filmed, therefore I am" might well be the new Cartesian motto of the modern high-performance athlete. With the rise of sport as a mass culture during the 1920s, sports photography did even more than to unveil, record, and celebrate the biomechanics of athletic movement. It recorded as well the cultural trends and historical forces of a tumultuous epoch. In Weimar Germany at this time, the simultaneous appearance of a mass entertainment industry, a new and dynamic type of political mobilization, and an unprecedented public interest in the display of the human body made sport a uniquely symbolic vehicle for values old and new. In the Soviet Union, propaganda-as-entertainment, mass mobilization across the breadth of the body politic, and a utilitarian approach to the physical potential of the masses created an analogous, but ideologically distinct, receptiveness to sport as a dynamic and therefore politically inspiring theater of human energy. In both Nazi Germany and the Bolshevist state, official doctrines proclaiming the creation of a "new man" required dynamic human images to serve as political models. Only in the German pictures, however, does race assert itself as a theme. For all these reasons many German and Soviet photographs of this period are filled with signs and portents that we can read with the sober, and sometimes sorrowful, wisdom of hindsight. In these images we find a turbulent mixture of utopian hopes, primitive impulses, fascination with the machine, and soaring ambitions for that mortal engine called the human body. Here the face of history can be read in the solitary explosion of physical effort, in the choreographed movements of the crowd, in the sheer determination of a human face.

A photograph by the German August Sander offers modern figures who are shadowed by historical forbears of great cultural import. In *Sport Association, Westerwald* (ca. 1924), (cat. 27, page 84) a large group of young athletes is attended by older men who are presumably their trainers. One senses a Prussian discipline in this German version of the sportive style of the 1920s. That this is a *Sportverein* (sports club) and not a *Turnverein* (gymnastics club) signals the victory of sport over the German gymnastics of the nineteenth century and the cultural conservatism it represented – a nationalism of grandiose dimensions, German racial identity, xenophobia, and a hatred of urban civilization and the effects of industrialization. "Sport" was an English import that arrived in Germany in the middle of the nineteenth century,[1] and for the rest of that century and well into the twentieth these competing physical cultures struggled for hegemony on German soil. This contest for the fit German body reproduced the fateful struggle for Weimar Germany itself: the Right against the Left, nationalist chauvinism against internationalism, the revanchists against the liberals who were eventually overwhelmed by Hitler's terror.

Over the course of a century this fundamental German schism expressed itself on the terrain of physical culture, for the ideal of the fit and robust German body played a role in German politics from the birth of German nationalism at the beginning of the nineteenth century until the end of the Nazi period.[2] The central figure of this tradition was Friedrich Ludwig ("Father") Jahn (1778-1852), originally a fervent Prussian patriot and later a German nationalist of enormous influence. Jahn established the first gymnastics ground (*Turnplatz*) in 1811, and he proceeded to make the gymnastics movement into a patriotic movement directed against the Napoleonic occupation of Germany. Jahn was also a xenophobe whose resentment of Frenchmen and Jews anticipated the upsurge in German racialistic thinking over the next century and beyond. His career as a political physical educator fused racial purity with corporeal aesthetics, German identity with the glories of nature and the great outdoors: "The soul of the gymnastics association (*Turnwesen*) is the life of the people itself (*das Volksleben*), and this thrives only in the open, in light and air." (Here is an early prototype of the sun-obsessed German nature-worship that produced the German nudism movement [*Naturismus*] at the end of the nineteenth century.[3] These strong bodies represented not merely fitness but an entire style of German masculinity: proud aggressiveness, ostentatiously rustic garb, and a self-consciously coarse German idiom that proclaimed its contempt for words of foreign origin.[4] It required little originality on the part of the Nazis to put this style in the service of the Third Reich.

Sanders's *Young Sport Pilot* (1925, cat. 30, page 83), while essentially independent of this tradition, is nevertheless an implicitly politicized figure. This young airman is an aeronautical version of the medieval knight on horseback, the man-of-action as a man-of-technology, the adventurer who takes physical risks to find another dimension of human experience — a male figure who has long figured as a German icon. Sanders's hero is, in effect, a modern Knight of Bamberg, the famous equestrian sculpture (ca. 1230) on display in the Bamberg Cathedral, who "was held – and by many still is held – to be the ideal German. His manner is regal, his gaze that of a free man, his features noble. A tender melancholy enhances an expression of perpetually youthful beauty."[5] In his essay on early aviation and German nationalism, Peter Fritzsche has pointed out the political significance of this figure's estrangement from the prosaic world of the bourgeois: "The notion that flying elevated the individual above the masses and prepared a new elite was commonplace in the 1920s and 1930s."[6] This young pilot is also a sportsman for whom the machine is an extension of both body and will. An important development of the period from 1910 to 1930 is that the automobile and the airplane became symbols of modernity through which a man could magnify his strength and speed *as a sportsman*. Thus the daring aviator became a popular figure across Europe just prior to the Great War of 1914-1918, amazing the crowds who witnessed his aerial maneuvers and heart-stopping landings. "Flying at that time was purely sport," a German memoirist recalls, "a favorite hobby of wealthy officers and gentlemen."[7] By the 1920s, however, the pilot represented an entire generation; he incarnated the cult of youth that followed the terrible slaughter of the Great War, in which pilots became heroes for the first time in history. At the same time, the pilot was a herald of the future. In Weimar Germany, a new generational vocabulary pointed to "the presence of a mass of young people who represented not merely an age-group but a new and radically different category of human beings."[8] Metamorphosed into a living example of the new man-machine relationship, the pilot and his aura suggested the possibility of an anthropological transformation and an extension of human capacities. As we will see in our discussion of Soviet sports photography of the 1920s, this imaginative synthesis of man and machine had been first popularized just before the war by the Italian Futurist movement and its charismatic leader, Filippo Marinetti.

Martin Munkácsi's *Aviation School in Training, Munich* (1928, fig. 1) is an outsider's stunningly candid portrait of a German phenomenon the historian Jeffrey Herf has called "reactionary modernism." Herf describes this ostensibly awkward synthesis as "a cultural paradox of German modernity, namely, the embrace of modern technology by German thinkers who rejected Enlightenment reason."[9] The clash between the primitive and the modern is heightened in the photograph by the unmediated juxtaposition of human and metallic skin. Here is a sudden regression from the visionary man-machine synthesis to a (now ironic) insistence on the difference between the two "organisms" that share the photograph. We assume these men are pilots, but they do not possess the modernistic persona of the aviator until they are actually integrated into the machine. The photograph can be read as a pictorial rendering of Oswald Spengler's argument in *Man and Technology* (1931), in which he "celebrates a virile antiintellectualism and forges links between technology and feudal images of nobles, soldiers, and adventurers."[10]

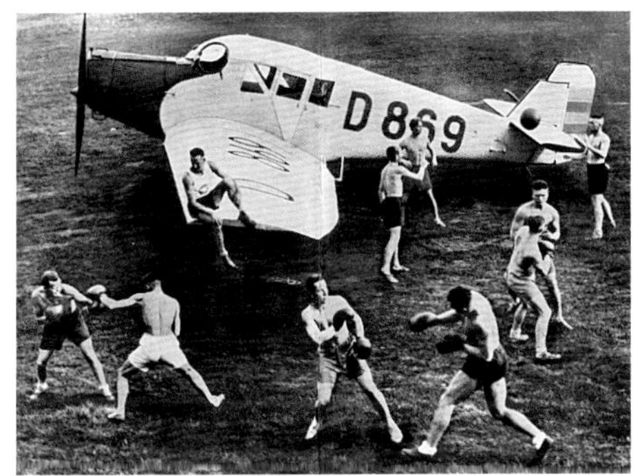

Fig. 1

MARTIN MUNKÁCSI
American,
born Hungary,
1896-1963,
*Aviation School in Training,
Munich*, 1928,
Gelatin silver print,
International Center
of Photography,
New York

The central issue, however, is the nature of such "links" between men and machines, metal and flesh. The startling character of Munkácsi's image confirms that imaginative *integrations* of mechanisms and human beings have a cultural familiarity that this stark juxtaposition does not: the arresting element is precisely the artist's refusal to reconcile the tensions created by the sheer contiguity of the machine and the almost naked men who are not "ready" to fly it. Indeed, their nakedness is the mystery contained in the picture, since in an age of technology, with their metal steed standing by, it seems to make no sense.

But this photograph contains more than an examination of modern man's relationship to technology. It also propounds a particular aestheticism of the body that must be seen in its cultural context. During the 1920s "sport" became a European *style* that seemed to energize life even beyond the stadium, and its acolytes wielded the confident authority of fashion. "But nowhere," John Willett has written, "was the myth of sport more potent than in Germany, where a whole series of sporting terms like 'k.o', 'training', 'form' and (as Brecht spelt it) 'panjjing ball' now entered the language."[11] "The body," one German observer wrote, "was the sensation [*Schlager*] of the hour. Sport was the coming thing. The commercial instinct of the decade scented the boom. Sport was promoted, demanded, and served up" to the masses.[12] How might we recreate for ourselves that period when "sport" emerged, not only as a mass culture, but as a dynamic metaphor for the excitement of modernity itself? How, after absorbing more than a half-century of sport and the spectacular achievements of high-speed sports photography, could we recapture such sensual innocence? What we do know is that within this unique moment in cultural time a sensibility flourished and was then transformed.

But if this unique experience blossomed and faded, its visual vocabulary has been absorbed into the sports idiom of our century. What is more, the sheer charisma of this idiom has proven to have almost limitless commercial applications. The triumph of the athletic shoe as an article of fashion, the advertising campaigns on behalf of expensive "sports watches," and the frequent use of athletic bodies to symbolize the dynamism of corporations signal a "sportification" of everyday reality comparable to the advent of sport-as-style back in the 1920s. The casual insouciance of the athlete lounging on the wing of the airplane recalls the endless series of comparably "virile" types featured in modern fashion advertising — maleness expressed as the sheer luxury of style, the refreshment of momentary idleness before plunging back into the maelstrom of "action" and its special satisfactions. Nor does this picture present pugilism as unrestrained ferocity; on the contrary, this is a posed and choreographed version of boxing that preserves the primacy of style over savagery. Germans have cultivated the "chivalric" ethos for centuries, and this sort of stylized combat — gentlemen at play — is part of the essence of "chivalry."

Munkácsi's stylized pugilist-aviators remind us that sport fascinated many intellectuals in Weimar Germany. The literary historian Wolfgang Rothe has maintained that "enthusiasm for sports, uncritical lionization of sports activities, prevails in the books of this period."[13] Many of the Weimar intellectuals were aficionados or athletically active, and among the former was the playwright Bertolt Brecht, who actually considered the sporting audience superior to that of the legitimate theater. Indeed, revolutionary dramatists like Brecht and Antonin Artaud[14] saw sport as an analogue to avant-garde theater. "There seems to be nothing to stop the theater from having its own form of 'sport,'" Brecht wrote. "If only someone could take these buildings designed for theatrical purposes . . . and treat them as more or less empty spaces for the successful pursuit of 'sport', then they would be used in a way that might mean something to a contemporary public that earns real contemporary money and eats real contemporary beef. . . . We pin our hopes on the sporting public."[15] For Brecht, John Willett has written, "sport was a form of entertainment whose principles ought to be taken over by the theater, with the stage as a brightly lit ring devoid of all mystique, demanding a critical irreverent attitude on the part of the audience."[16] Brecht underlined the aesthetic equivalence of sport and art by appearing in public with the boxing champion Paul Samson-Körner. His fascination with sport has since been emulated by many writers and artists for whom the athletic body represents a mysterious domain of experience diametrically opposed to their own. This reverential attitude toward athletic self-expression on the part of many artists is yet another confirmation of sport's status as a style of existence that permeates modern consciousness.

Yet Munkácsi's picture is also a profoundly political document. For beneath the polish and superficiality of its men's-magazine style, this pugilistic tableau evokes a brutal past and an even more brutal (and imminent) future. As an evocation of the German past, it is a modernized por-

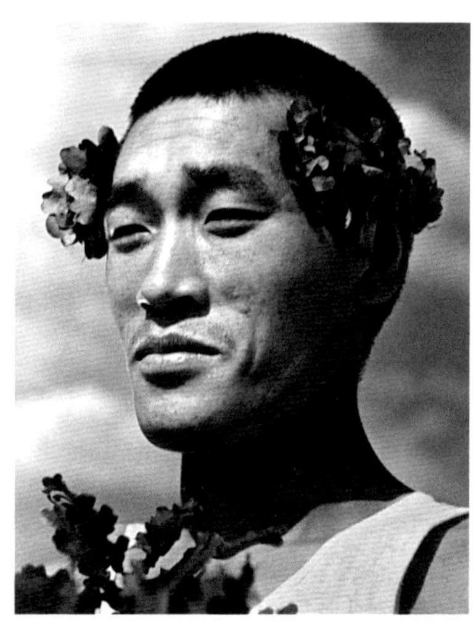

Fig. 2

LENI RIEFENSTAHL
German, born 1902,
*Kitei Son, Marathon Winner,
Berlin Olympics,* 1936,
Gelatin silver print,
11 3/8 x 9 1/8 in.
(28.9 x 23.2 cm.)
Collection of the
Division of Prints
and Photographs,
Library of Congress,
Washington, D.C.;
Courtesy Leni
Riefenstahl-Produktion,
Pöcking, Germany

trait of the *"furor teutonicus,* the age-old, elemental aggressive mania of the Germans";[17] at the same time, it points ahead to the imminent triumph of the atavistic impulses of the Nazi movement and its male ideal – a "new type of man correctly proportioned in body and soul."[18] Indeed, boxing was Hitler's idea of a politically wholesome sport – an antidote to "peaceable aesthetes and bodily degenerates" – and it was accorded pride of place within Nazi physical culture.[19] Hitler's taste for boxing was, in fact, a conspicuous symptom of his own "reactionary modernism" – a syndrome that easily accommodated uninhibited glorification of the male order (*Männerorden*) and its privileges. The public celebration of masculinity was, in turn, a way to sanctify the German war experience (*Kriegserlebnis*) hallowed by a generation of veterans who had endured a bitter defeat at the hands of the decadent West. In Munkácsi's photograph, the threat presented by this cult of the male order to the fragile political and social structures of the Weimar Republic is there for all to see.

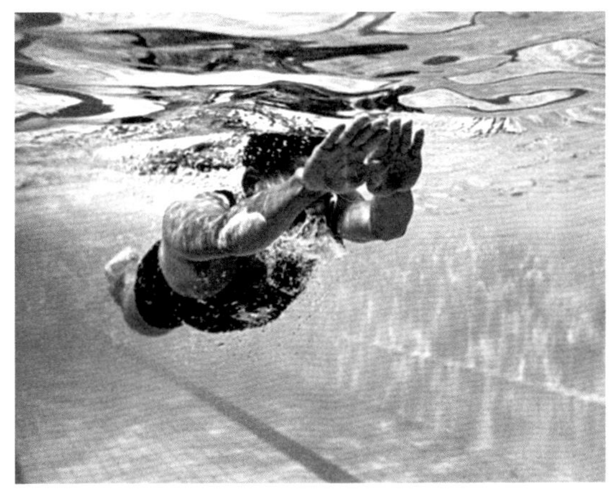

Fig. 3

LENI RIEFENSTAHL
German, born 1902,
*Starting Dive
Photographed Underwater,
Berlin Olympics,* 1936,
Gelatin silver print,
9 x 11 1/2 in.
(22.9 x 29.2 cm.)
Collection of the
Division of Prints
and Photographs,
Library of Congress,
Washington, D.C.;
Courtesy Leni
Riefenstahl-Produktion,
Pöcking, Germany

Leni Riefenstahl's portrait of *Kitei Son, Marathon Winner, Berlin Olympics* (1936, fig. 2) suggests a racial cosmopolitanism wholly at odds with the Nazi regime that sponsored the famed filmmaker and photographer.[20] As the official film documentarist of the 1936 Berlin Olympiad, Riefenstahl enjoyed an unprecedented opportunity to contemplate, record, and finally shape the aesthetics of sport. "To say that sports cinematography was in its infancy before August 1936 is metaphorically as well as factually inaccurate," Richard Mandell has written, "since self-conscious sports cinematography was introduced to the world by Leni Riefenstahl."[21] The Olympic Games presented her with a visual encyclopedia of human forms and movements, and the two-part film that resulted (*Olympia*, 1938) is widely regarded as a classic testament to the aesthetics of the human body. The racial cosmopolitanism of the Olympic film – in stark contrast to the fervent Aryan mythologizing of her propagandistic *Triumph of the Will* (1934) – is grounded in the universalism of the human body that every Olympiad makes clear.

Officially sanctioned race-mixing at the "Nazi Olympics" was, of course, an innovation for Hitler's Germany, and it did not come to pass without a struggle between the most extreme racial purists and more pragmatic types within the Nazi movement.[22] Hostility to sports internationalism went back to the earliest days of National Socialism. Later (in 1928) the Nazi ideologist Alfred Rosenberg called the Olympic Games a crime on account of their international character. In 1932 the *Völkischer Beobachter* commented: "Negroes have no place at an Olympiad. Unfortunately, one finds today that the free man must often compete against unfree blacks, against Negroes, for the victory wreath. This is an unparalleled disgrace and degradation, and the ancient Greeks would turn in their graves if they knew what modern men have made out of their holy National Games."[23] In 1933 Hitler finally accepted Olympic multiracialism in exchange for the public relations value of the Games, and the International Olympic Committee (IOC) was happy to oblige him.[24]

Riefenstahl may thus have seen her portrait of the marathon champion as a quiet gesture of ideological subversion, as an act of aesthetic seduction. The effect is that of a polished stone bust:

the ancient Greek wreath seems welded to an oriental face of beatific tranquillity – the "spiritu-ality" of the East, the "serenity" of a smiling Buddha – achieving an implicit fusion of races and cultures that is emblematic of Olympic cosmopolitanism. At the same time, we sense a supreme contentment after the heroic testing of human limits. "The human body can do so much," Kitei Son said after his great victory. "Then the heart and the spirit must take over."[25] This photo-graph may contain, then, two separate ironies: the non-Aryan racial icon presented as German art, and serenity as the transcendental afterglow of agonizing physical effort.

Riefenstahl's *Starting Dive Photographed Underwater, Berlin Olympics* (1936, fig. 3) portrays a different sort of iconic figure. While the study of Kitei Son presents the athlete *as* his face, the swimmer

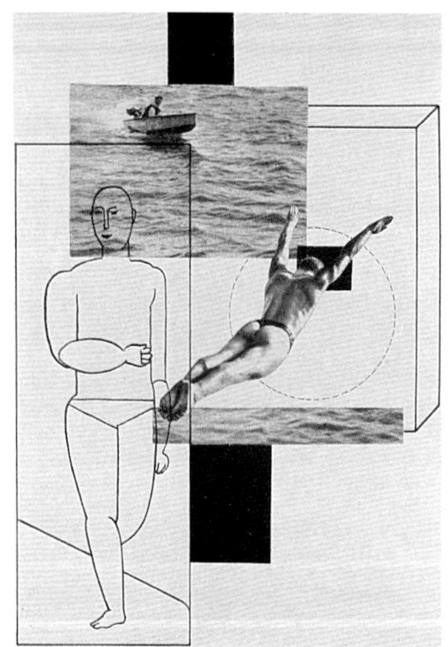

Fig. 4

WILLI BAUMEISTER
German, 1889-1955,
Diver, ca.1926,
Gelatin silver prints,
pencil drawing,
and ink collage,
Courtesy
Archiv Baumeister,
Stuttgart,
(Work destroyed
during the Second
World War)

in this photograph lacks a face altogether. If Kitei Son is the generic spiritual hero-ism of the athlete, then this figure is the generic body of the athlete which has be-come a projectile and the instrument of willpower. The anonymity of the swimmer makes him less a person than a human submarine and thus the personification of *streamlining* – one of the signature stylistic devices of an Age of Speed. In this way the photographer has managed to conjure up the Spirit of Technology in the absence of both metal and the machine, and one result is the subtle dehumanization that also accompanies the merger of man with the machine that catapults him far beyond the limits of his own physical powers. For Riefenstahl's swimmer, too, is an explorer fig-ure who makes his way through an alien realm: out of his element in a literal sense, he is also figuratively out of bounds like the pilot who has rocketed into the inhos-pitable cold and mystery of the upper atmosphere. Neither man can breathe, but each plunges on in fulfillment of his mission.

Willi Baumeister's *Diver* (1927, fig. 4) and *Athlete* (1926), (not shown in this exhibi-tion) attempt to deconstruct or subvert the sheer corporeal immediacy that gives Rie-fenstahl's submarine-body (and, indeed, most sports photography) its dynamic ap-peal. On a superficial level, the line-drawings turn the three-dimensional, flesh-and-blood athletes into semiological formulas comparable to the symbolic stick-figures that identify the various sports at a modern Olympiad. On a deeper level, the montage of sculpted photograph-ic bodies and their hypersimplified geometrical reductions abruptly subvert the dynamic-athletic principle by calling into question the muscled body in its dramatic immediacy. Particu-larly in *The Diver*, the function of the line-drawing is to challenge the newly fashionable author-ity of muscle with a cubist playfulness that dissolves and amputates its massive and solid quali-ty. This kind of minimalistic treatment of the athlete punctures Riefenstahl's submission to the charisma of the body, which reasserted itself many years after the Berlin Games in her photo-graphs of magnificent Nuba wrestlers.[26] Its geometricism also evokes the mathematical dimen-sion of movement, the possibility of a "solution" that might be expressed in the abstract sym-bols of physics. In this sense Baumeister points (no doubt unconsciously) to the scientific investigation of high-performance athletics that, having begun in the 1890s, was now well un-derway, above all in Germany.

Let us take a more detailed look at how the scientific imagination could be applied to the body of the athlete at this time. As Baumeister experimented in his studio, the prominent industrial psychologist Robert Werner Schulte was hard at work in his "psychotechnical" laboratory in Berlin, where he subjected athletes to a battery of physiological or psychological testing procedures in his search for athletic "aptitudes." Schulte tested visual and auditory acuity, analyzed blood and urine, and measured respiratory capacity, the hardness of the muscles, the athlete's tendency to tremble, the coordination of eye and hand, even courage and willpower. He spoke of "psychological electrodiagnostics," "psychochemistry," and mathematically calculable performances.[27] The hyperbolic aspect of this early sports science is not to be denied. At the same time, however, its flights of fancy illuminate an imaginative process that had seized upon the athlete as an object of scientific analysis. Like Baumeister's art, Schulte's physiology probed and dissected the athlete and pointed to a theoretical "solution" that might define the biomechanical phenomena "behind" the performance.

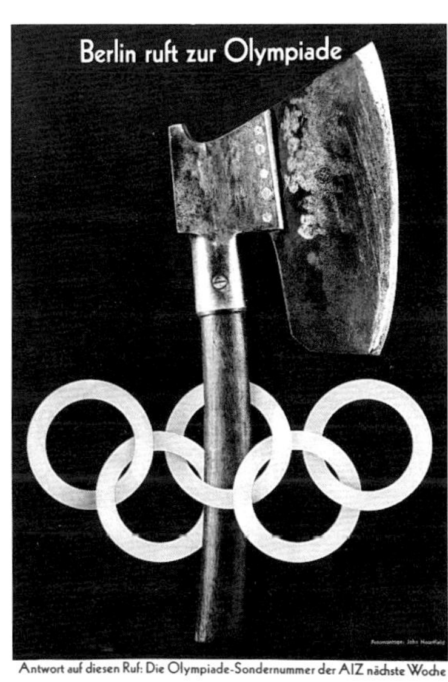

Fig. 5

JOHN HEARTFIELD
Berlin ruft zur Olympiade
(Berlin calls to the
Olympiad), from *Die*
Arbeiter-Illustrierte-Zeitung
(The Workers' Illustrated
Newspaper), 25,
no. 26, June 24, 1936
(back cover)
Collection of The
Museum of Fine Arts,
Houston; Museum
purchase with funds
provided by Isabell
and Max Herzstein

John Heartfield's *Berlin calls to the Olympiad* (1936, fig. 5) proclaims the fraudulent character of Nazi internationalism with a brutal simplicity. Penetrating and violating the Olympic rings, the ancient warrior-axe incarnates the ancient *furor teutonicus* and its contempt for the subjugated racial alien. Published in the socialist *Arbeiter-Illustrierte-Zeitung*, Heartfield's photograph was an eloquent shot fired in the German Left's rear-guard propaganda offensive against their Nazi conquerors. In addition, this political critique of the Nazi Olympiad expressed an alternative Olympic ideal that – unlike the "bourgeois" IOC – would not have accommodated the Nazis in any circumstances. The German workers' sport movement (*Arbeitersportbewegung*) was the largest branch of the Socialist Workers' Sport International (SWSI), which attempted to create a distinctly socialist sports culture and Workers' Olympiads to celebrate it.[28] These impressive festivals were held in Prague (1921), Frankfurt (1925), Vienna (1931), and Antwerp (1937). According to one German socialist, the Workers' festivals were distinguished from their "bourgeois counterparts" by the fact that the socialist Games were "based on genuine international solidarity, not on national pride."[29] Heartfield's image thus challenged Nazi contempt for internationalist fraternalism and pointed by implication to a utopian internationalism that would be made possible only by a socialist transformation of the world.

The Marxist transformation of sport during the 1920s took two forms. In Europe the SWSI attempted to create a new socialist ethos of sport that emphasized cooperation, education, and the preservation of athletes' health. At the same time, the Bolsheviks in Russia were practicing social transformation on a much larger scale, and a utopian belief in the transforming power of technology became a popular dogma that would later be exploited by Stalin and his successors. The role of the human body in this technological project was a subordinate one, as is clearly shown in photographs by Alexander Rodchenko (*Wheel, Gymnastics Festival, Red Square, Moscow*, 1936, cat. 62, page 97) and Georgi Zelma (*Champions of Moscow on Red Square*, 1938, cat. 70, page 96). Both pictures illustrate – and celebrate – the integration of human bodies into metal frames whose forms signify their utilitarian function: the wheel and the skyscraper. No less than the geometrical rigor of Rodchenko's marching column of athletes (*Dynamo Sports Club*, 1930, cat. 48, page 96), these man-machine syntheses glorify the collectivistic discipline that is evident in every Soviet image, including those that appear to feature individual athletes.

The significance of the athletic body in Bolshevist Russia during the 1920s thus transcended competitive sport in two ways. On the one hand, it could be absorbed into a geometrical structure to symbolize the subordination of human autonomy to the machine and Stalinist industrialization. Admittedly, the integrations of human and machine forms presented in the Rodchenko and Zelma photographs are ambiguous, since the observer may see these bodies being energized as well as (or instead of) being absorbed by the structure into which they have been fitted. The ideological viewpoint of the observer will, in effect, determine how this dilemma is resolved. A modern variation on this theme is Zdeněk Lhoták's *Untitled* from the "Sparta Series" (1978-88, cat. 125, this page), which combines the athletic dynamism of many bodies with an abstract pattern that "tames" the individuals by weaving them together. But rather than political discipline, this photograph evokes technology itself. We seem to be looking at a photomicrograph of a textile – the microscopic warp and woof of an artificial fabric, and here too we detect a loss of interest in the individual. The important difference is that this exercise in geometricism, unlike its obviously functional antecedents of the 1920s and 1930s, suggests an abstract playfulness quite distinct from the literalism of wheels and steel buildings. This is a post-Spartakiad human sculpture that has left Soviet discipline behind in order to pay homage to the geometrical mysteries of art.

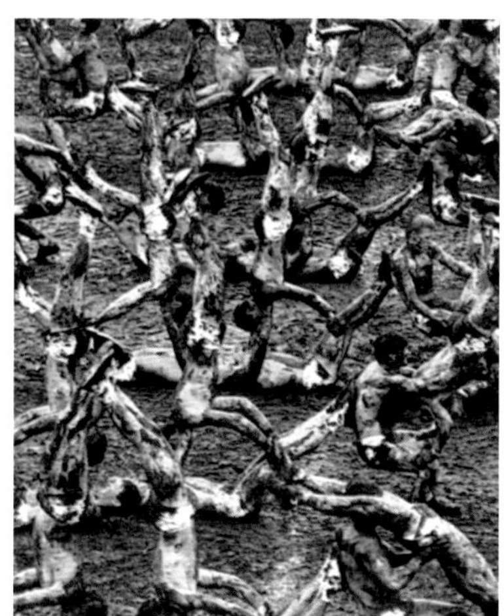

Cat. 125

ZDENĚK LHOTÁK
Untitled, from the series "Sparta," 1978-1988
Courtesy of the artist and The Witkin Gallery, Inc., New York

The athletic body of the early Bolshevist period also transcended sport by serving as a paragon of perfected motion. For the visionary social planners of this period, the efficient movements of the sportsman were a model for streamlining the labor process, and the extreme wing of this approach to boosting productivity was the so-called mechanists. The most important of these thinkers was Aleksei Gastev, head of the Central Institute of Work in Moscow. Gastev, who dreamed of turning men into machines that would build a new industrialized civilization, was one of "the modern ecstatics of rationalism" described by an astonished Western visitor in 1926. These were people who "labour to become like the machine and finally to be absorbed into bliss in a structure of driving-belts, pistons, valves, and fly-wheels. People began eagerly to investigate the mechanical elements in man himself, the technical foundations of the bodily organism, which must in the future be encouraged and religiously developed."[30] Gastev saw athletic skill as a necessary component of this new anthropological type: "He especially admired the skill of sportsmen and circus artists and greatly enjoyed watching performances of jugglers, acrobats, and magicians. He regarded their dexterity as a result of practice, proof that muscles and reflexes could be trained to perform phenomenal feats of precision and agility." He dreamed of training children starting at the age of two: "The new age demands a generation with tempered nerves, strong physiques and unreflective agility. To do this we must develop a system of precise exercises" – as perfect a prescription for scientifically developing the high-performance athlete as anyone could imagine.[31]

Gustav Klucis's untitled postcards (1928, cats. 39, 40, 41, page 45) are devoted to the first of the great Soviet sports festivals. That each of these images is a montage facilitates their common political message: the individual athlete performs for the state, the individual performance dissolves in the political collective. In the first image, the shot-putter who appears to stand astride the marching column "like a colossus" is held in check and diminished by Lenin's ferocious stare. The second photograph recalls the militarization of physical culture during the years immediately following the 1917 Revolution.[32] Every figure belongs to a disciplined and militant subgroup within the photograph as a whole. In the third photograph, Lenin's baleful visage casts its paternalistic and controlling authority over the most dynamic and individualistic figures in the entire series: the vaulter, the leaper, the equestrian, the cyclist, and the motorcyclist. Yet another photograph (not in this show) exhibits the same construction with the apparent exception of a diver. Yet he, too, is deindividualized by the geometrical progression of the dive: he is a one-man team of clones whose silhouettes diminish out to the horizon of the frame. A decade later Stalin, too, would cast his own paternalistic aura over an entire series of para-athletic heroes: the record-breaking Stakhanovite super-worker, the aviator, the parachutist, the long-distance skier.[33] In summary, every one of the Soviet photographs has harnessed human energy to the State.

The German and Soviet sports photographs discussed above, like most sports photography, pay homage to energy and a dynamic principle for which the athletic body in motion has become a universal symbol. If sport is not "the Esperanto of the races" (Jean Giraudoux), then which other medium is? But the body of the athlete did not evolve into an icon in a state of cultural isolation. Time and time again, we have seen this dynamic figure conjoined with (or somehow imitating) the machine, and it is only natural to inquire into the sources of this symbolic integration of muscle and metal, mechanism and mind. In retrospect, we can see that this conjunction was mandated by the pursuit of the record-breaking performance and its ethos of unlimited linear progression into unknown realms of experience. Machines, after all, are better suited than men to this pitiless quest. But it is men and not machines who are the protagonists of drama, and the pursuit of record performances is one of the defining dramas of modern man. Small wonder that the German expressionist playwright Georg Kaiser declared in a manifesto in 1929: "The purpose of being is the attainment of record achievements. Record achievements in all areas. The man of record achievements is the dominant type of this age, which will begin tomorrow and never end."[34]

The pioneering texts of this ethos were written by the madcap Italian Futurist Filippo Marinetti (1876-1944), who spread his doctrine of radical modernism, adoration of the machine, and athletic imagery across Europe during the years just before the First World War. In his "Manifesto of Futurism" (1909), Marinetti proclaimed: "Up to now literature has exalted a pensive immobility, ecstasy, and sleep. We intend to exalt aggressive action, a feverish insomnia, the racer's stride, the mortal leap, the punch and the slap." What is more, the automobile and the airplane now made possible an entirely new sensibility that expressed the new technological civilization: "We say that the world's magnificence has been enriched by a new beauty; the beauty of speed." But the full range of Marinetti's imagination – and its political dimension – emerges only at the end of the "Manifesto":

> We will sing of great crowds excited by work, by pleasure, and by riot; we will sing of the multicolored, polyphonic tides of revolution in the modern capitals; we will sing of the vibrant nightly fervor of arsenals and shipyards blazing with violent electric moons; greedy railway stations that devour smoke-plumed serpents; factories hung on clouds by the crooked lines of their smoke; bridges that stride the rivers like giant gymnasts, flashing in the sun with a glitter of knives; adventurous steamers that sniff the horizon; deep-chested locomotives whose wheels paw the tracks like the hooves of enormous steel horses bridled by tubing; and the sleek flight of planes whose propellers chatter in the wind like banners and seem to cheer like an enthusiastic crowd.[35]

Marinetti visited both Berlin (in 1913) and St. Petersburg (in 1914),[36] and his legacy can be found in most of the photographs discussed above: the mobilization of "excited" masses on behalf of "revolution," the metaphorical fusions of men and machines, the ambition to release unprecedented energies on behalf of unimagined goals, sheer dynamism as a self-evident virtue, athleticism as a fundamental idiom to express the modern. Surrounded, surfeited, and disoriented by the proliferation of such images in our own experiential universe, we may well envy Marinetti his presence at the birth of this new world, as well as the seminal powers, the ecstatic freshness of vision, that witnessed its creation.

ENDNOTES

1. Arnd Krüger, *Sport und Politik: Von Turnvater Jahn zum Staatsamateur* (Hannover: Fackelträger-Verlag, 1975), 24.
2. This tradition continued, although in a less primitive and overt fashion, after 1945. The former German Democratic Republic's extraordinary investment in high-performance sport continued the nationalistic exploitation of the German athlete under the ideological auspices of Marxism-Leninism. Nor should one underestimate the political importance of the (state-funded) sports establishment of the Federal Republic, its hunger for Olympic medals, and its long and unhappy athletic competition with the East German state it has now absorbed.
3. See Giselher Spitzer, *Der deutsche Naturismus* (Ahrensburg bei Hamburg: Verlag Ingrid Czwalina, 1983).
4. Hans Kohn, *The Mind of Germany: The Education of a Nation* (New York: Harper Torchbooks, 1965), 85-86.
5. Hermann Eich, *The Germans* (Briarcliff Manor, N.Y.: Stein and Day, 1965), 12.
6. Peter Fritzsche, "Planes, Pilots and Patriots: Aviation and German Nationalism," *Tel Aviver Jahrbuch für deutsche Geschichte* 18 (1989), 432.
7. Werner Forssmann, *Experiments on Myself: Memoirs of a Surgeon in Germany* (New York: Saint Martin's Press, 1974), 21.
8. Robert Wohl, *The Generation of 1914* (Cambridge, Mass.: Harvard University Press, 1979), 43.
9. Jeffrey Herf, *Reactionary Modernism: Technology, culture, and politics in Weimar and the Third Reich* (New York: Cambridge University Press, 1984), 1.
10. Ibid., 66.
11. John Willett, *Art & Politics in the Weimar Period: The New Sobriety 1917-1933* (New York: Pantheon Books, 1978), 102.
12. Willy Meisl, *Sport am Scheidewege* (Heidelberg, 1928), quoted in Siegfried Moosburger, *Ideologie und Leibeserziehung im 19. und 20. Jahrhundert* (Ahrensburg bei Hamburg: Verlag Ingrid Czwalina, 1972), 113.
13. Wolfgang Rothe, "When Sports Conquered the Republic: A Forgotten Chapter from the 'Roaring Twenties,'" *Studies in Twentieth Century Literature* 4 (1980), 9.
14. "The actor," says the quasi-mystical Artaud, "is an athlete of the heart. . . . What the athlete depends upon in running is what the actor depends upon in shouting a passionate curse, but the actor's course is altogether interior. All the tricks of wrestling, boxing, the hundred yard dash, high-jumping, etc., find analogous organic

bases in the movement of the passions; they have the same physical points of support." See Antonin Artaud, *The Theater and its Double* (1938; New York: Grove Press, 1958), 133.

15. Bertolt Brecht, "Mehr guten Sport," *Berliner Börsen-Courier,* February 6, 1926.

16. John Willett, *Art and Politics in the Weimar Period* (New York: Pantheon Books, 1978), 103.

17. Eich, *The Germans*, 65.

18. Nazi interior minister Dr. Wilhelm Frick, quoted in Gilmer W. Blackburn, *Education in the Third Reich: Race and History in Nazi Textbooks* (Albany: State University of New York Press, 1985), 97.

19. Hajo Bernett, ed., *Nationalistische Leibeserziehung* (Schondorf bei Stuttgart: Verlag Karl Hoffmann, 1973), 22; Winfried Joch, *Politische Leibeserziehung und ihre Theorie im Nationalsozialistischen Deutschland* (Frankfurt am Main: Peter Lang, 1976), 26.

20. For a well-known critique of Riefenstahl as an amoral aesthete and political opportunist, see Susan Sontag, "Fascinating Fascism," in *Under the Sign of Saturn* (New York: Farrar, Straus & Giroux, 1980), 73-105.

21. Richard D. Mandell, *The Nazi Olympics* (New York: Macmillan Company, 1971), 258.

22. For an account of this conflict, see John Hoberman, *The Olympic Crisis: Sport, Politics and the Moral Order* (New Rochelle, N.Y.: Aristide D. Caratzas, 1986), 103-4.

23. Quoted in Arnd Krüger, *Die Olympischen Spiele 1936 und die Weltmeinung* (Berlin, Munich, Frankfurt am Main: Verlag Bartels & Wernitz KG, 1972), 33.

24. "That the success of the eleventh Olympiad gave Hitler an enormous boost, both moral and political, nobody could deny. The world came to Berlin, and, with the exception of a few cynics, the world was overwhelmed with admiration for what it had seen." See Duff Hart-Davis, *Hitler's Games: The 1936 Olympics* (New York: Harper & Row, 1986), 228.

25. Quoted in Mandell, *The Nazi Olympics*, 218.

26. See, for example, Sontag, "Fascinating Fascism," 88-90.

27. Robert Werner Schulte, *Eignungs- und Leistungsprüfung im Sport* (Berlin: Verlag Guido Hackebeil A.-G., 1925).

28. On the Workers' Olympiads, see Hoberman, *The Olympic Crisis*, 107-8.

29. Helmut Wagner, *Sport und Arbeitersport* (1931; Cologne: Pahl-Rugenstein, 1973), 181.

30. René Fuelopp-Miller, *The Mind and Face of Bolshevism* (1926; New York: Harper Torchbooks, 1965), 24-25.

31. Kurt Johansson, *Aleksej Gastev: Proletarian Bard of the Machine Age* (Stockholm: University of Stockholm, 1983), 104, 112.

32. See James Riordan, *Sport in Soviet Society: Development of Sport and Physical Education in Russia and the USSR* (Cambridge: Cambridge University Press, 1977), 68-81.

33. Katerina Clark, "Utopian Anthropology as a Context for Stalinist Literature," in *Stalinism: Essays in Historical Interpretation*, ed. Robert C. Tucker (New York: W.W. Norton & Company, 1977), 182, 187, 190-91.

34. Georg Kaiser, "Man in the Tunnel," in *Anthology of German Expressionist Drama*, ed. Walter H. Sokel (Garden City, N.Y.: Anchor Books, 1963), 13-14.

35. Filippo Marinetti, "The Founding and Manifesto of Futurism" [1909], in *Marinetti: Selected Writings*, ed. R.W. Flint (New York: Farrar, Straus & Giroux, 1972), 41-42.

36. Peter Gay, *Weimar Culture* (New York: Harper Torchbooks, 1970), 6; Anna Lawton, introduction to *Russian Futurism through its Manifestoes, 1912-1928*, ed. Anna Lawton and Herbert Eagle (Ithaca and London: Cornell University Press, 1988), 16-17.

Protocols of Innocence
Photography and the American Sports Fan

He was rawboned and taciturn, the farm boy who was the best athlete in the semi-rural high school where he was a senior and I was in seventh or eighth grade in the middle of the 1950s. A miserable transplant from a large city, I could hardly distinguish him from the local louts whose answers to the problem of small-town boredom included making my life a small-town suffering. Then I saw a photograph in the school paper. It was an action shot taken with flash at a track meet at dusk of him high jumping, straining over the bar in the penultimate moment of the old scissors kick. He had no style to speak of, just strength and will. His face and limbs were grotesquely contorted – sinews popping out in places I didn't know someone could have sinews – as he made his body a slack-jawed ungainly thing to clear the barrier. The high-contrast photograph was fearfully ugly, with livid whites of flesh bleached by the flashbulb and black shadows of muscles. It had a nakedness about it, and a bravery. Its use in the paper had to signify "school spirit," recognizing a feat on "our" behalf, and, indeed, I felt one of my occasional frail surges of loyalty to that town I hated. But the picture also unclenched wilder stuff: emotions of social alienation and yearning, perhaps, and sexual intimidation and fascination, among other syndromes of my adolescence. In streets and hallways thereafter I would furtively stare at him, trying to find in his ill-favored appearance the heroic aspect it had in the photograph. I couldn't. The violent glamor of the image remained rather an abstract attribute of his person, or else his person persisted as an awkward pendant to the image. Though the school was small, I never spoke to him, because I didn't dare, and he never spoke to me, because why should he?

I have begun this essay on sports photography with my memory of a successful sports photograph. In my case, you might say the photograph was exceptionally successful. The photographer can scarcely have hoped for so extravagant an effect, but the effect was no mere fantasy on my part. All vocational photographers, like all artists and media artisans of any sort, angle to catch souls, whether they are conscious of it or not. Most photographers are not conscious of it, mechanically deploying motifs that, having once caught souls, linger as clichés. But even the tiredest convention may ignite somebody's spirit if, for instance, the person is young and grasps the convention's primitive content for the first time as if suddenly understanding something in a foreign language. Part of my memory is a confused awareness of my participation in the power of the image: I was making it happen, somehow, even as it made something happen in me. (I couldn't actually believe this. I had to test it by looking for the whole cause of my thrill in the athlete.) That was a moment of initiation. I entered into an ordinary mystery, an open secret, of my culture, a mystery of innocence vested in the contemplation of sports. We will not comprehend much about sports in the United States, and about the photography and other media that weave them into many lives, if we do not appreciate their character as protocols of innocence, preserving and amplifying guileless raptures into adulthood. Like certain kinds of artistic experience, grown-up sports fandom is a subterranean escape hatch to untrammeled early states of mind. Thinking about the protocols' unconscious patterns will help us gauge the conscious departures of some exceptional photographers in this exhibition, who bring shadowy meanings of sport into the light of art.

The high jump picture was a very American type of shot, an example of what I will call the *Sports Illustrated* paradigm: combining admiration of a particular athlete with connoisseurship of a moment peculiar to a given sport (see cats. 101, 106, 174, pages 46, 55). Glance at any sports magazine or newspaper sports page in this country. What Americans like in sports photography is a fused double concentration on the dancer and the dance. The second baseman leaping to elude a sliding runner while turning a double play, the basketball player soaring for a dunk — images ever the same and new, like Byzantine icons. What we don't like is anything extraneous to dancer and dance. Suppressed especially in the *Sports Illustrated* paradigm is the detailed presence of other observers, whose alternative angles on the action would spoil the illusion that we have the uniquely privileged view. Shallow depth of field, like fast film, is a technical given, presenting a thin slice of the world's space in a splitsecond of time. Nothing could be less like how humans normally see. Unaided eyesight is approximate, an affair of constant, darting refocusings in space and, in time, of awareness that slides back and forth over the beat of the present: into the past, absorbing what has been seen, and into the future, anticipating what will be seen next. Only the camera can afford undistracted instantaneous vision, memorializing lightning-quick crises of action that we otherwise sense without really seeing. This superiority of photography to the human sensorium is the basis of its value for the sports fan. Is what I am saying true of any photography of motion? Yes, but minus the aspect of ritual that marks the work of the sports photographer (as also the work of the television slow-motion replay director, whose decisions throughout a game can seem a flowing encyclopedia of photographic conventions). The aspect of ritual binds pictorial craft to a practice of observation that is also an *observance*.

It has been said before that modern spectator sport is not just served by photography but is photography's creation. Such is plainly the case of *professional* sport, whose city-based franchises travesty the communal identifications that give people an emotional stake in amateur contests. (Amateurism in sport of course becomes ever rarer in fact than in name as our culture of spectacle burgeons; think only of the corporatizing of college football.) To be effective in mass culture — professional culture, made not by artists with passions but by specialists with job descriptions — sport must be mediated, because it is not in itself a medium. Consider the experience of a fan at a ballpark. What I witness has features of theatrical performance (that of the circus, say), but unlike theater it is not structured for effect. It is not aimed at me. It is self-contained and self-directed, just baseball occurring — a *game* that grown men are toiling at, essentially oblivious to an audience. (Fans tend to resent players who showboat for the crowd, rupturing the game's containment; though certain stars, contained in their own signature auras, are indulged.) The game happens in a kind of transparent bubble from which I am excluded. My irrelevance to it is, in a real way, absolute. (That I am a customer helping to pay the players' salaries hardly constitutes a bond; it is disenthralling, if anything.) For how long could I bear my exclusion and irrelevance if I had no relief from them? But there is relief. The next morning I open the newspaper and see the game I attended spread out in pictures, words, and statistics. I savor these slowly, sinking into the warm flow of irrational caring — innocence regained — that is fandom. Modern fandom is an artificial agreement of the individual with the mass, an agreement to pretend to care, in ways ideally indistinguishable from true caring, about something insignificant. The agreement would wither in a year if deprived of media irrigation.

What, then, of the mystery I found, and through memory can find again at will, in the high-jump picture? But for its tincture of "school spirit," my response to the image had nothing directly to do with fandom. I was no more then than I am now a fan of track-and-field events. It had to do with an aroused susceptibility of mine that, together with the craft and luck of the photographer, constituted the image as a symbol. In other words, the picture functioned for me like a work of art. The memory of it gives me a mental pivot on which to turn from conventions of sports photography to the searching qualities of many photographs in this show which in quest of specific truths disdain to reinforce the fan's pretense of caring. These photographs reflect the nature of thematic art (work both really thematic and really art), which is to be inside and outside its subject at the same time. The picture I remember satisfied this definition, albeit accidentally, as at once a celebration of the high-jump and an estrangement from it. It showed me the idiosyncrasy of an athlete and the character — the technique, the ordeal — of a sporting event, but with powerful detail transcending the event. (The detail was intrinsically photographic, peculiar to a Weegee-like use of flash in darkness.) Photographs in the present exhibition achieve analogous effects on purpose, identifying with some essence of a subject even, or especially, while distancing it. As sports pictures, they do so with a purity unavailable to other genres. The purity derives from the nature of sport as an activity already, like art, aesthetic and gratuitous, though lacking art's forming consciousness. The serious photographer of sports must introduce that consciousness without destroying the innocent absorption, like a sleepwalker's trance, that makes sport interesting enough to photograph in the first place.

Consider one perfect picture, Stephen Shore's 1978 view of New York Yankees star Graig Nettles practicing batting in the cage of a pitching machine (cat. 128, page 58). The immediate focus is on the resplendently uniformed player, fiercely concentrated in his batting stance. Note the straight diagonal line through his bat and down his left side to the ground. He is shifting his weight to his left foot in the first phase of a classically articulated swing. The figure might as well be an image razored out of the photograph of an actual game in a roaring stadium. Nettles could not bat an iota more beautifully if the World Series were on the line. But the figure is not in a game. He performs in autistic solitude amid a bizarre maze of pitching-machine cages, which in turn occupies an indifferent landscape. (It is Fort Lauderdale, Florida, during spring training.) These testifying data — someone to all appearances playing baseball, paraphernalia for simulating baseball, and a swatch of the wide world oblivious to baseball — are a laminate of realities, a three-tone scale from inside to outside the game. Fans and non-fans alike, I think, must respond to the delectable strangeness of the image. Fans of a traditional sort may find it vaguely upsetting. Shore's eye for fissures among disparate realities coolly exposes what a fan of course knows but cringes from admitting: the meaninglessness of the game. (Speaking of fissures, remember the 1989 World Series, interrupted by an earthquake? The two games that followed the disaster, exposed in their triviality, were spiritless and grueling for all concerned.) The style of Shore's photograph is exact to the late seventies, when younger American artists and intellectuals, with or without boosts from critical theory, became caught up in skeptical attitudes toward mass culture. On a vernacular level, the shift in sensibility fostered, among other things, eighties-style David-Lettermanish hipness about popular genres: sort of "I-love-how-ridiculous-it-is-to-love-this." Shore's photography announces an apparent end to innocence, but it leaves open a sophisticated recourse of innocence to the protective coloration of irony (the facetiousness dissembling passion that is the common tone of sports talk among educated folk nowadays). Shore, an artist, got all of this in one disenchanted and riveted glance, and I am glad to pay tribute to a great photograph that has haunted me ever since I saw it reproduced at the time. It helps me find another meaning in my high-jump picture. Like Graig Nettles's uncanny focus on a ball popping out of a gismo, the preposterousness of the jumper's exertion, in clearing a barrier that bars no one, was part of the image's crazy appeal. No worldly activity other than sport, except maybe war, entails as an obligatory matter of course such desperate spasms of effort.

Shore's photograph is subtly anti-heroic – deflating its subject from mythic status to a representation of skilled professionalism – in a way always somewhat typical of American sports fandom and increasingly definitive of it. Fans no sooner fixate on a star player than they seek to measure the mere person behind the reputation. American sports journalism sometimes resembles a seminar in amateur psychology and character analysis. The scrutiny is rarely prying and malicious in the manner of celebrity gossip (though edgier tones have crept into sports columns with the astronomical growth of players' salaries and presumptions). Rather, the attention seems bent on democratically bringing down to regular human scale, if possible, incidental aspects of an athlete's personality, the better to contemplate with undistracted admiration the eminence of the athlete's performance. American fans adore (with due allowance for twinges of envy) the superiority of the star athlete, but do so fairly strictly on the basis of talent and of efficiency and grace in fulfilling the talent. Apparent exceptions – Babe Ruth, Muhammad Ali (cat. 108, page 114) – are larger-than-life individuals whose charisma spills beyond sport and disarms the fan's scrutiny. Such meta-stars dominate mediation by inventing the terms on which they will be regarded, leaving fans no choice but simply to worship them – we fans perhaps laughing a bit with embarrassment at our subjection, but delighted nonetheless. (Michael Jordan, Platonic model of the American sports star, does not fit this description. An unassuming man, Jordan can seem as much an interested spectator of his own incredible ability as we are.) Nickolas Muray's 1927 portrait of Babe Ruth, the vision of a primeval beast in a baseball uniform (with phallic bat enfolded by huge paws), is a great American document because, try as one might, one cannot avoid the feeling that Ruth himself, not the photographer, authored it (cat. 36, page 88). (At the Baseball Hall of Fame in Cooperstown, New York, there is a deliriously entertaining wall of publicity photographs of Ruth, his gargantuan aplomb triumphing over improbable circumstances including *cowboy regalia* and a *Girl Scout cookie drive.* Photographers who pointed cameras at the Babe took the best pictures of their careers.) Muray's photograph jumps out at me with undimmed freshness equal to Shore's, signaling the permanence of its truth. For an instructive contrast, consider the jolting dissonance of the 1941 photograph by W. Eugene Smith, *American Football* (cat. 76, page 98). The heroizing low-angled composition of a quarterback firing a pass while surrounded by hurtling bodies is like a frieze of Achilles launching a fatal spear. The picture's qualities of abstract and balletic form give it a chilly exaltation, at once gorgeous and, apropos American sport, all wrong. For an antidote, look at Garry Winogrand's eye-level sideline football shot (cat. 116, page 106), dispassionately taking in the helter-skelter of an unusually dispersed play (a screen pass?) from behind the substantial rear end of a crouching referee in a crowded stadium on an autumnal Saturday in Texas, U.S.A.

The protocols of innocence in American sport, of which journalistic sports photographs are more or less calculated instruments and signs, depend on rigid separation of games from other spheres of life. But those other spheres may be freely projected and reconstituted in the arena, the transparent bubble. My high-jump picture could function for me as a soul-stirring symbol — of masculinity feared, desired, despaired of — precisely because it was contained by rules of a sport and conventions of the sport's representation. The important part of the story, for me, is that I wanted and failed to reconcile the hero of the picture with the senior carrying books in the hall. (His name was Gale Sprute.) I had yet to develop the benignly schizophrenic American knack for enjoying mass culture, sports especially: a play of real feelings secured by the tacit irreality of their object. Like dreams, sports engage one's full emotions while underway, then dissipate to nothing. In calling this pattern benign, incidentally, I do not mean to gloss over its routine cynical exploitation. A lot is done with our feelings while they are in the molten projected state. Mostly, they are flavored with gross admixtures of commercialism. (All of us are inured to the hucksterization of sport up to a point. I draw the line at a beer company that obliges television baseball announcers to salute home-team home runs as occasions for another dose of malted alcohol: "Hey, [name of homerun hitter], this [beer]'s for you!" Advertisers who defile the bliss of a home run, when the best sportscasters instinctively fall silent, would insinuate messages into our lovemaking, if they could.) Less frequent in the United States are attempts to inject fandom with political content beyond occasional generic patriotism. The 1991 Super Bowl halftime show, replete with yellow ribbons for "our troops in the Gulf," was as politically charged as American sports mediation gets. While repelling some of us, it wasn't exactly Leni Riefenstahl.

In art that involves photography, we are emerging from a period that, beginning in the late seventies, has been obsessed with exposing mass-cultural manipulations. Much of the work, naively skeptical, simultaneously belabors the obvious (not lost on mass culture's seasoned consumers) and misses its point (the consenting-adult transactions I term protocols of innocence). But some work in this vein is unnervingly brilliant at revealing the mechanics of media psychology, the triggers of our dreamlike collective pleasures, without imposing tedious judgments. Such is the work of Jeff Koons, whose series of cunningly altered Nike advertising posters of basketball stars is undeservedly much less well known than his sculpture (cat. 165, page 62). The posters must be viewed in person to be comprehended, because Koons's physical alterations of the images, rendered with the same printing screens by the same commercial firm that did the originals, vanish in reproduction, their use of sumptuous oil dyes instead of inks on snowy linen instead of paper. The subliminal effect of these substitutions is to kick up the seductiveness of the posters just enough to send it over the top of a viewer's habituated resistance to commercial blandishment, exciting the mental reflexes that the ad campaigners counted on. (The Nike campaign in question communicated to a target audience of basketball-addicted boys the feel-good conceit of a superstar aristocracy defined by cool nicknames, such as Silk, and of course de rigueur footwear.) By amplifying, rather than deconstructing, the American blurring of fandom and consumerism, Koons affords no refuge of an intellectually detached point of view. To look at his posters is to experience at full force and in untippable balance the tug and the repulsion of media that play so finely on our feelings to such crude ends. Thus humiliating viewers' pride in their immunity to kitsch, this artist has often been condemned in the way of a messenger blamed for the message he delivers. We would do better simply to swallow Dr. Koons's medicine of queasy consciousness, say thank you, and get on with our grievously equivocal lives.

Having begun this essay with a reference to a sports photograph in a Midwestern town, I end with another, David Graham's *The Post Bulletins Practicing at Graham Park, Rochester, Minnesota,* 1988 (cat.182, cover). A decidedly unformidable gridiron team takes posture instruction from an off-camera coach in an industrial neighborhood crowned by a water tower shaped like an ear of corn. The salad of realities somewhat recalls Stephen Shore's Graig Nettles picture, except that in Graham's shot the disjunctions are far from crisp. The amateur players approximate professional, let alone mythic, ideals of football only wishfully, in their own minds. (They are adorable.) They are not spiritually separate from the background factories, whose workaday quiddity defines them more than their helmets and pads do. The photographer's choice to center his composition on the water tower pronounces an ambiguous judgment: *corny.* This is a corny culture whose pursuits can only be corny. How we feel about that – in what measure alienated, in what measure resigned – is a choice given by the picture's ambiguity. The choice is anything but rich or dignified, but it represents freedom of a sort that must satisfy those of us determined both to share in our nation's available joys and not to insult our own intelligences more than we absolutely have to. There is something to be said for it. The willful foolishness of immersion in sports culture harbors an always present potential of transcendence, when some reverberating truth – some symbol – bursts clear of ordinary contingency. One of Graham's desultory footballers may on a given afternoon do or experience, in ragged play, something unforgettable for which he has no word or model. Or some such thing may register in the eye of an onlooker. Or some such thing may even emerge in the developing tray of a photographer of the event, an image to set the blood racing. A lover of sport, as of art and ultimately of life, can make no preparation for such epiphanies except jealously to maintain an appetite for awe.

GUSTAV KLUCIS
Untitled, 1928
Collection of W. Michael Sheehe, New York (cats. 39, 40, 41)

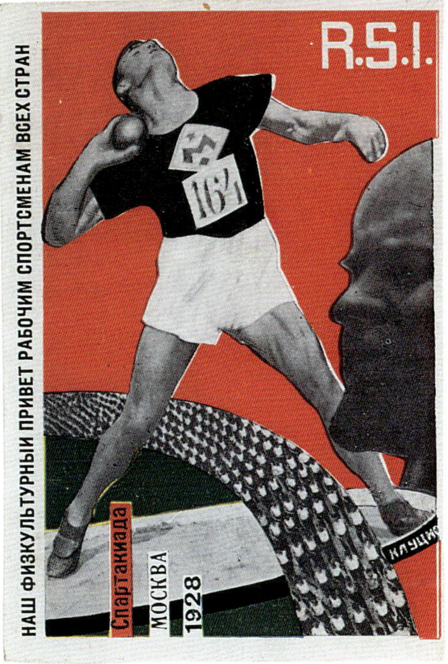

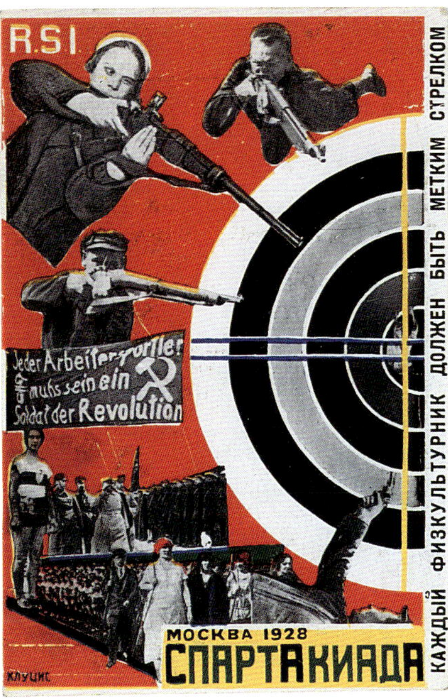

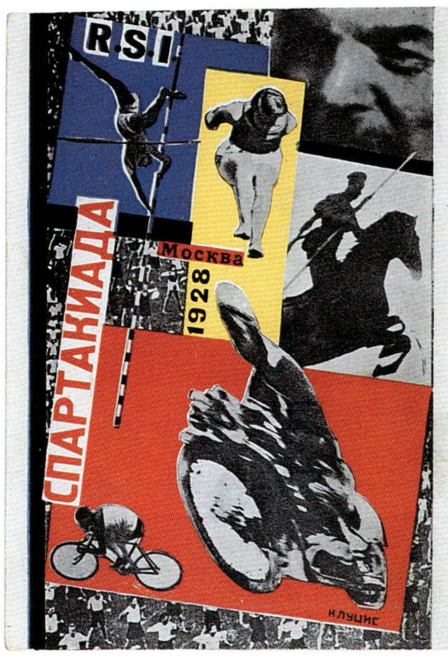

JOHN G. ZIMMERMAN
Toronto Maple Leafs Goalie Johnny Bower Kicks Away a Goal-bound Puck,
1962, printed later
Courtesy of the artist and *Sports Illustrated* (cat. 101)

NEIL LEIFER
Ali vs. Liston II, Lewiston, Maine, 1965, printed later
Courtesy of the artist and *Sports Illustrated* (cat. 106)

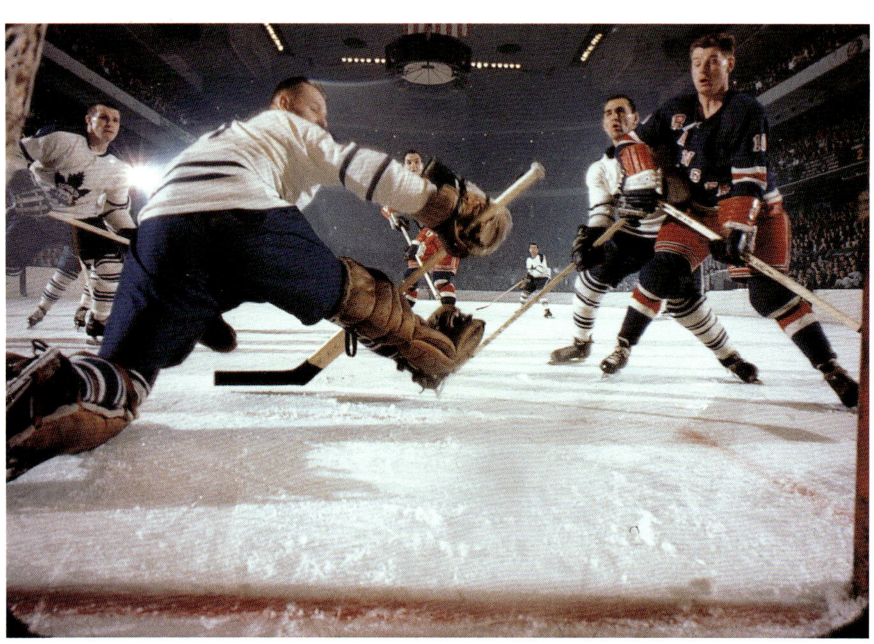

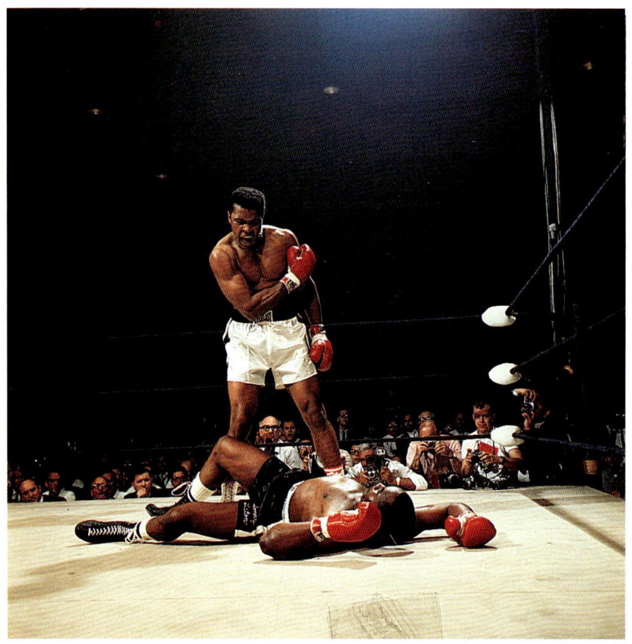

JOHN BALDESSARI
Box (Blind Fate and Culture), 1987
Collection of the Fondation Asher Edelman,
Musée d'Art Contemporain, Pully/Lausanne (cat. 178)

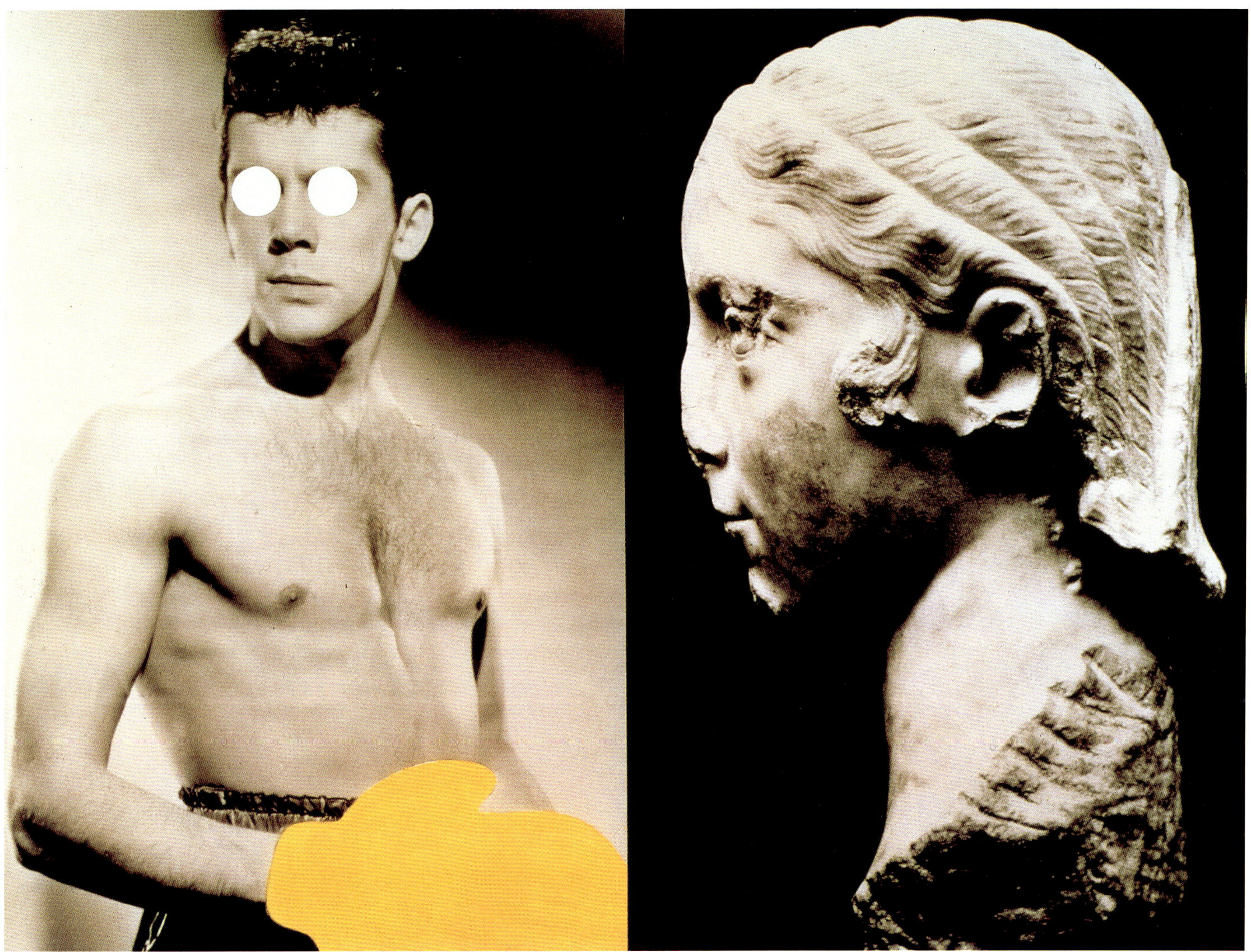

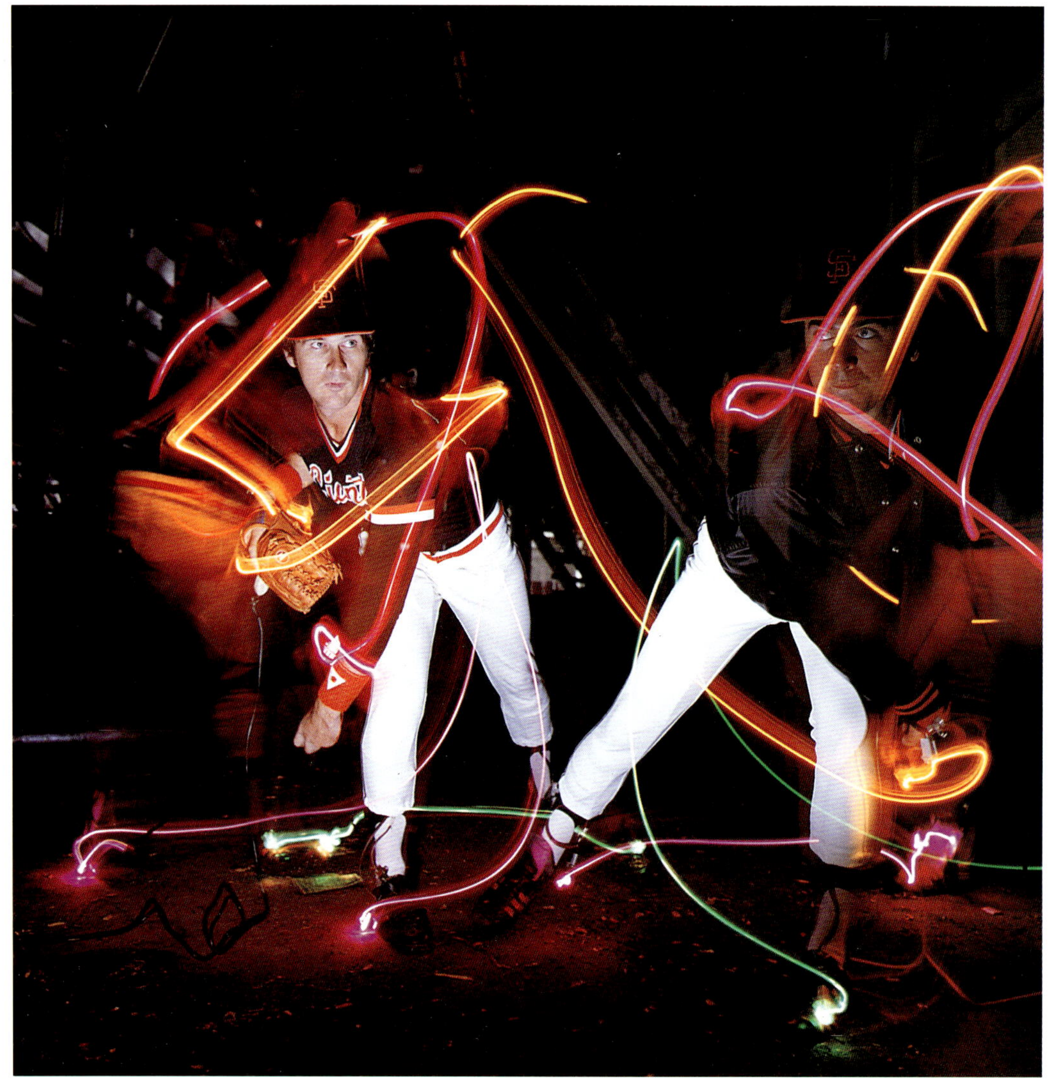

DAVID HOCKNEY
The Skater, New York, December 1982, #13, 1982
Courtesy of the artist (cat. 145)

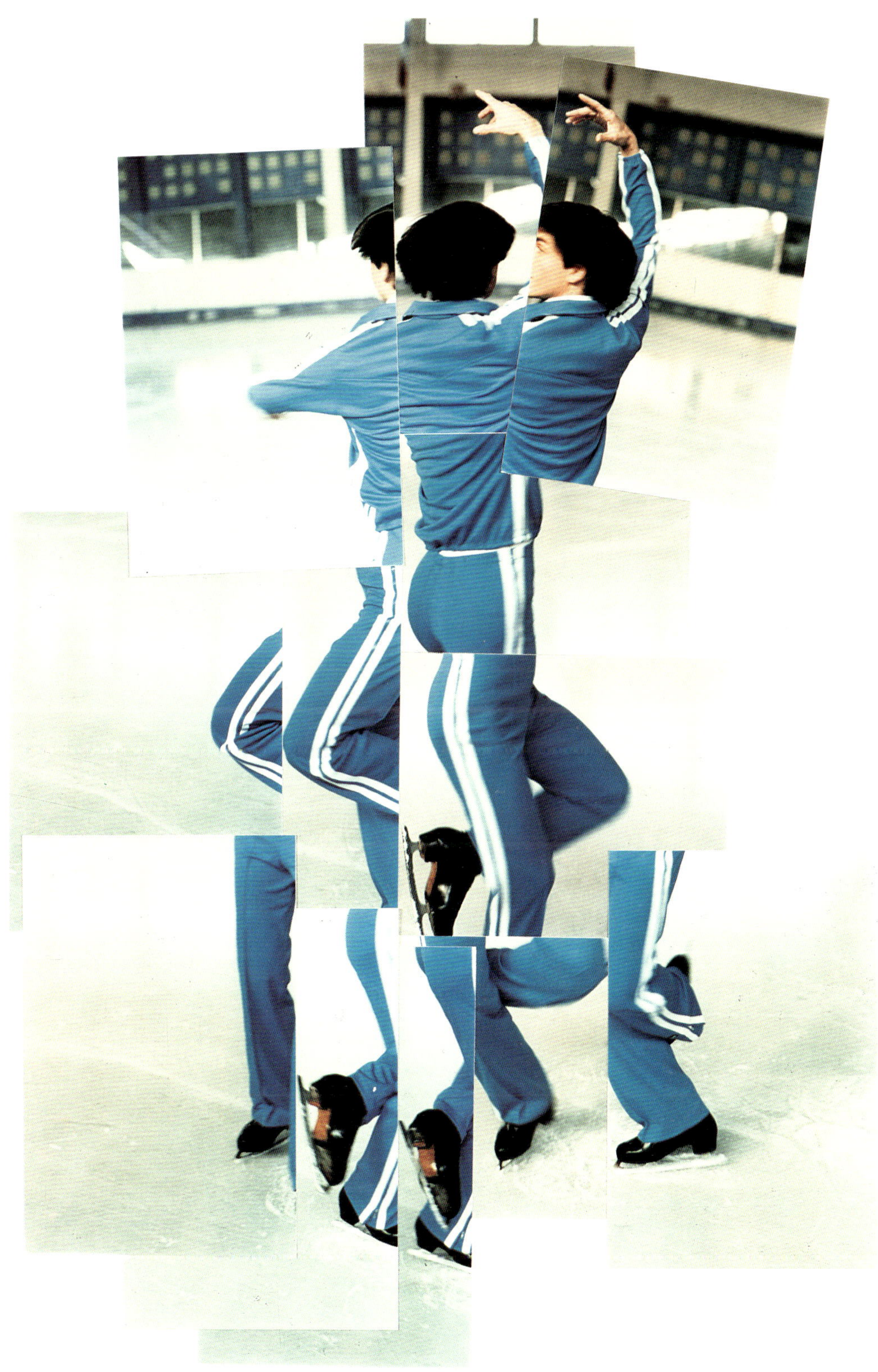

JERRY GORDON
The Breakers Hotel, Palm Beach, Florida, 1979
Collection of the High Museum of Art, Atlanta;
Gift of Lucinda Bunnen (cat. 134)

TINA BARNEY
Untitled from the album "Swimming," with text by Tina Howe, 1991
Courtesy Janet Borden, Inc., New York (cat. 193)

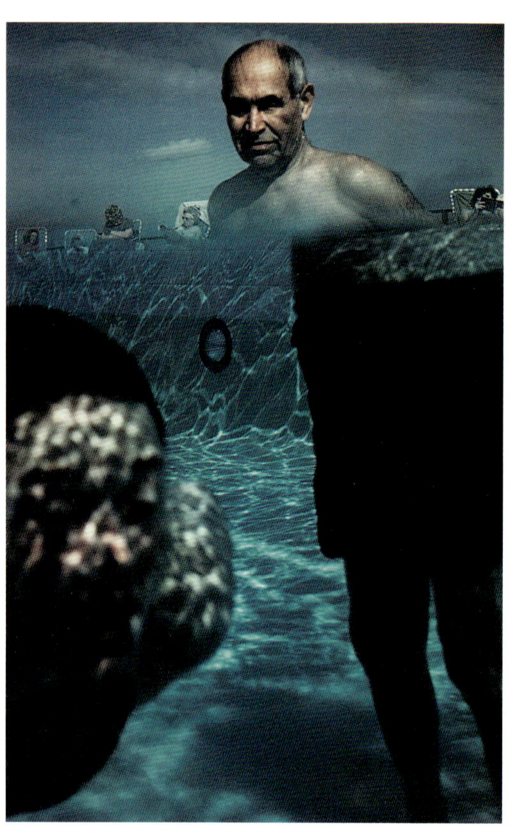

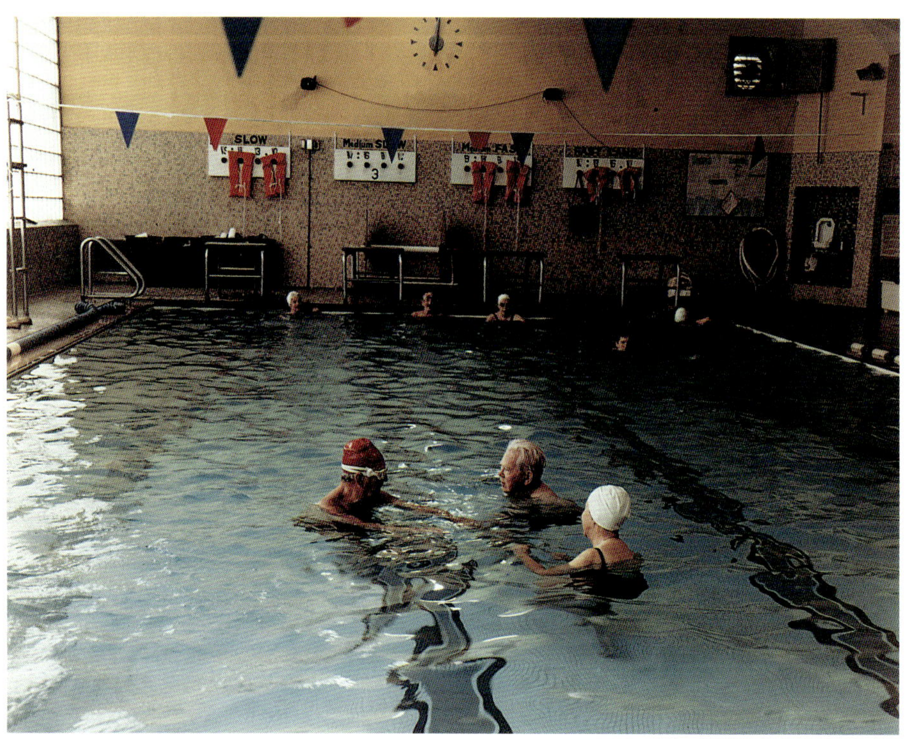

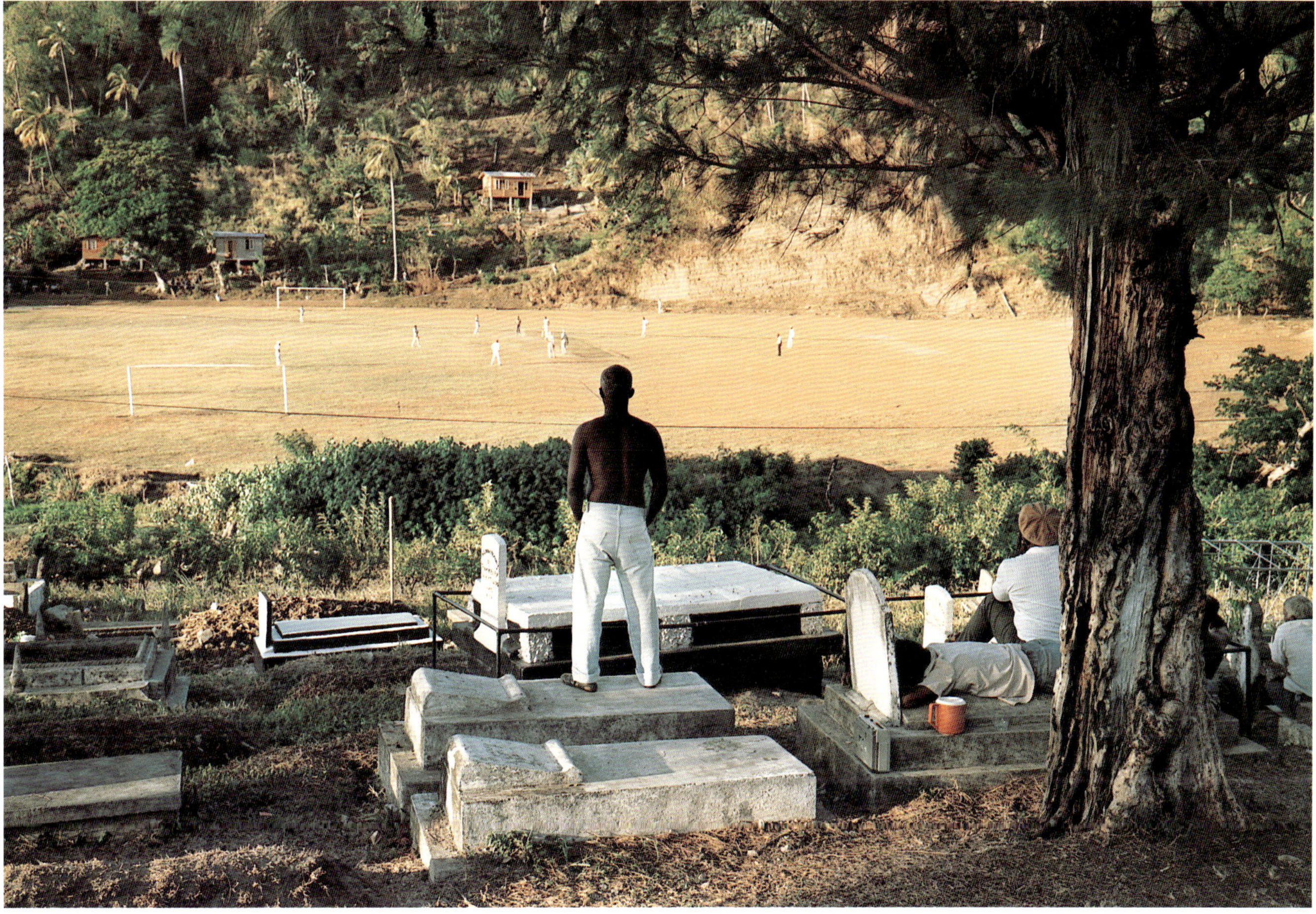

Sunday Cricket Match, Gouyave, Grenada, 1987
Courtesy of the artist (cat. 175)

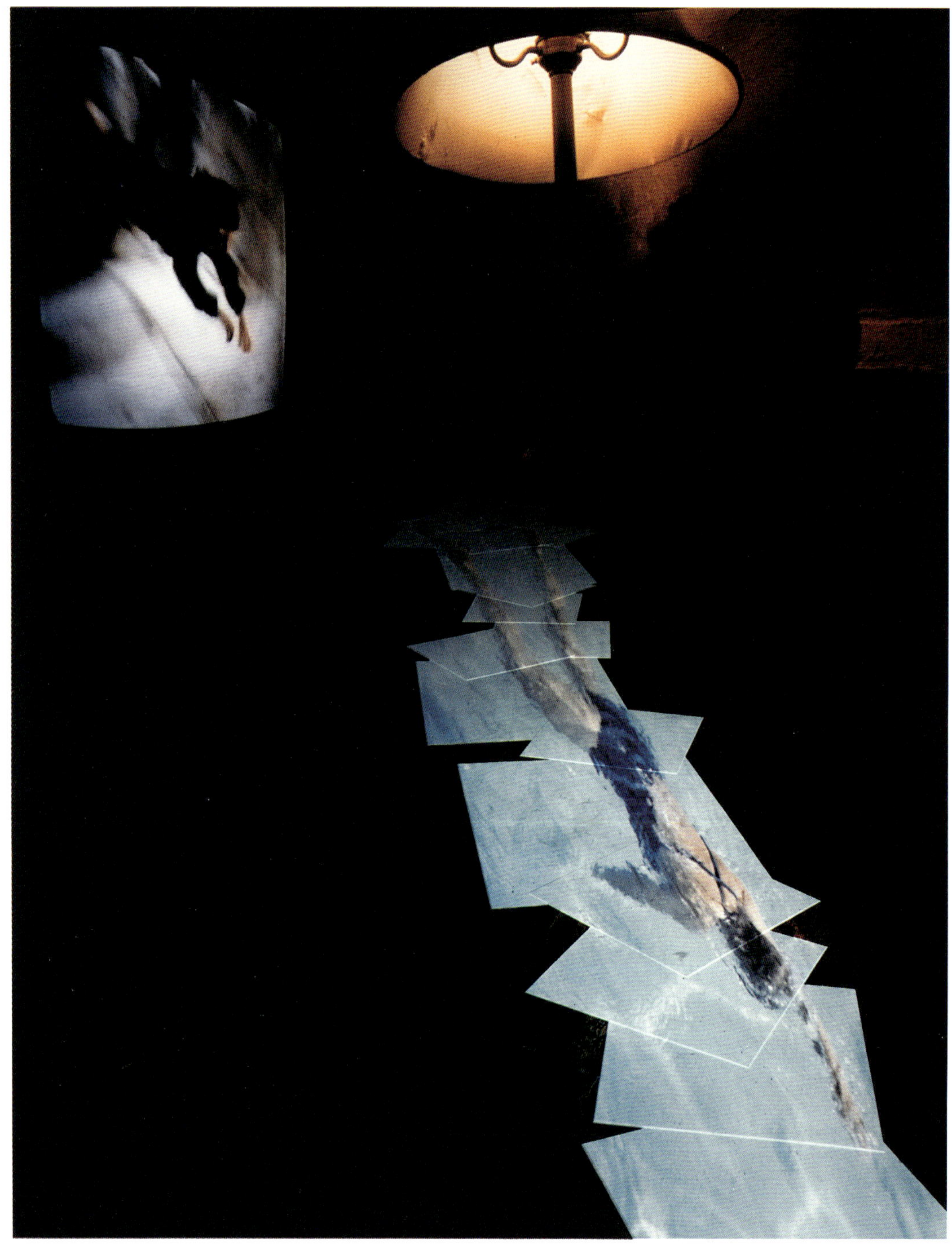

LORIE NOVAK
False Starts, 1986
Courtesy of the artist (cat. 167)

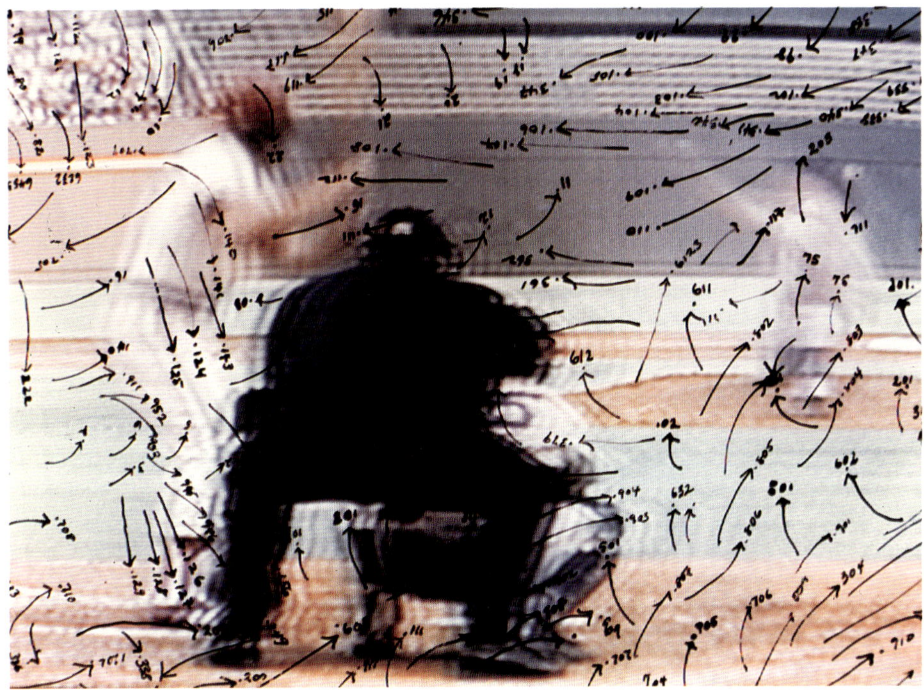

HOWARDENA PINDELL
Untitled (Video Drawing: Baseball), 1974, printed 1979
Courtesy of the artist (cat. 118)

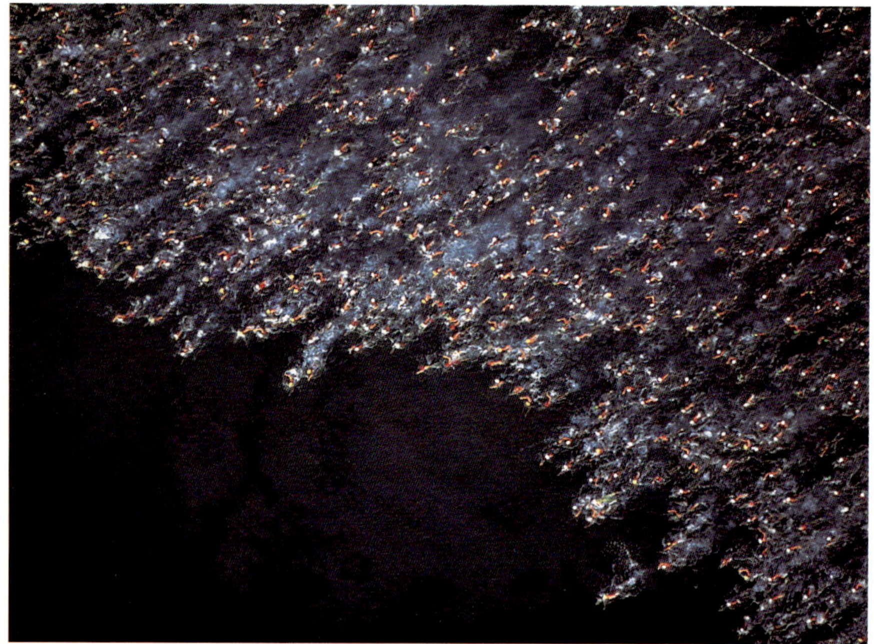

WALTER IOOSS, JR.
Michael Jordan Practicing at Illinois Benedictine College,
Lisle, Illinois, 1987, printed later
Courtesy of the artist and *Sports Illustrated* (cat. 174)

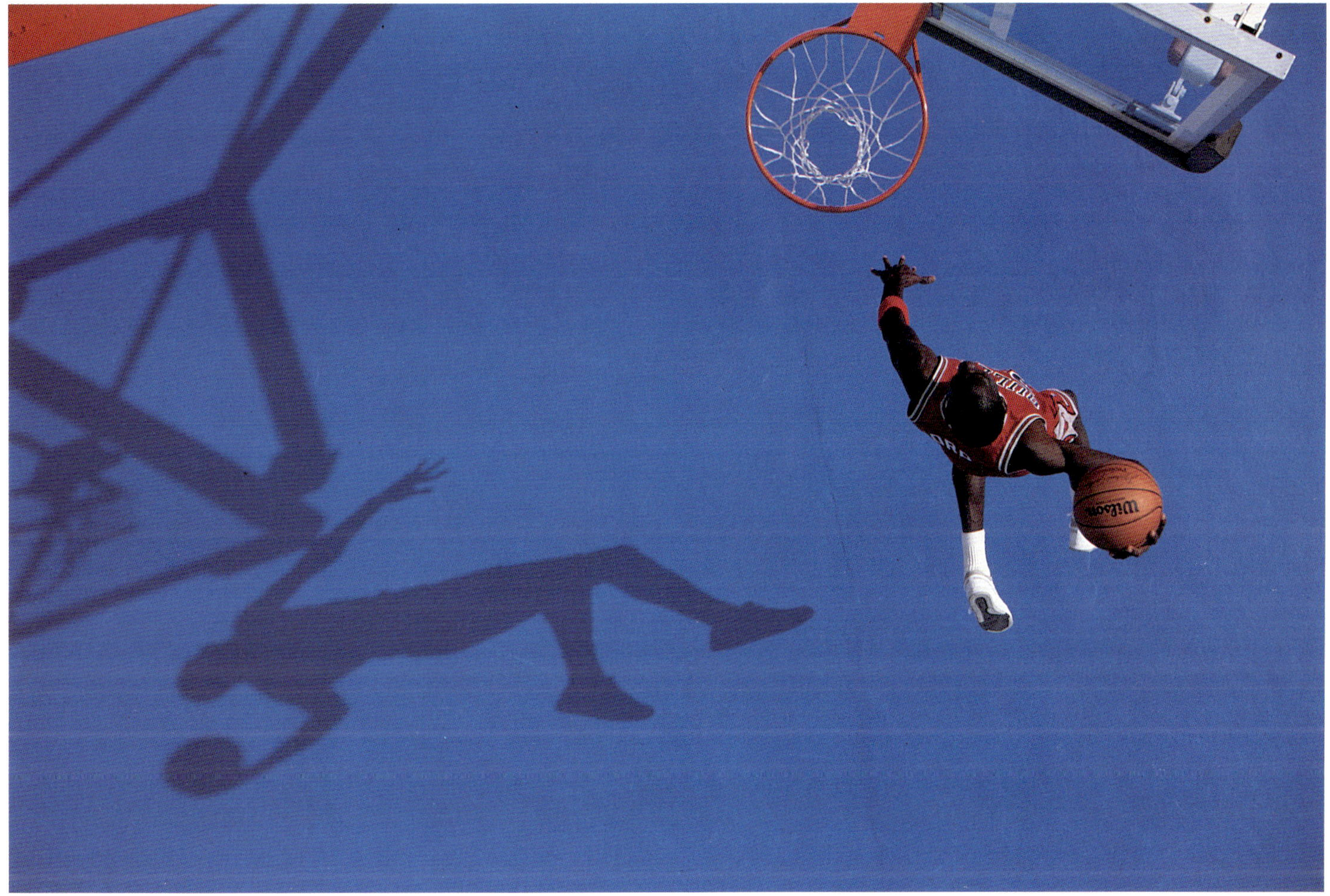

JOEL MEYEROWITZ
Atlanta, 1988
Courtesy James Danzinger Gallery, New York (cat. 184)

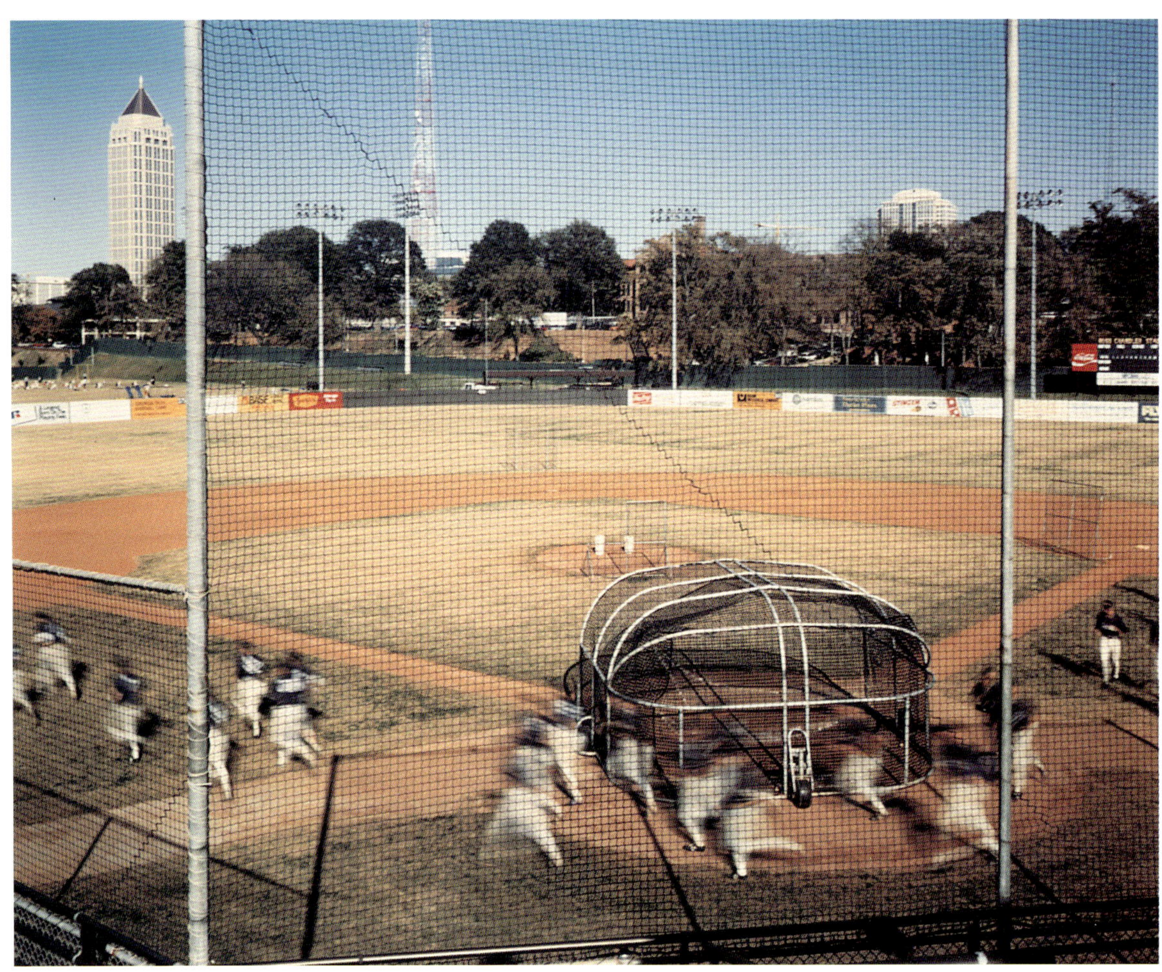

CHRIS HAMILTON
The Winning Move (Dominique Wilkins, Atlanta Hawks), 1991
Courtesy of the artist (cat. 195)

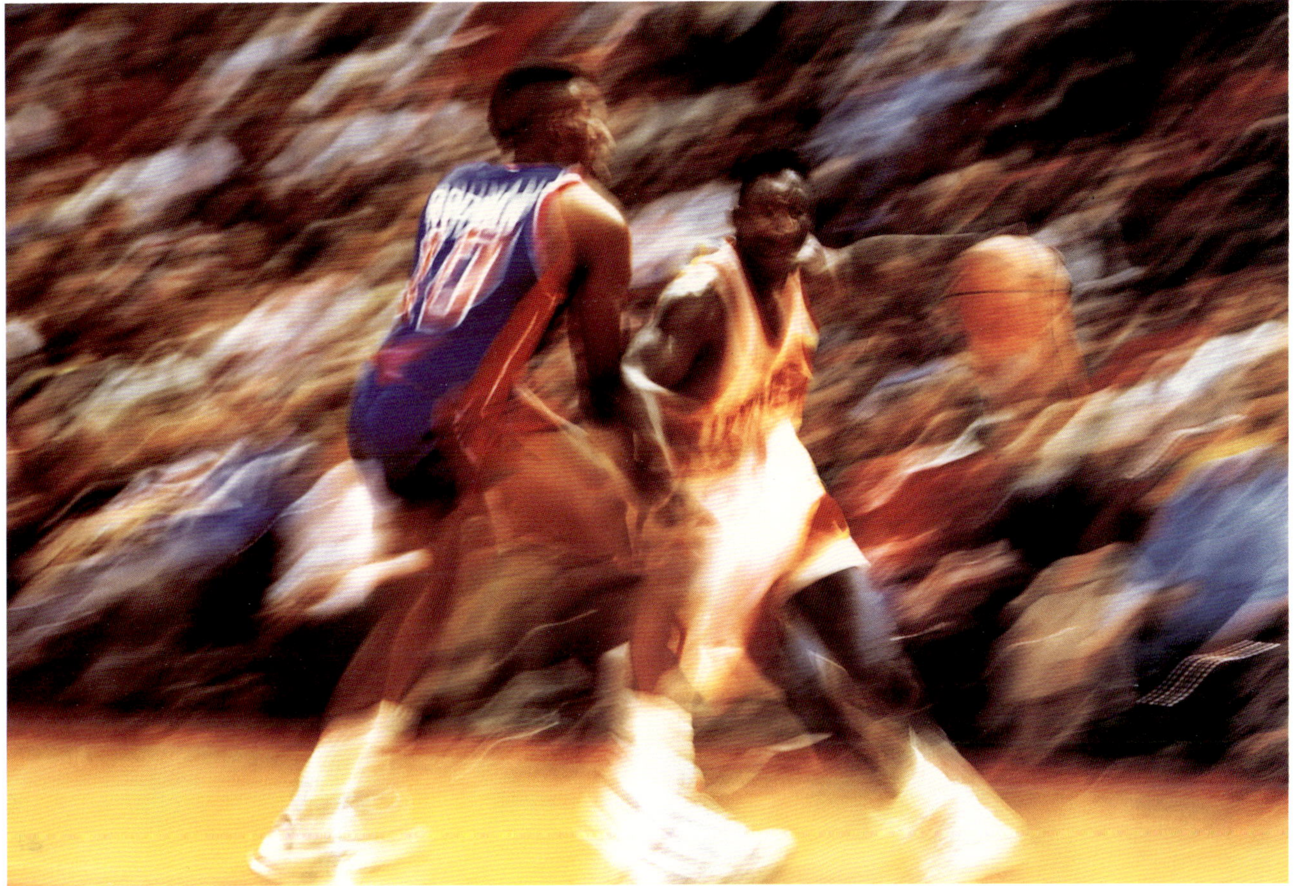

STEPHEN SHORE
*Ft. Lauderdale Yankee Stadium, Ft. Lauderdale, Florida
(Graig Nettles)*, 1978
Courtesy Pace/MacGill Gallery, New York (cat. 128)

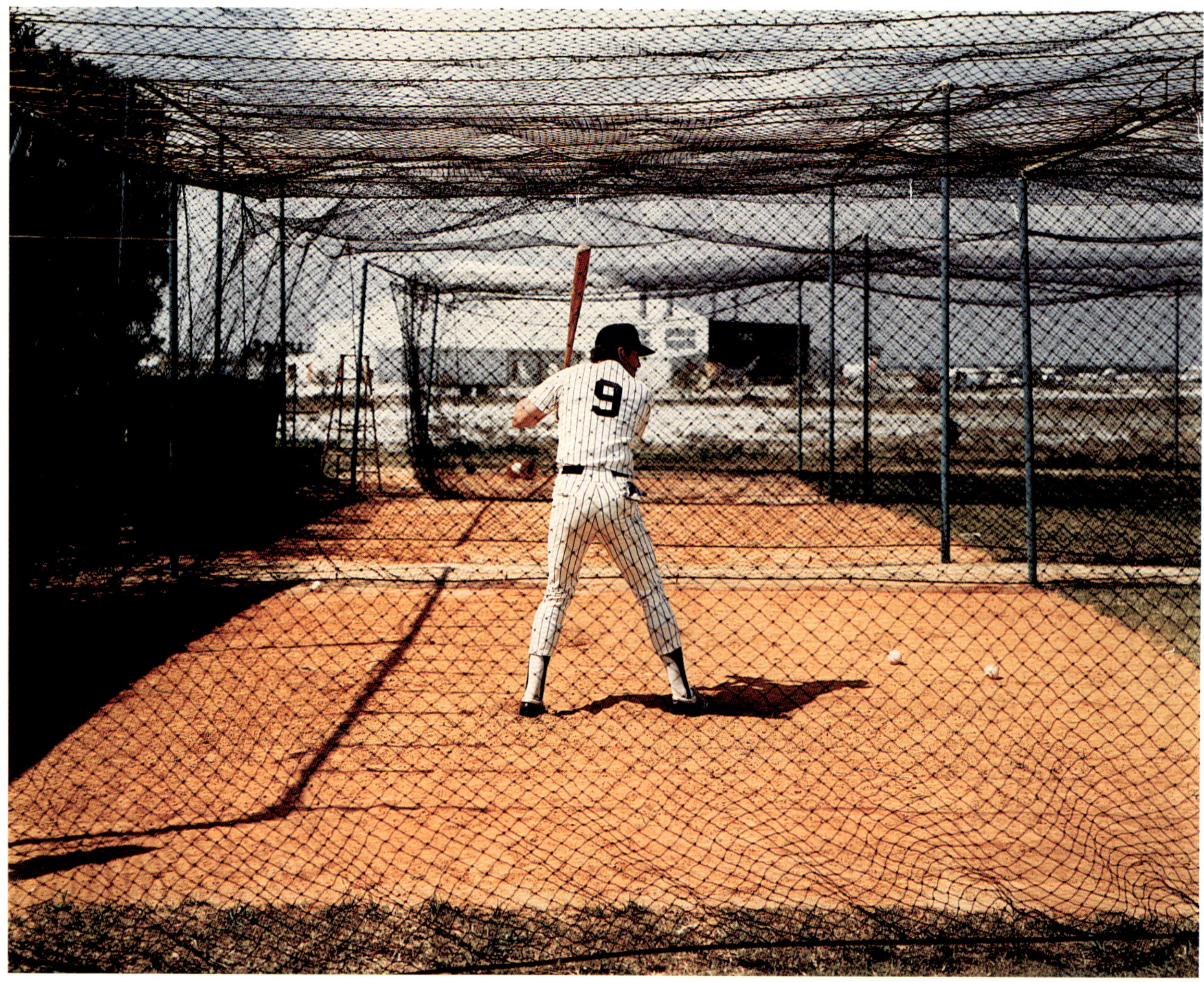

JIM DOW
Veterans Stadium, Philadelphia, 1980
Courtesy Janet Borden, Inc., New York (cat. 141)

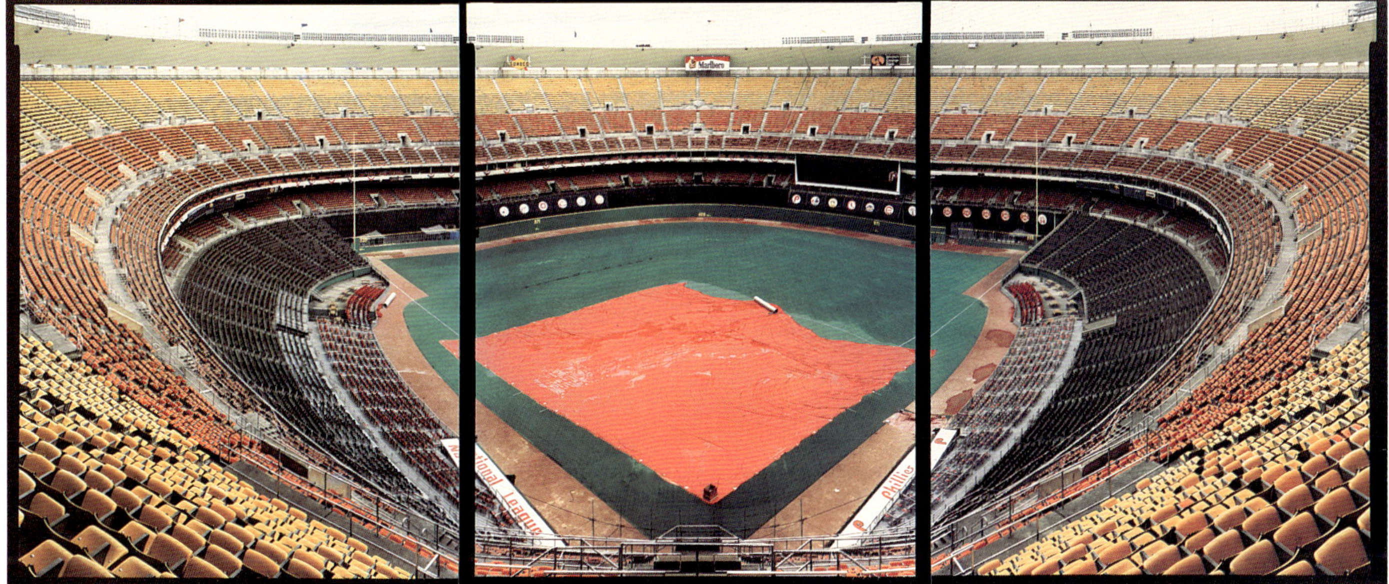

JOEL STERNFELD
Atlanta, Georgia, 1983
Courtesy Pace/MacGill Gallery, New York (cat. 150)

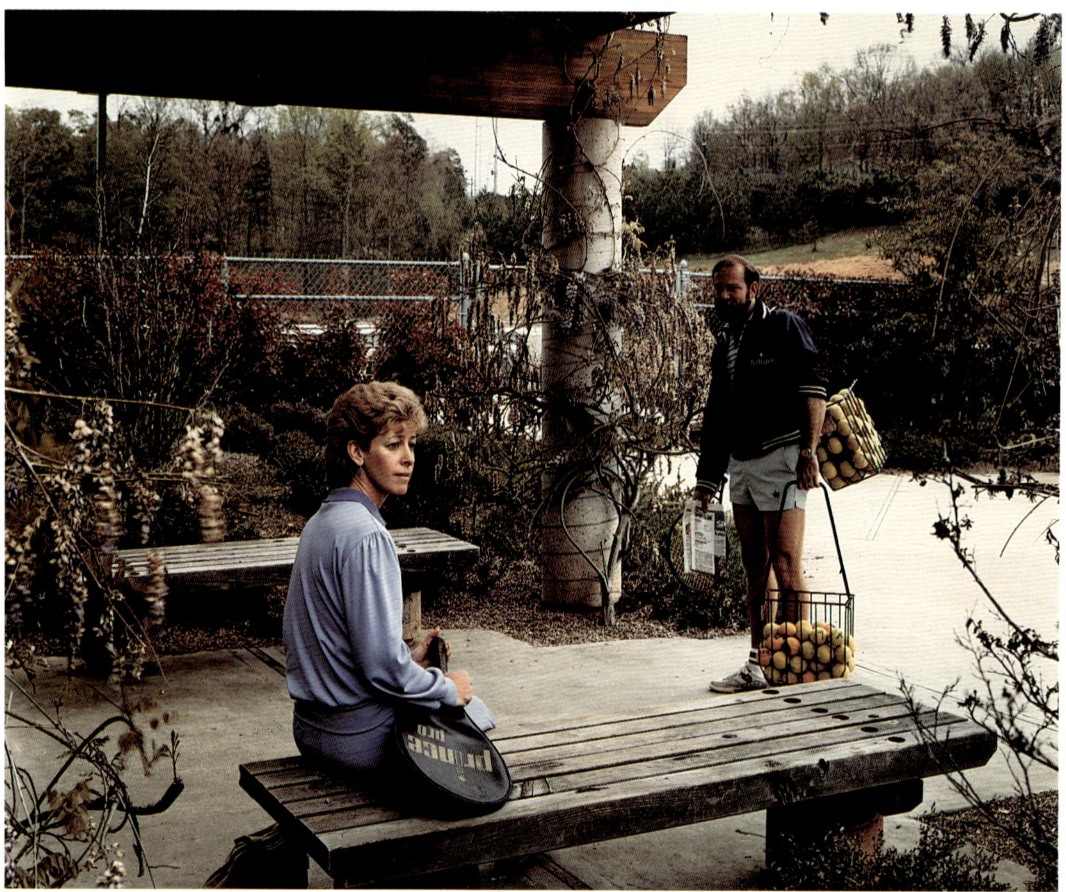

LARRY SULTAN
My Mother Posing for Me, Palm Springs, California,
from the series "Pictures from Home," 1984
Courtesy Janet Borden, Inc., New York (cat. 162)

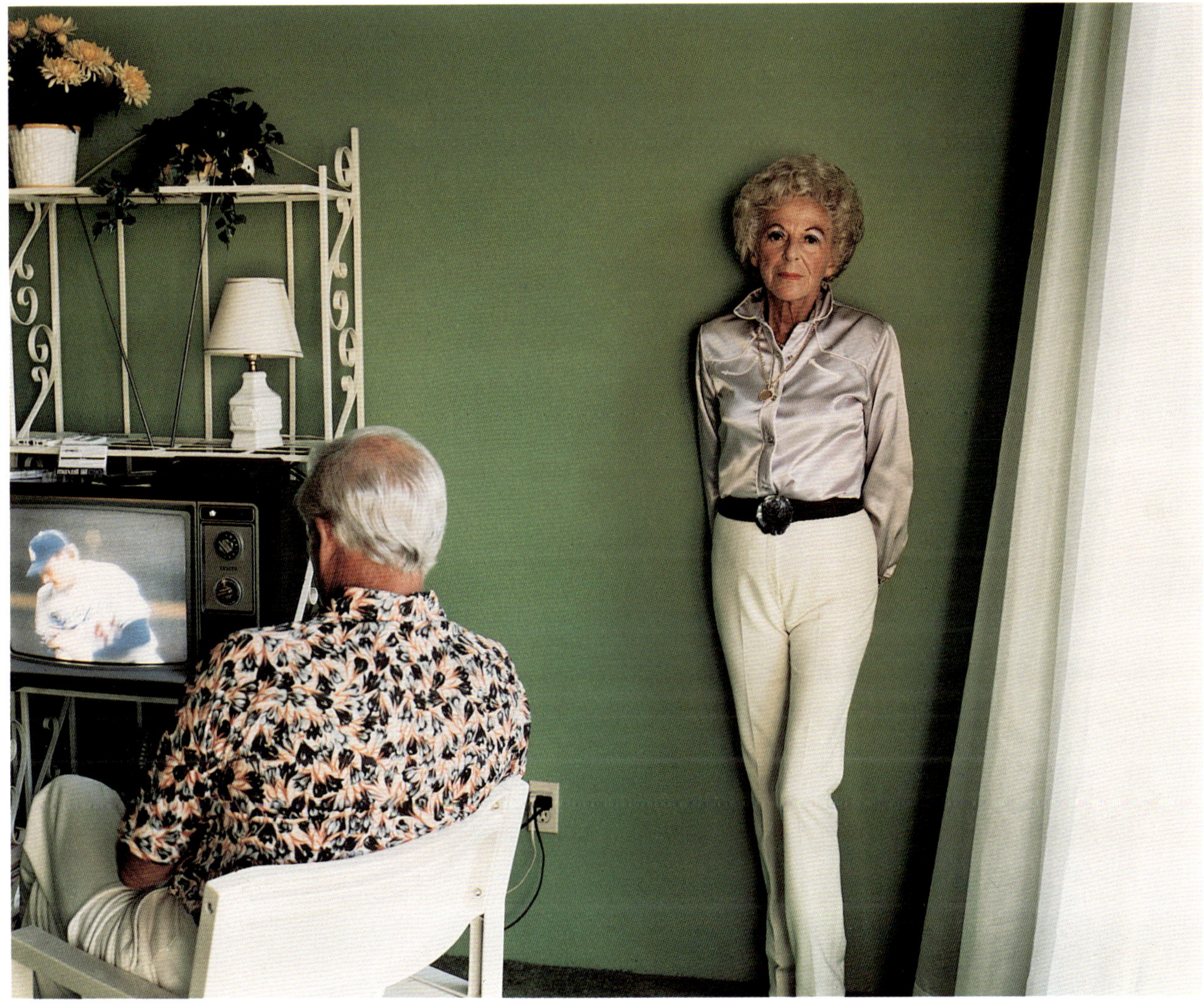

JEFF KOONS
SILK, 1985
Lehmann Collection, Geneva;
Courtesy Sonnabend Gallery, New York (cat. 165)

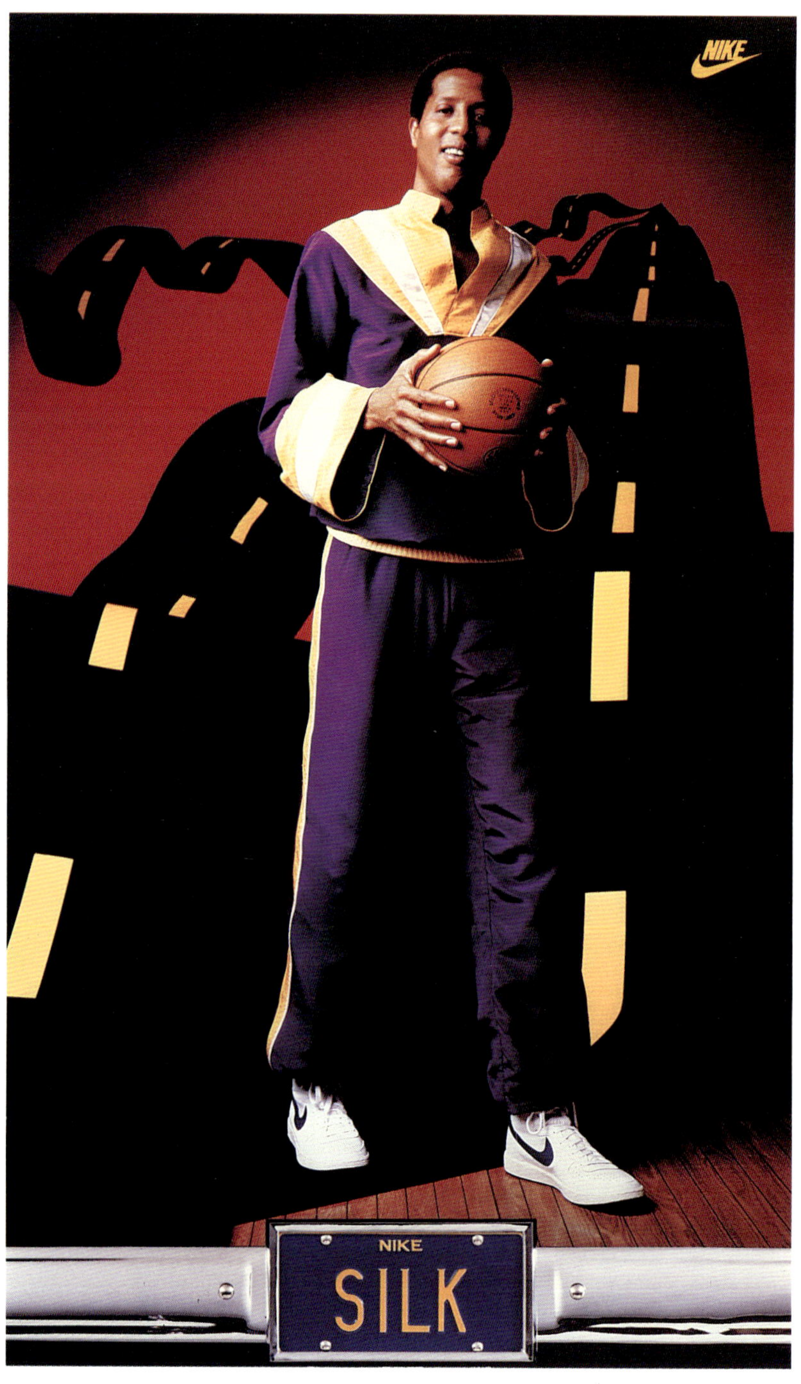
NIKE
NIKE
SILK

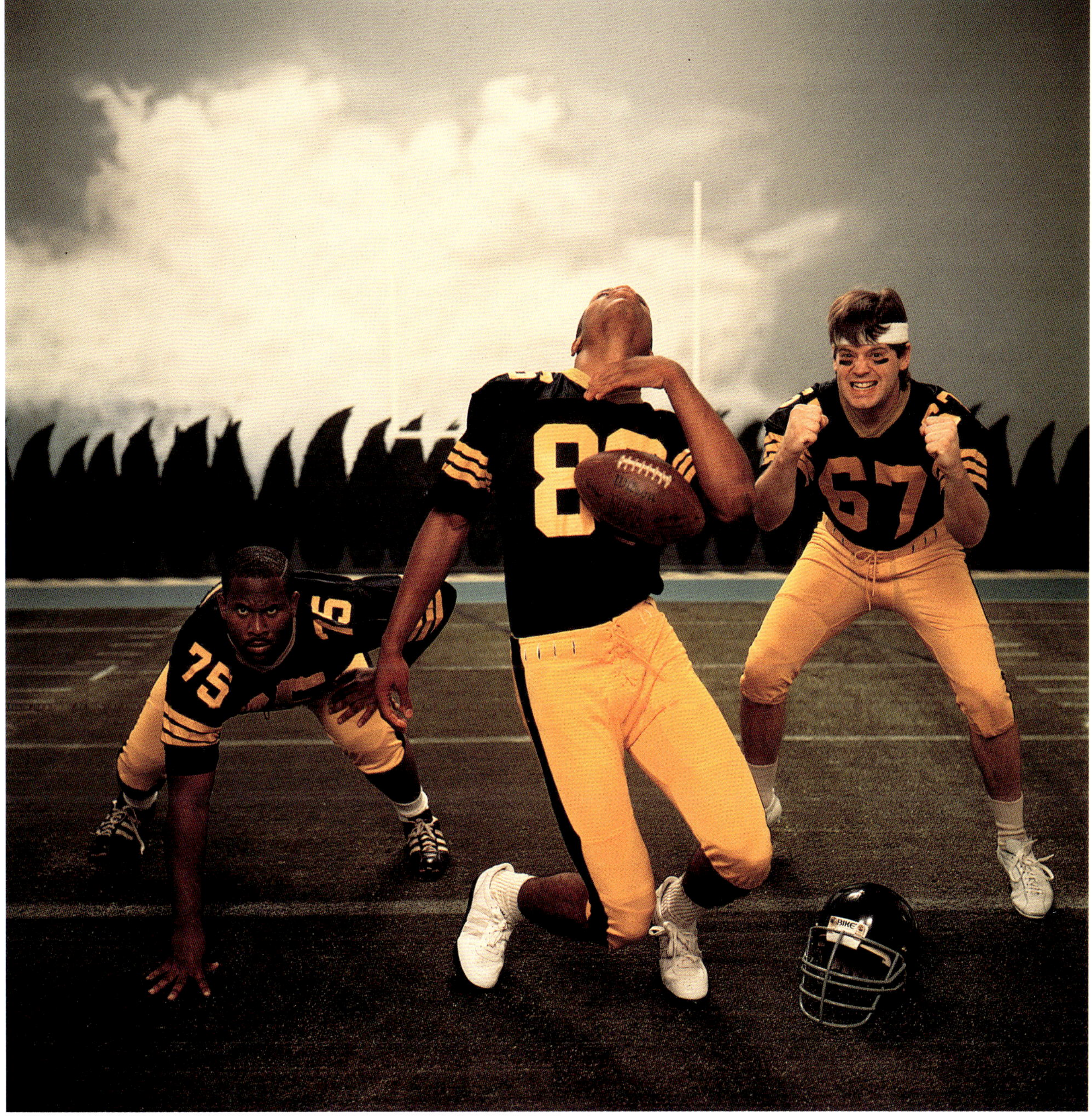

JAN STALLER
Batting Practice Facility in Jersey City, New Jersey, 1987
Courtesy of the artist and Lieberman & Saul Gallery, New York (cat. 172)

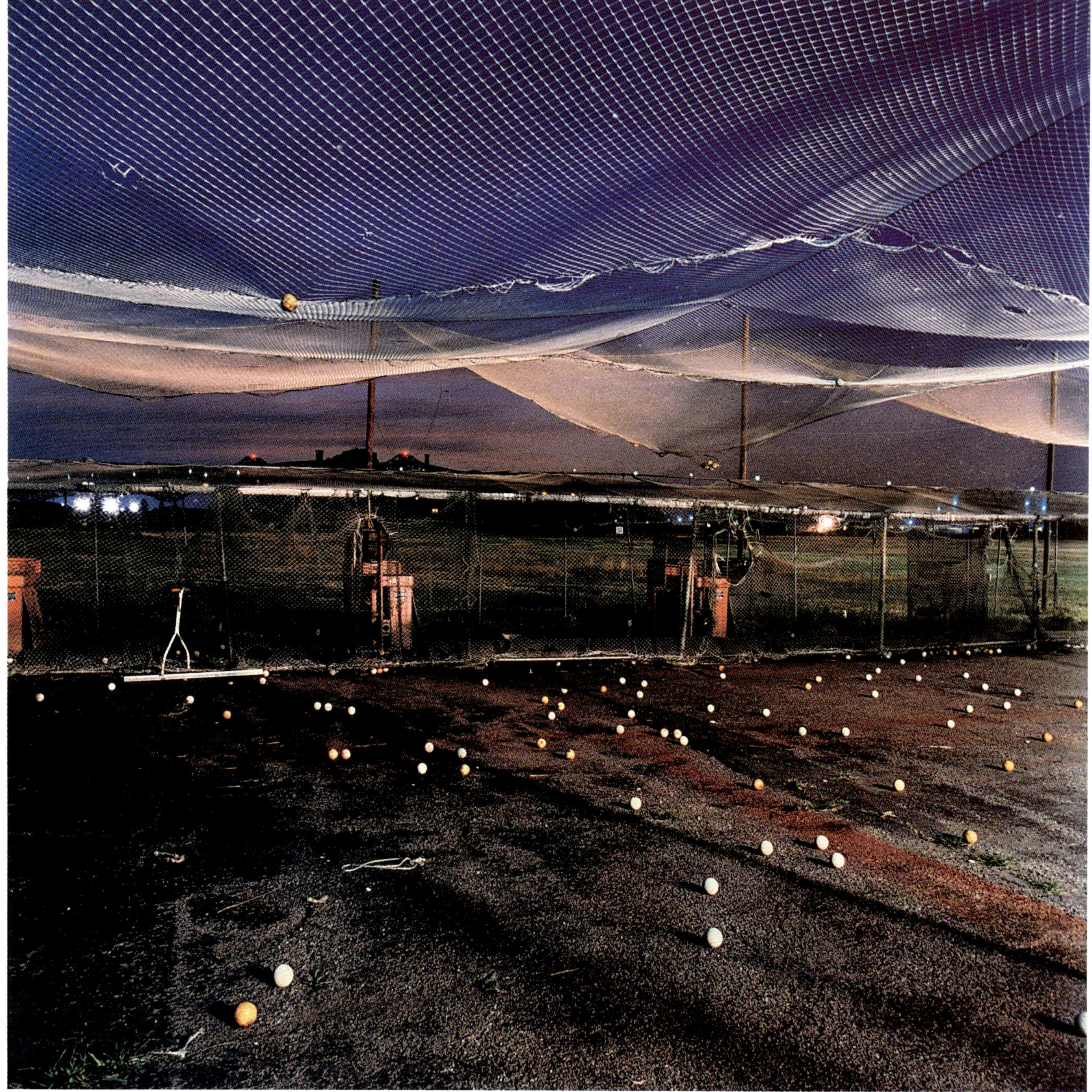

ANNIE LEIBOVITZ
Tom Seaver, Greenwich, Connecticut, 1987
Courtesy James Danzinger Gallery, New York (cat. 173)

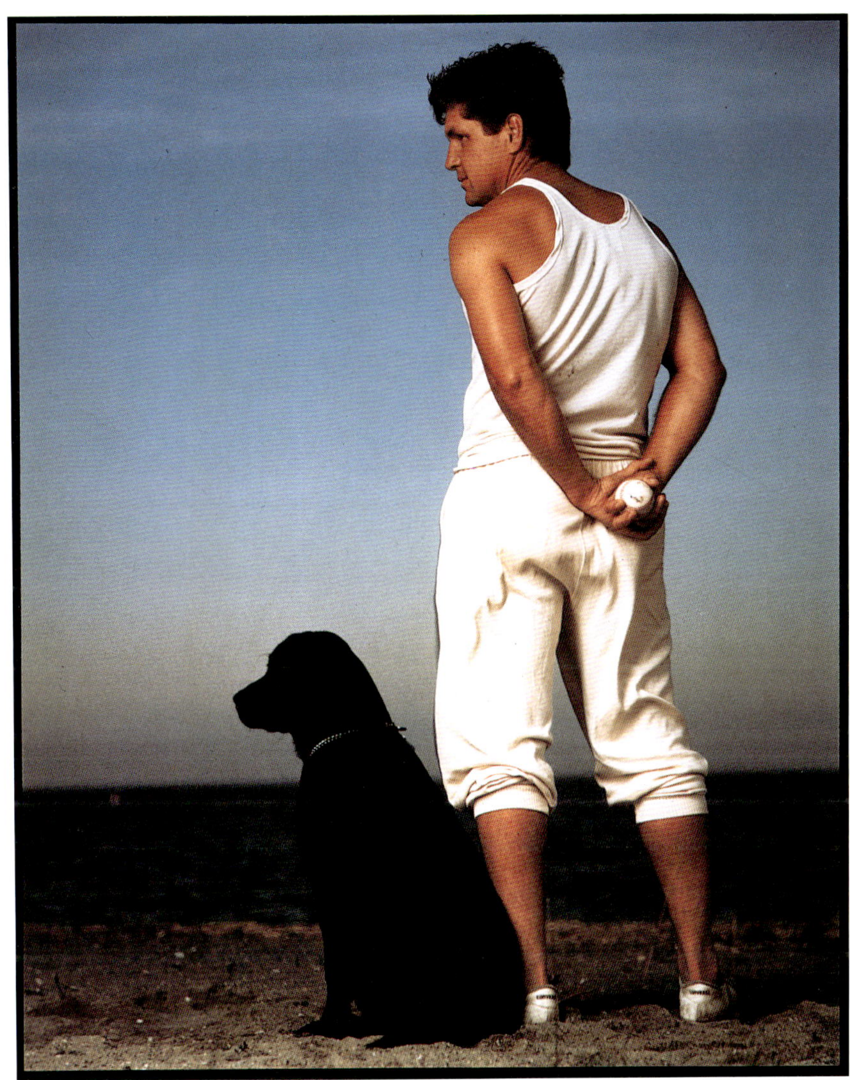

CHRISTOPHER JAMES
Running Track/Cambridge #7, 1980
Courtesy of the artist and The Witkin Gallery, Inc., New York (cat. 139)

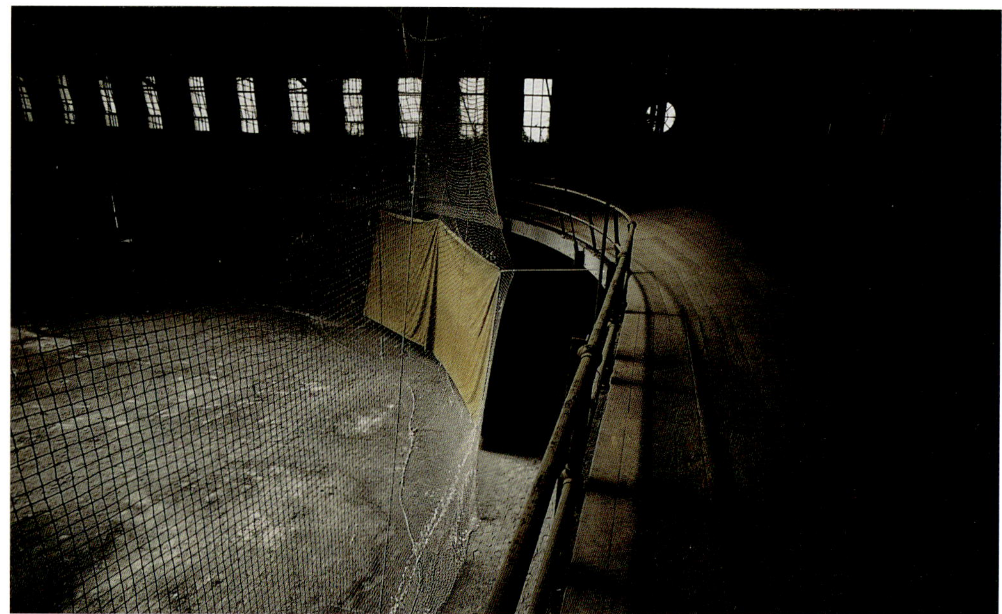

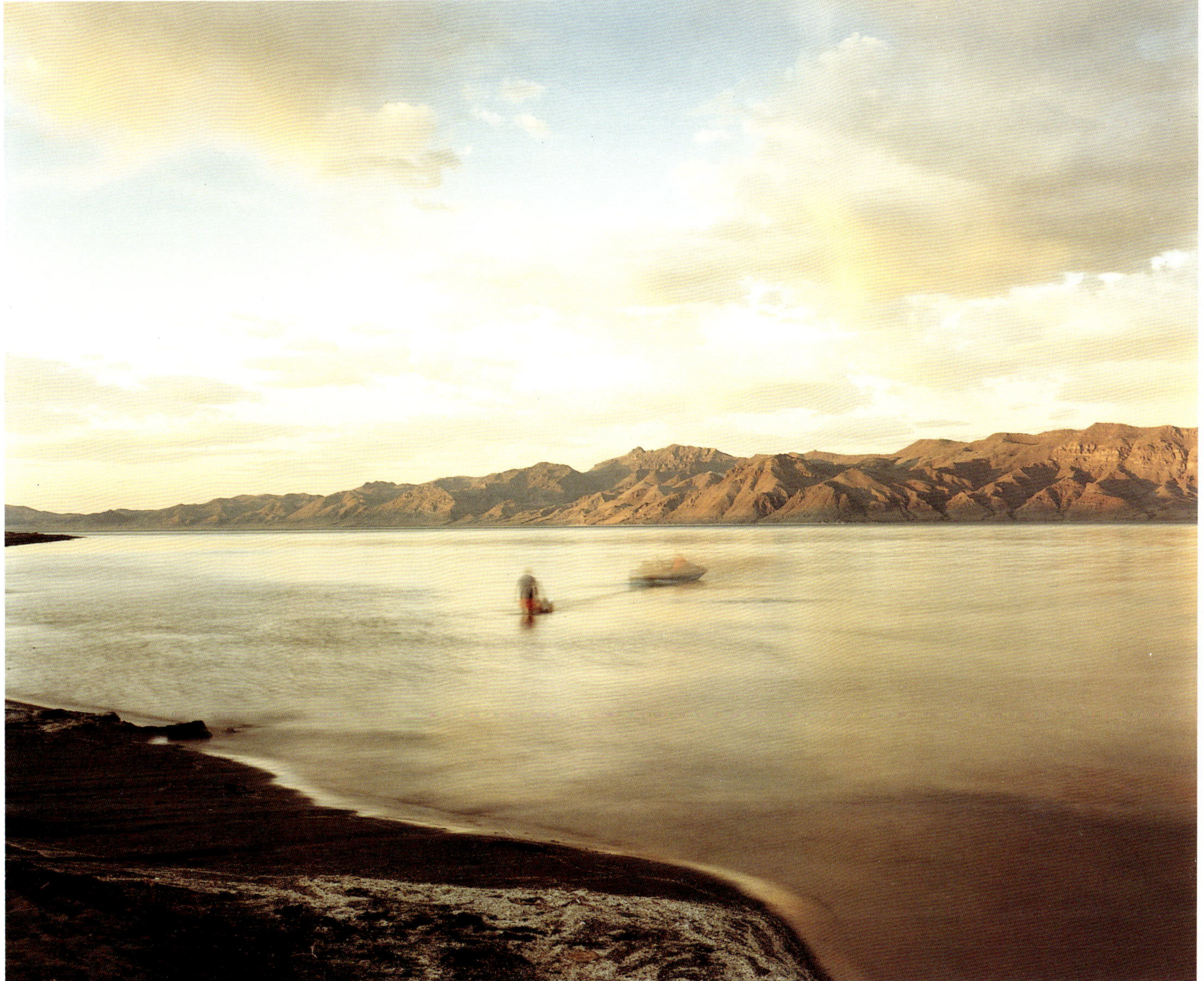

RICHARD MISRACH
Water Skiing, Pyramid Lake Indian Reservation, Nevada, 1991
Private Collection; Courtesy Fraenkel Gallery, San Francisco (cat. 192)

DAVID GRAHAM
The Post Bulletins Practicing at Graham Park,
Rochester, Minnesota, 1988
Courtesy Laurence Miller Gallery, New York (cat. 183)

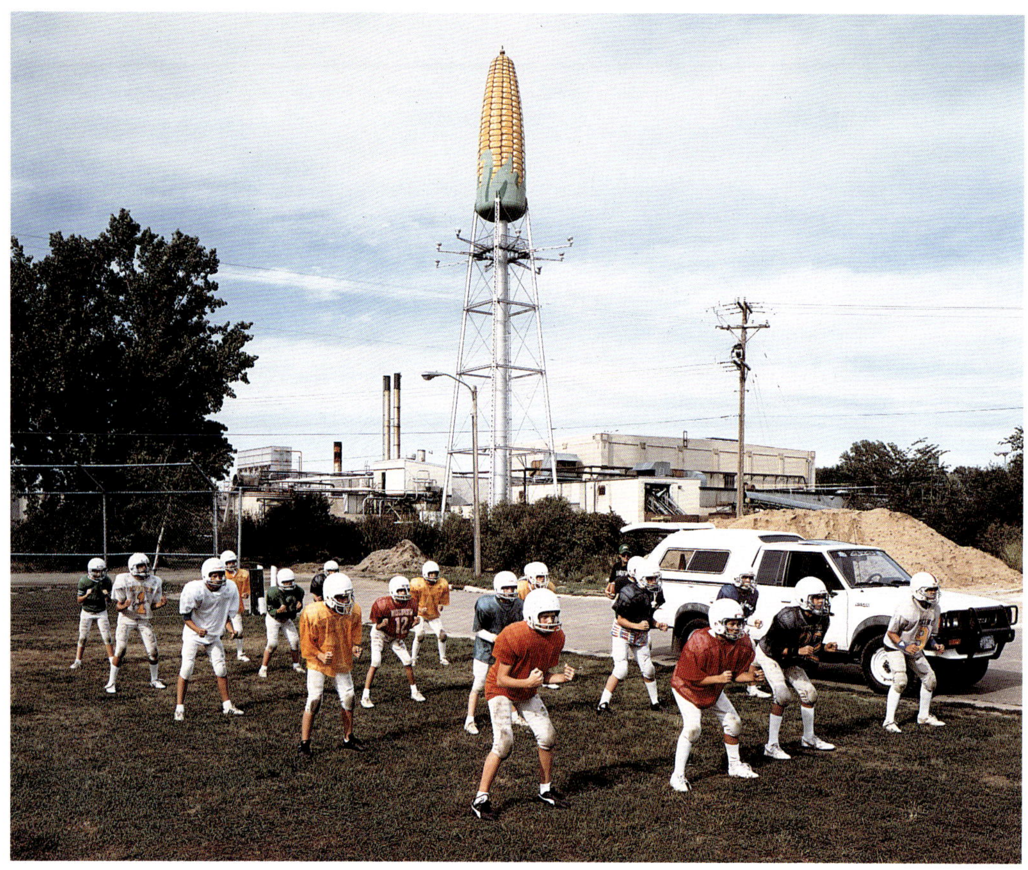

SKEET McAULEY
Navajo Tribal School Near Goulding, Utah, 1984
Courtesy of the artist and Barry Whistler Gallery, Dallas (cat. 161)

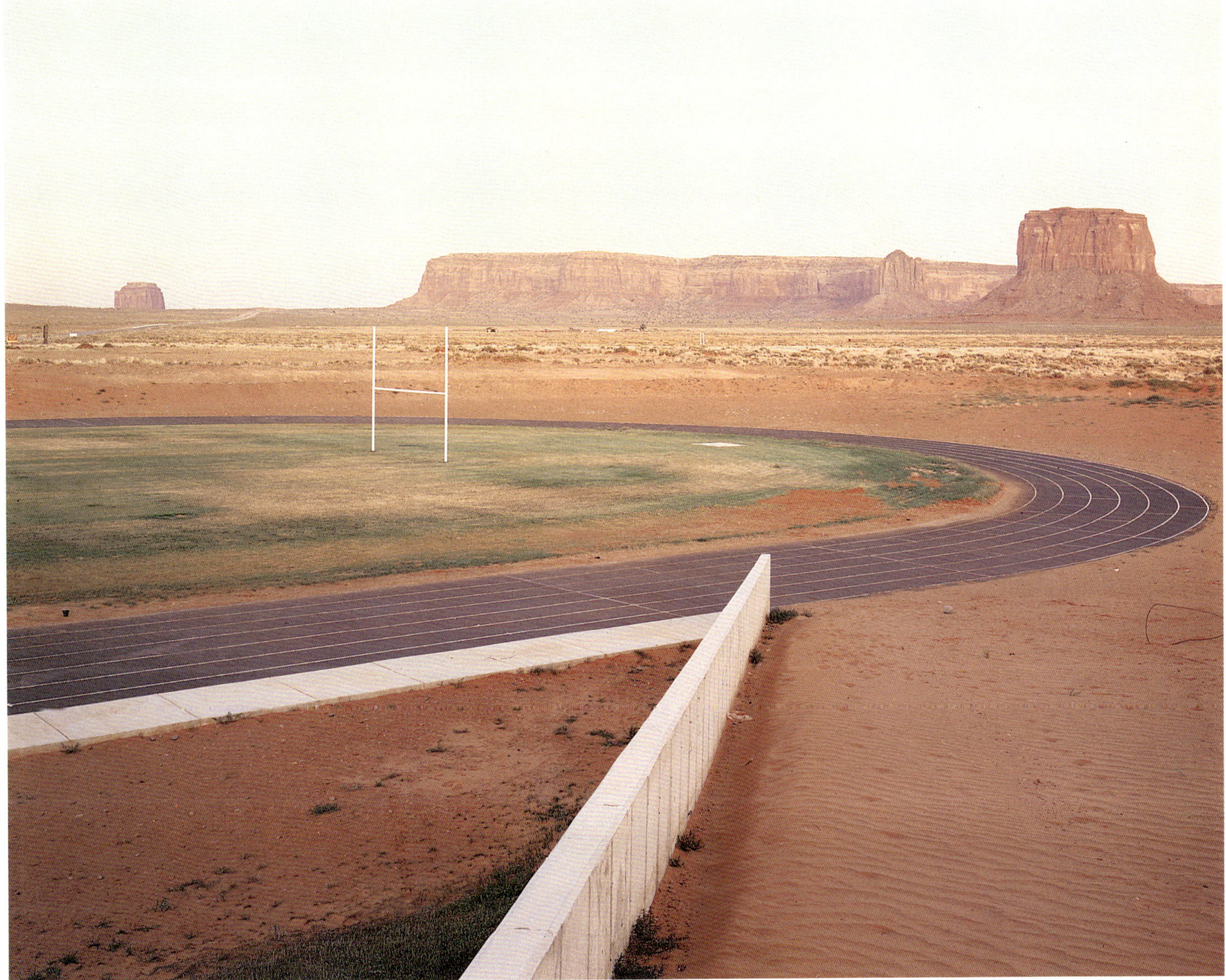

FRANK MAJORE

Welcome to the Club, 1986
Collection of Jill and Richard Schloss, New York;
Courtesy Holly Solomon Gallery, New York (cat. 171)

Ultra, 1989
Collection of the Butler Institute of American Art,
Youngstown, Ohio (cat. 187)

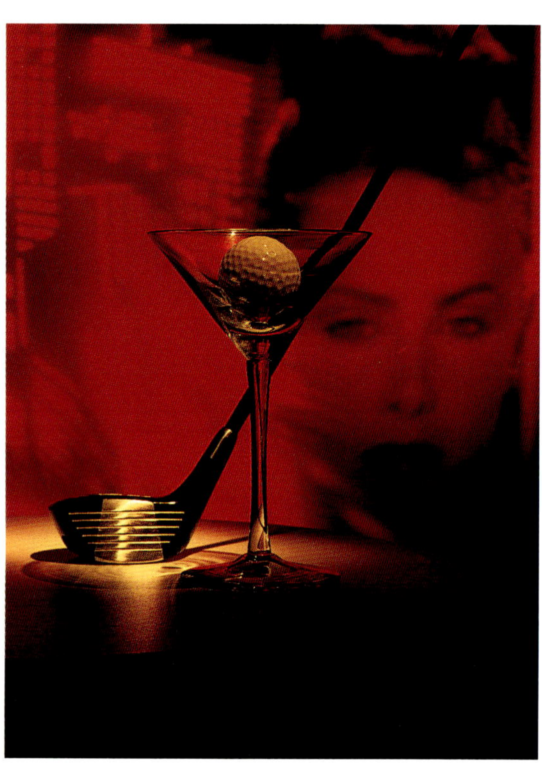

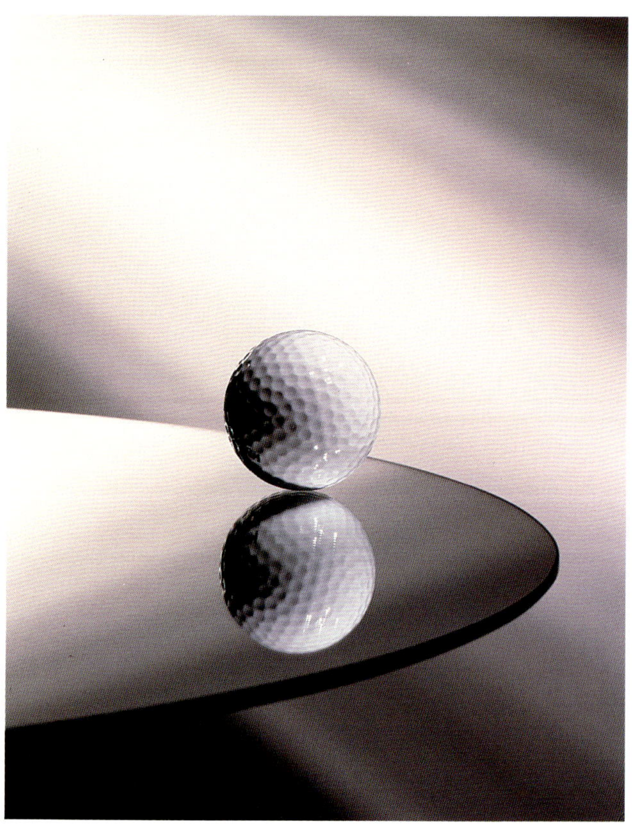

NEIL WINOKUR
Football, from the series "Self-Portrait:
An Installation," 1990
Courtesy Janet Borden, Inc., New York (cat. 190)

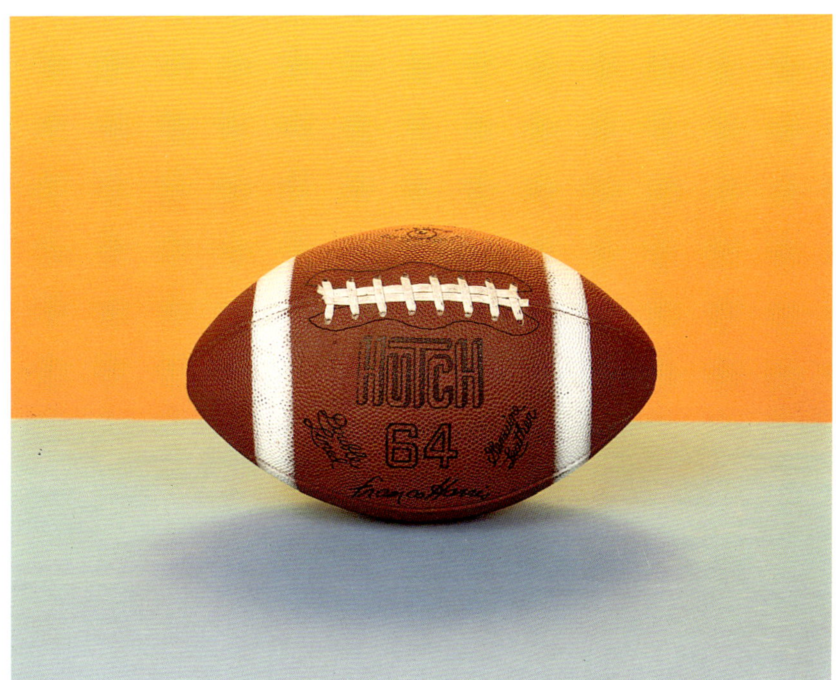

JACK CARNELL

Mike Schmidt, Camera Night, Philadelphia, 1987
Courtesy of the artist (cat. 181)

Photographers, Track and Field, Summer Olympics, Los Angeles, California, 1984
Courtesy of the artist (cat. 158)

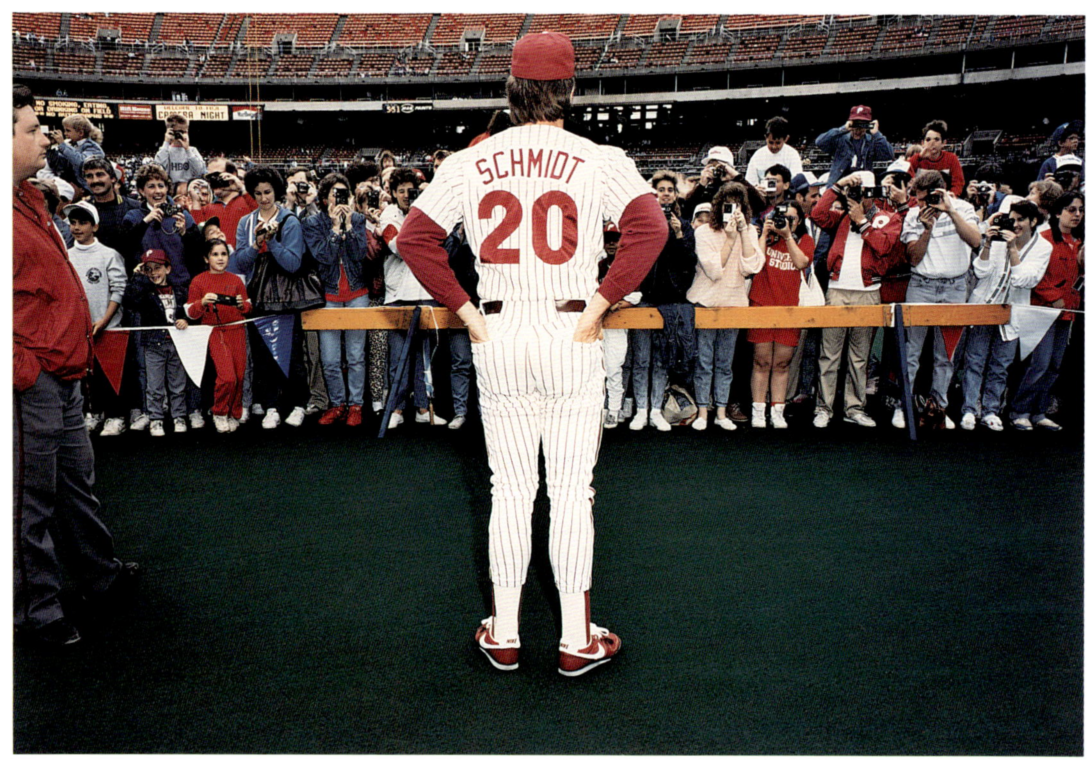

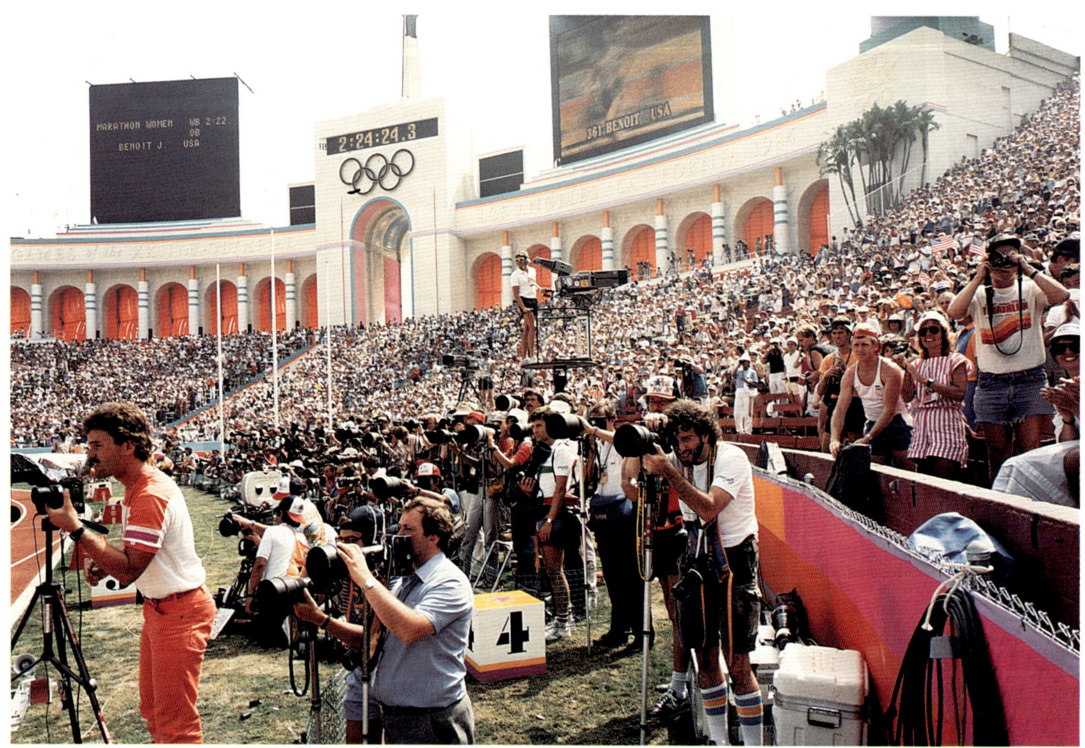

EADWEARD MUYBRIDGE

*"Abe Edgington," owned by Leland Stanford; driven by C. Marvin,
trotting at 2:24 gait over the Palo Alto track,* June 15, 1878
Collection of the Division of Prints and Photographs,
Library of Congress, Washington, D.C. (cat. 1)

THOMAS EAKINS

Marey Wheel Photographs of George Reynolds, 1884
Collection of the Hirshhorn Museum and Sculpture Garden, Smithsonian
Institution, Washington, D.C.; Gift of Joseph H. Hirshhorn, 1966 (cat. 3)

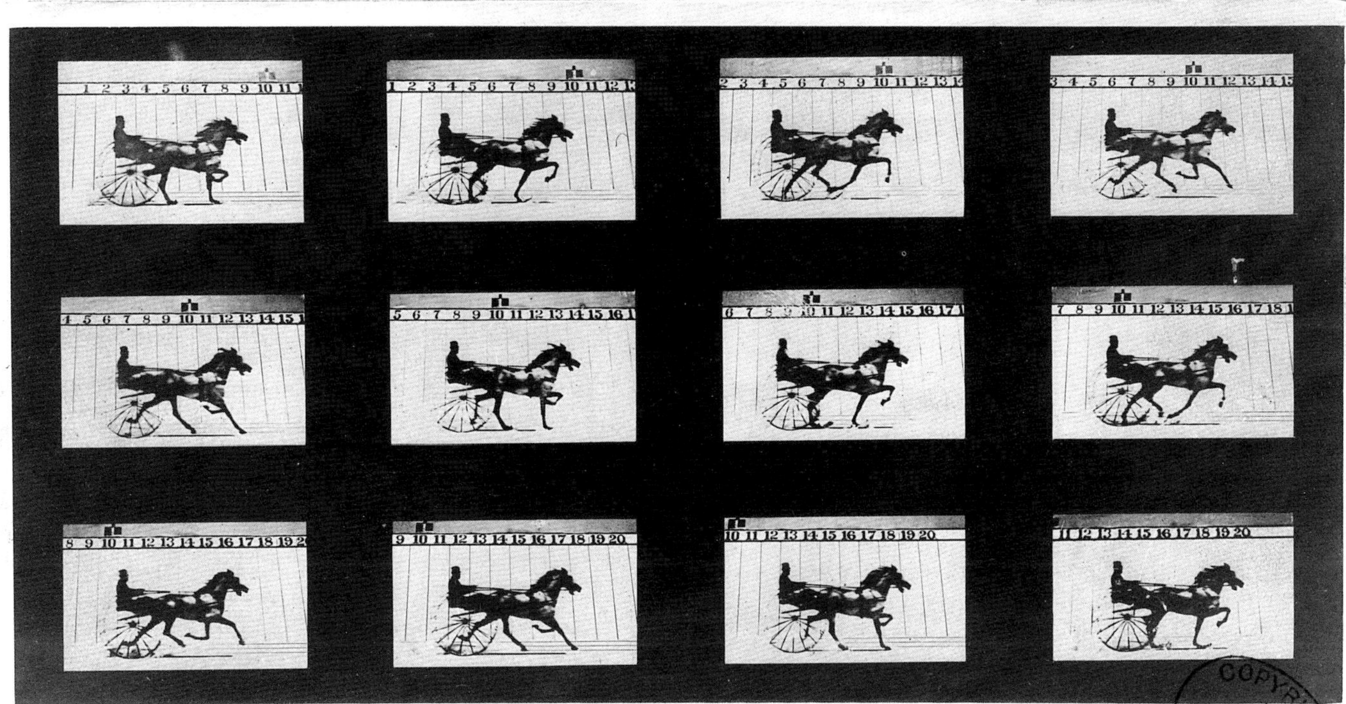

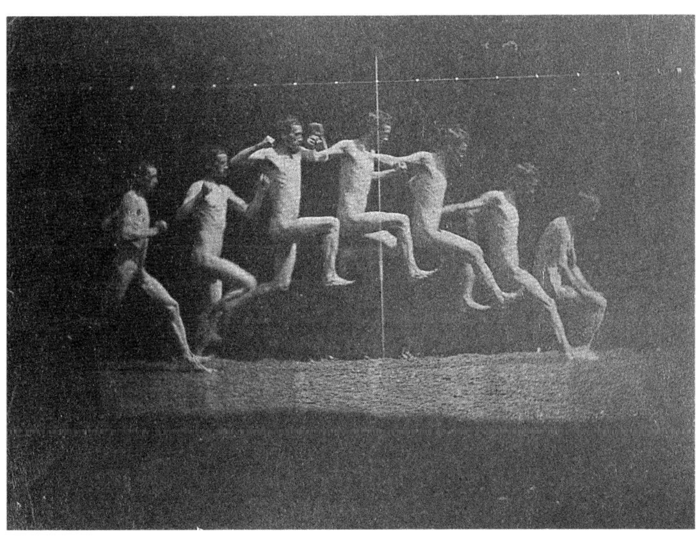

EADWEARD MUYBRIDGE
Untitled (man throwing a discus),
from "Animal Locomotion," plate 307, 1887
Collection of The Metropolitan Museum of Art, New York;
Gift of The Philadelphia Commercial Museum, 1938 (cat. 6)

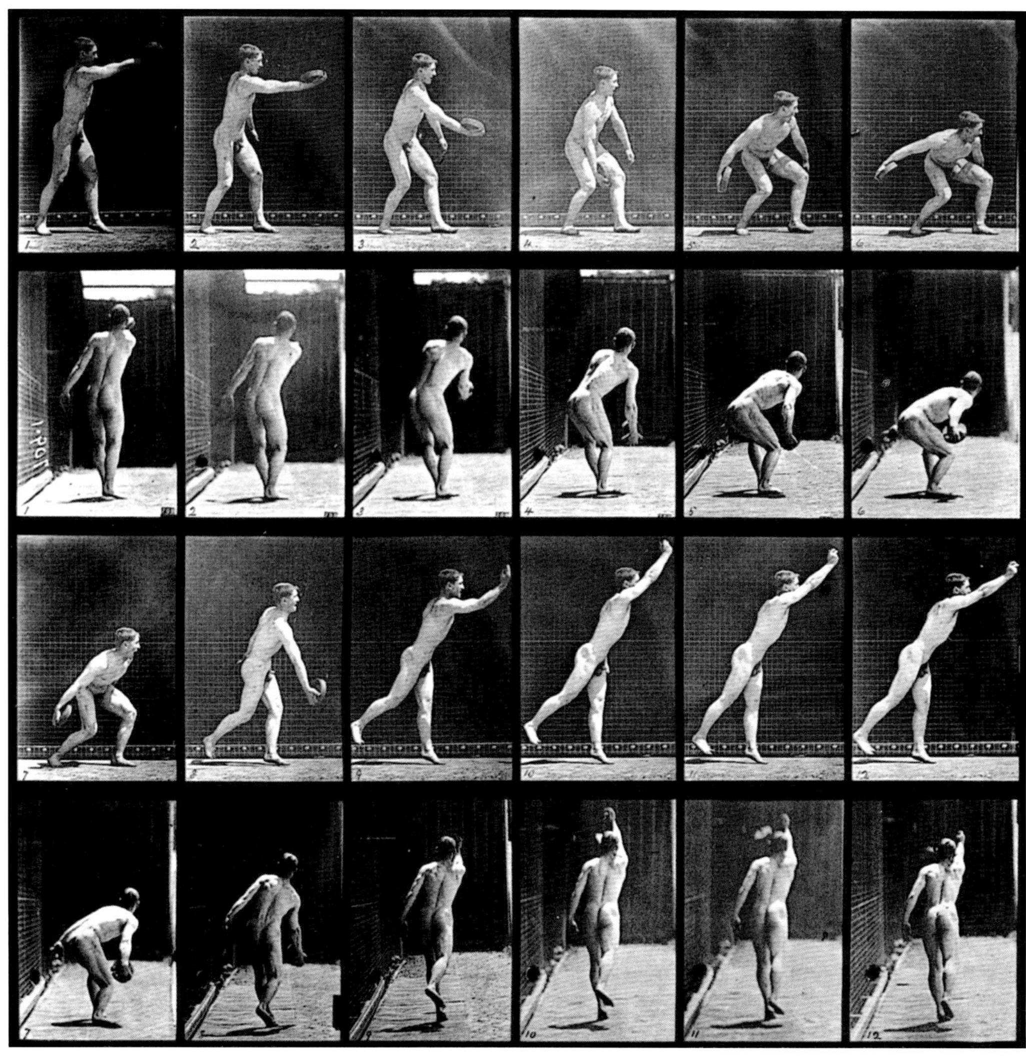

WILLIAM HENRY JACKSON
Trout Fishing at Wagon Wheel Gap, 1883
Collection of The Colorado Historical Society, Denver (cat. 2)

ALICE AUSTEN
Untitled (tennis scene), ca. 1884
Alice Austen Collection, Staten Island Historical Society, New York (cat. 5)

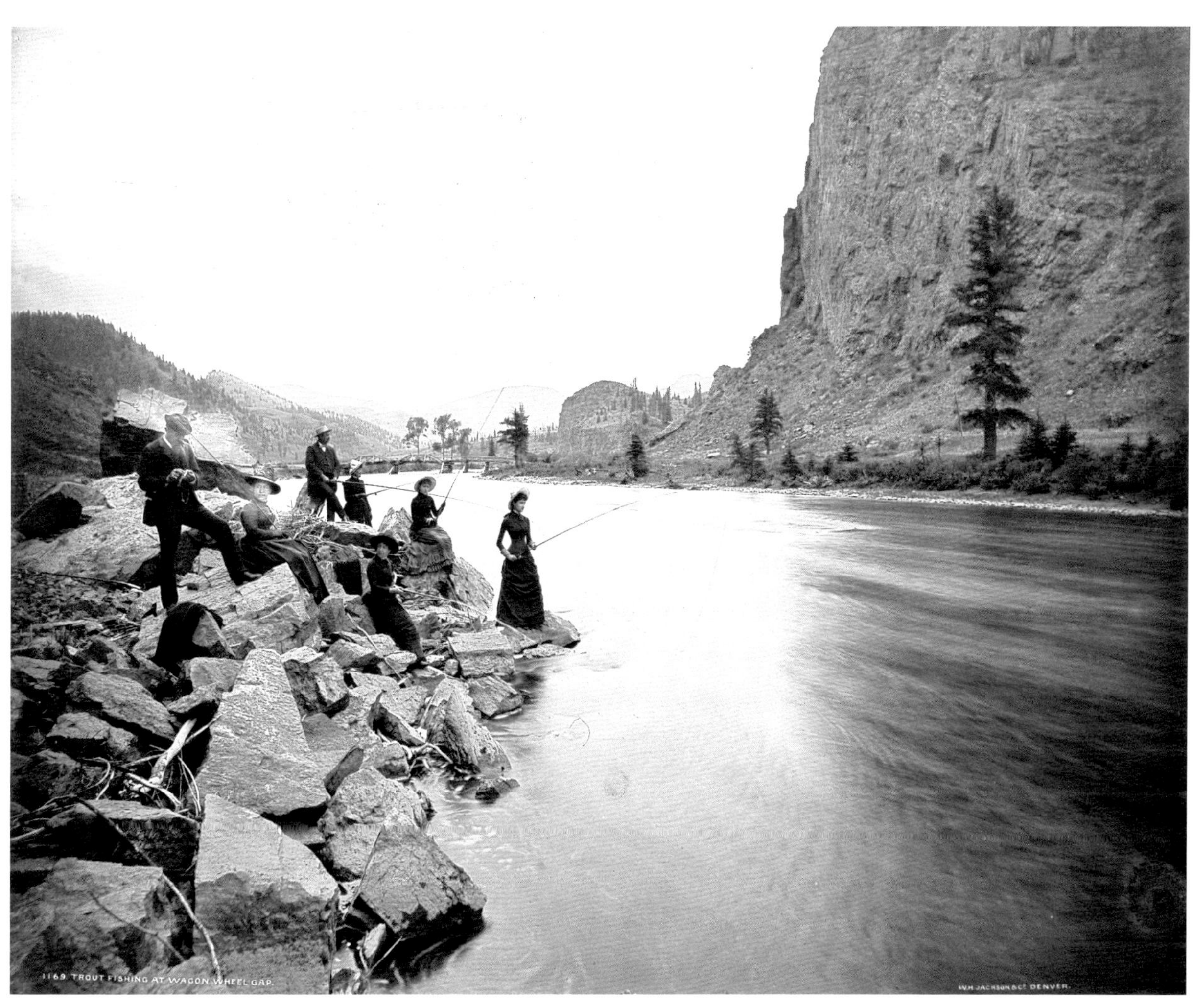

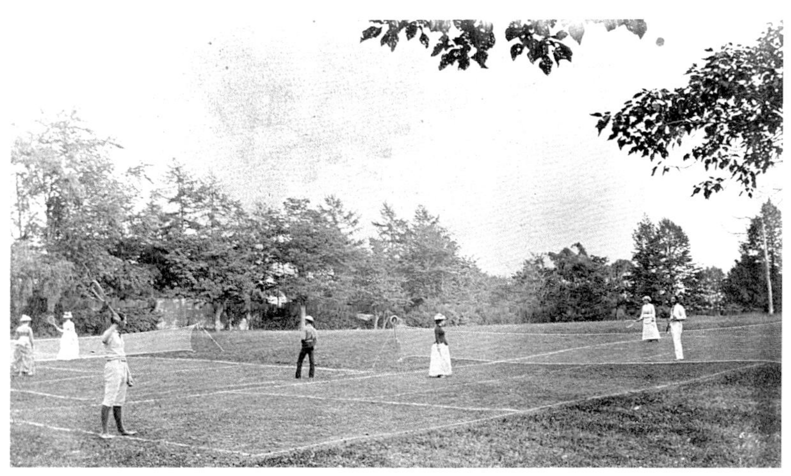

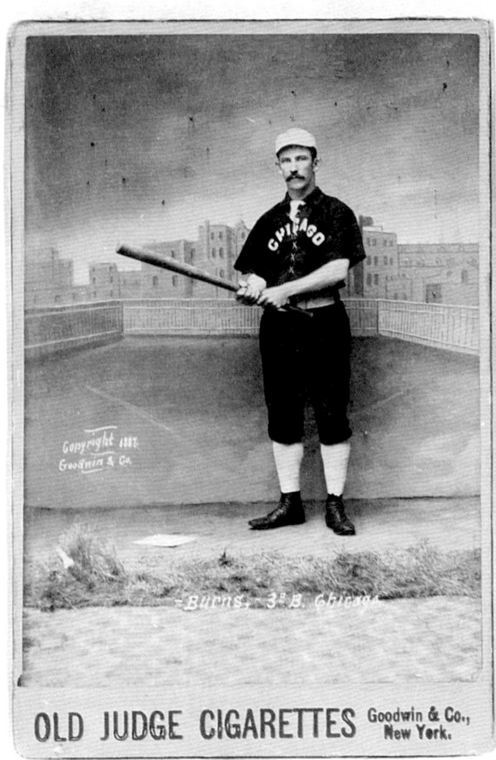
CHICAGO
Copyright 1887.
Goodwin & Co.
Burns, 3ᵈ B. Chicago.
OLD JUDGE CIGARETTES Goodwin & Co.,
New York.

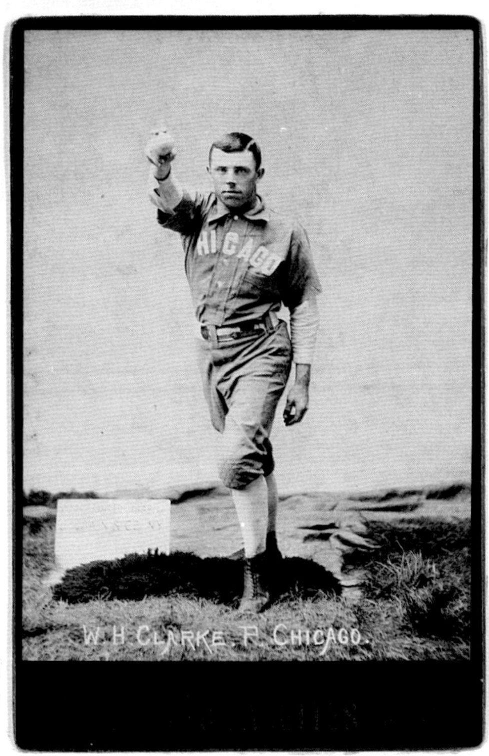
CHICAGO
W. H. CLARKE. P. CHICAGO.

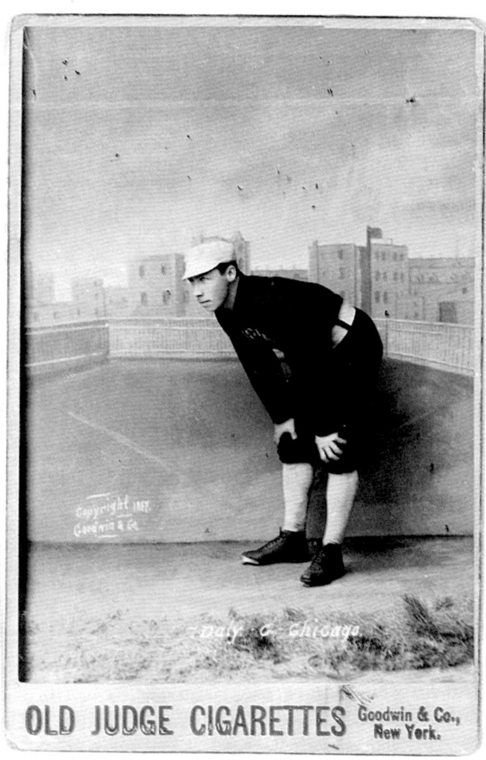
Copyright 1887.
Goodwin & Co.
Daly, C. Chicago.
OLD JUDGE CIGARETTES Goodwin & Co.,
New York.

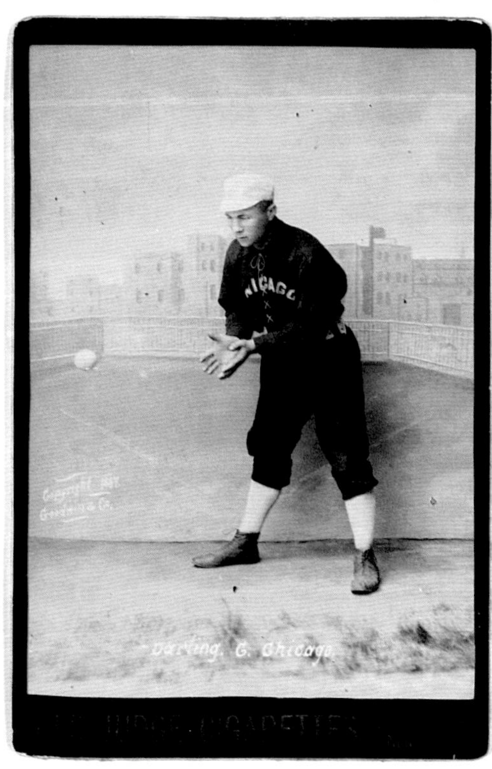
CHICAGO
Copyright 1887.
Goodwin & Co.
Darling, C. Chicago.

KUHNS FAMILY
Girl with a Bicycle, ca. mid-1890s
Collection of the Atlanta Historical Society, Inc. (cat. 12)

ATTRIBUTED TO CARLETON E. WATKINS
Hotel del Monte, Swimming Tanks, ca. 1889
Collection of Wm. B. Becker (cat. 11)

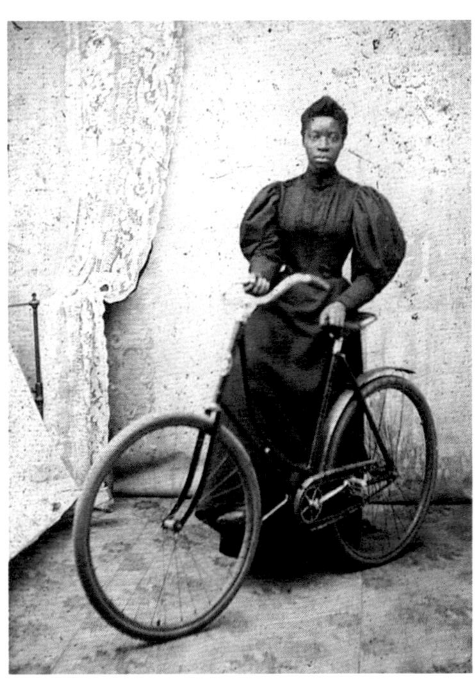

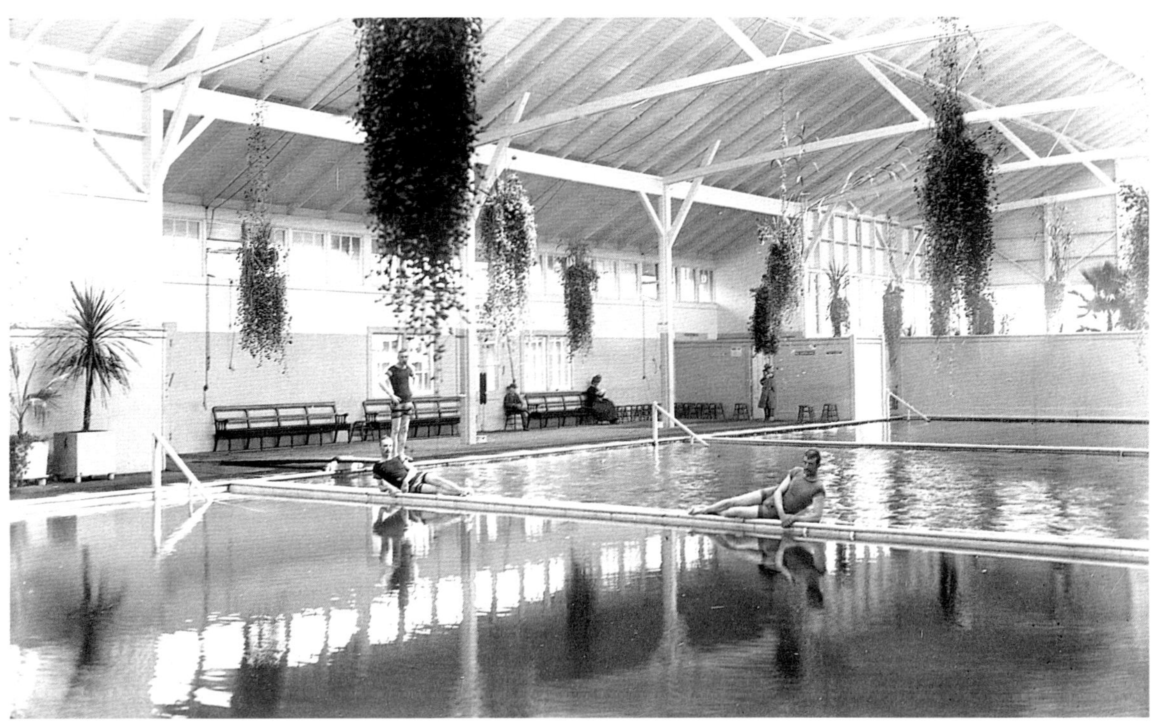

FRANCES BENJAMIN JOHNSTON
A Football Team, from an album of photographs documenting
The Hampton Institute, Hampton, Virginia, 1899-1900
Collection of The Museum of Modern Art, New York;
Gift of Lincoln Kirstein (cat. 15)

ANONYMOUS
Fulton Bag and Cotton Mill Team, Atlanta, 1910
Collection of Michael W. Griffith, Lilburn, Georgia (cat. 20)

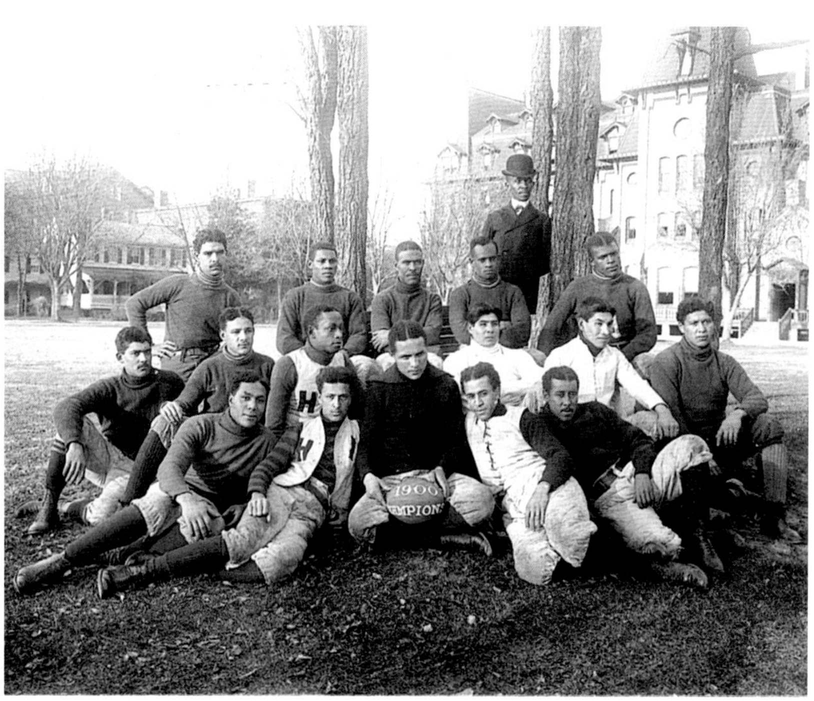

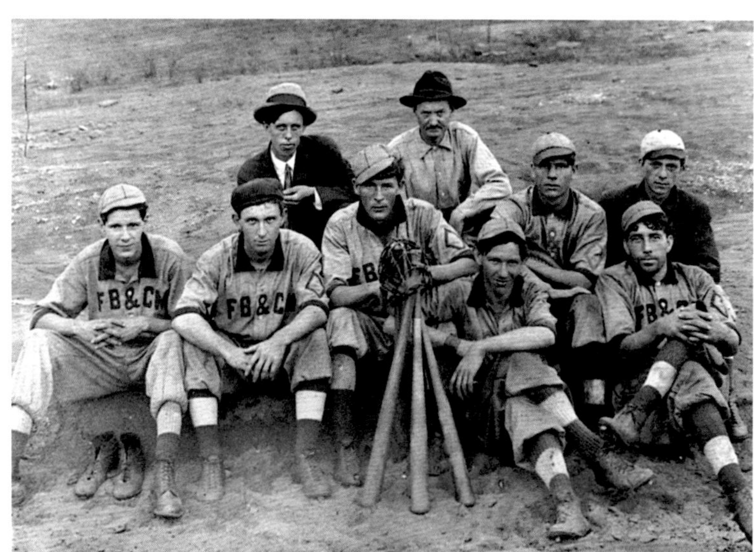

JOSEPH BYRON
Skating, Van Cortland Park, New York City, 1897
The Byron Collection,
Museum of the City of New York (cat. 14)

ALFRED STIEGLITZ
Going to the Start, 1904
Collection of The Metropolitan Museum of Art,
New York; Gift of J. B. Neumann, 1958 (cat. 17)

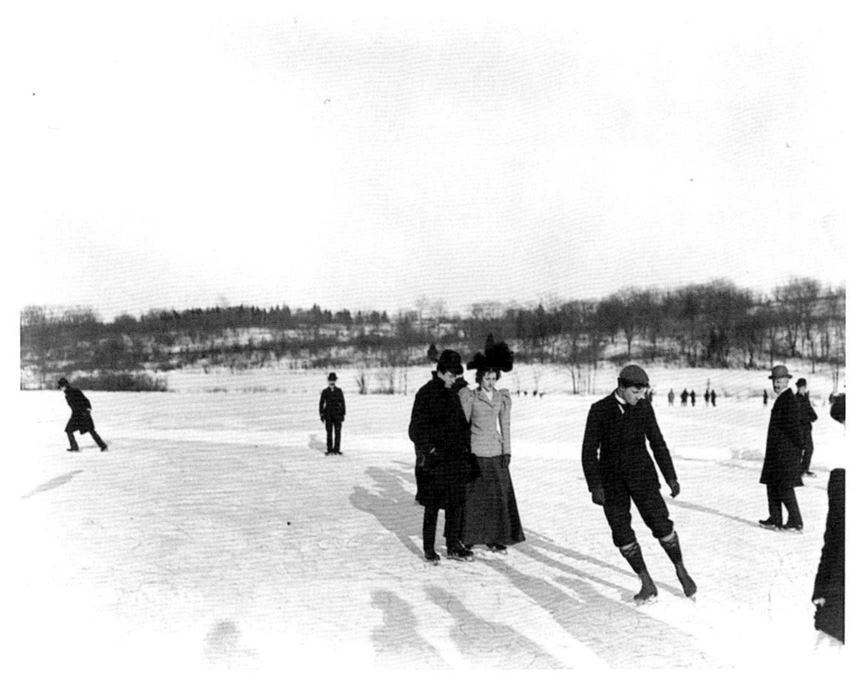

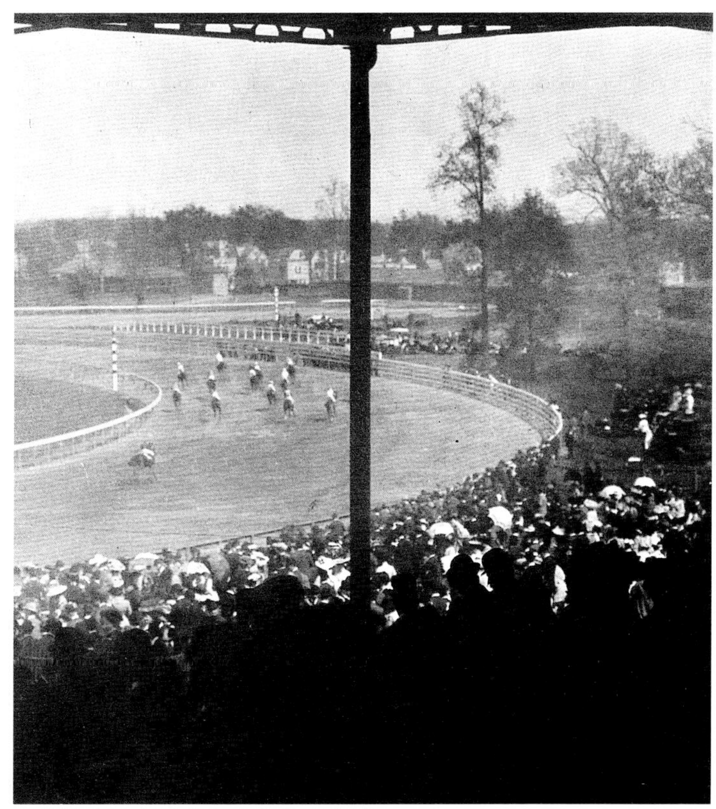

JACQUES-HENRI LARTIGUE

The Day of the Races at Auteuil, 1910, printed 1984
Collection of the High Museum of Art, Atlanta; Purchase
© Association des Amis de Jacques-Henri Lartique (cat. 23)

Grand Prix of the Automobile Club of Paris, 1912
Collection of the International Museum of Photography at
George Eastman House, Rochester, New York; Purchase
© Association des Amis de Jacques-Henri Lartique (cat. 24)

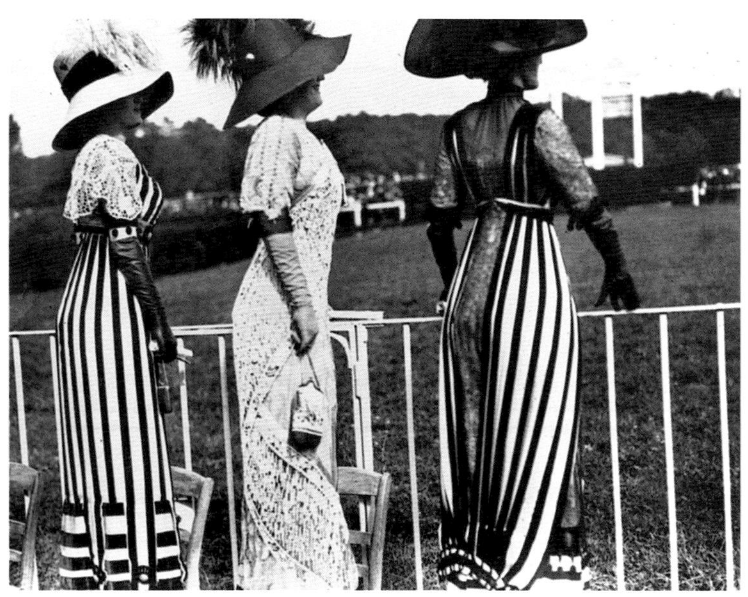

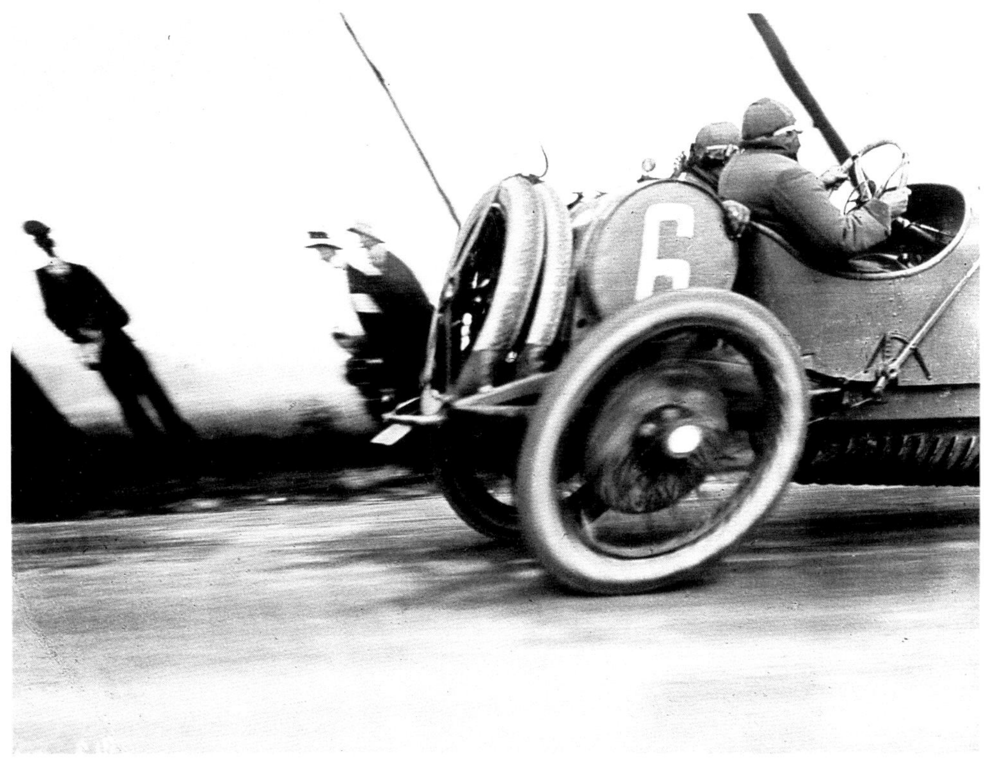

ANDRÉ KERTÉSZ

Underwater Swimmer, Esztergom, Hungary, 1917, printed 1973
Collection of the High Museum of Art, Atlanta;
Purchase with funds from a Friend of the Museum (cat. 25)

Swimming, Duna Haraszti, September 14, 1919, printed 1973
Collection of the High Museum of Art, Atlanta;
Purchase with funds from a Friend of the Museum (cat. 26)

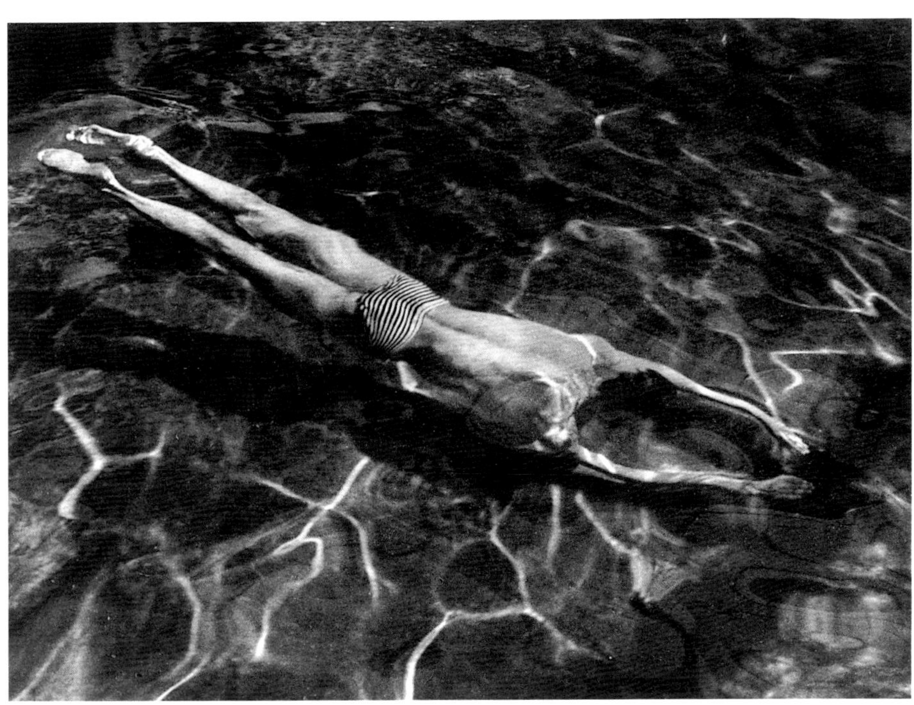

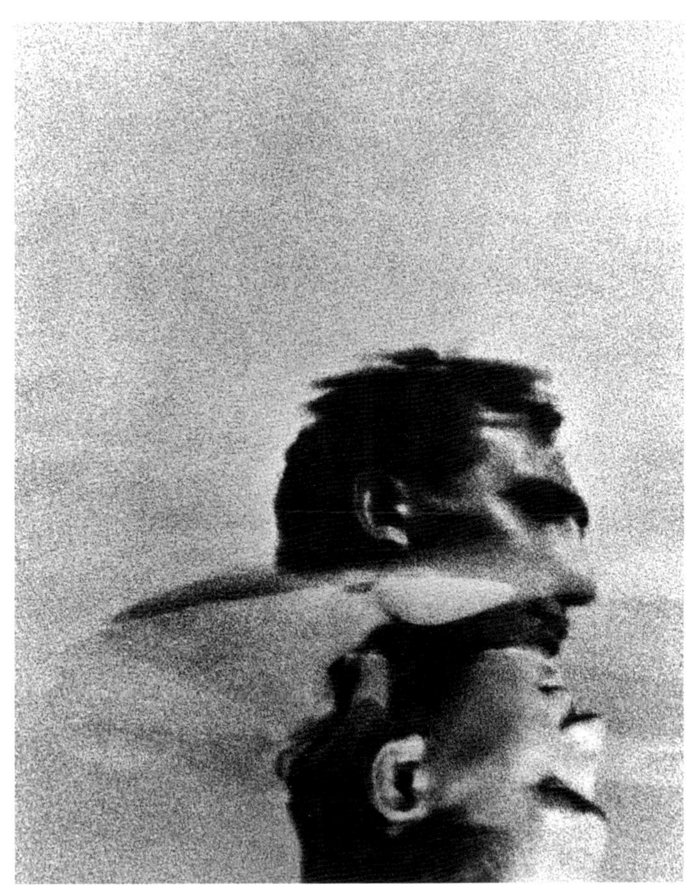

AUGUST SANDER
The Boxer Heinz Heese, 1928
Collection of The Metropolitan Museum of Art, New York;
Warner Communications Inc. Purchase Fund, 1978
© August Sander Archive, Cologne (cat. 37)

ARTHUR GAY
Untitled, from the portfolio "Bodybuilders," 1925, printed later
Courtesy Lewis Lehr, New York (cat. 29)

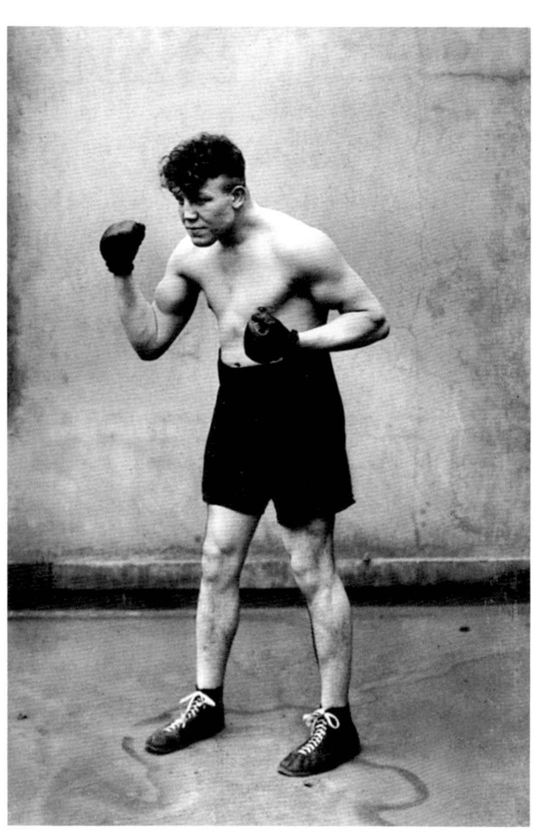

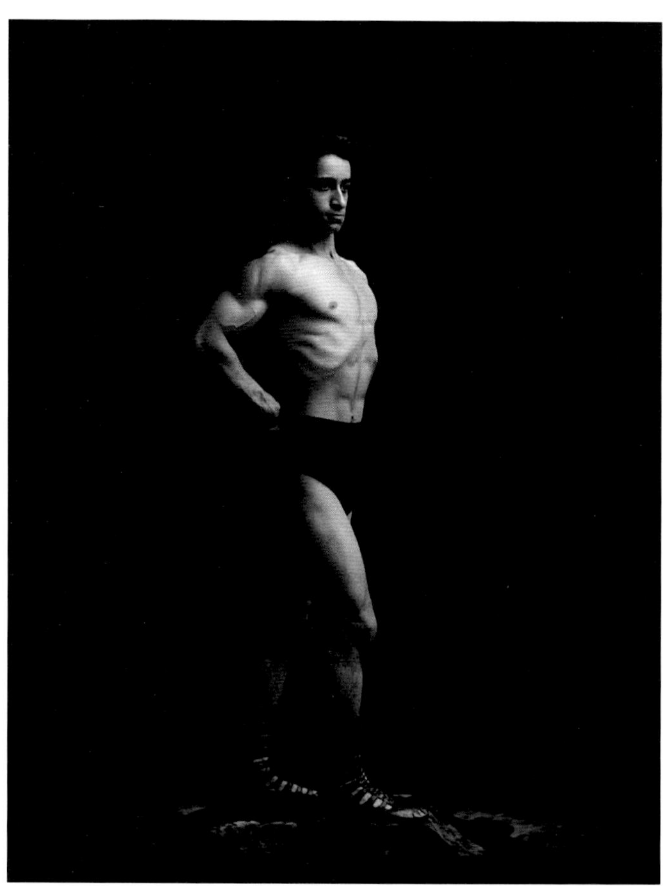

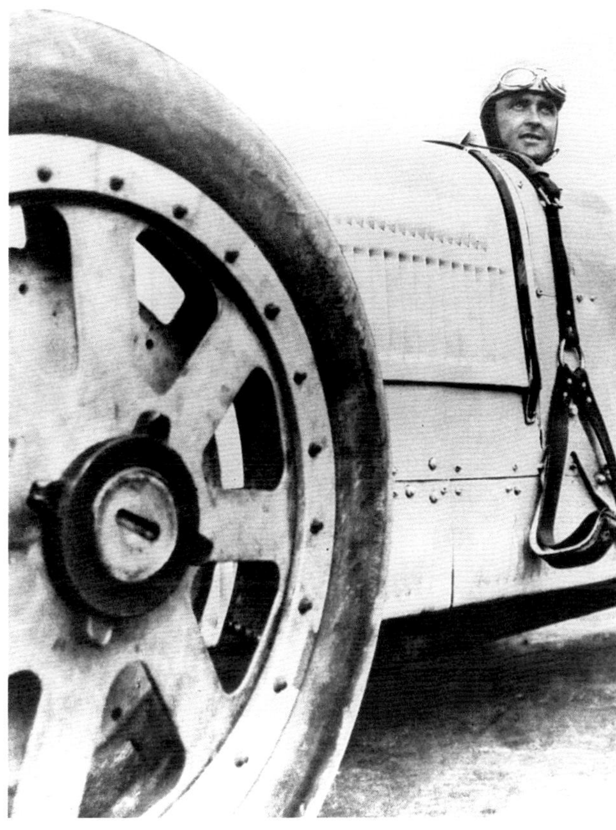

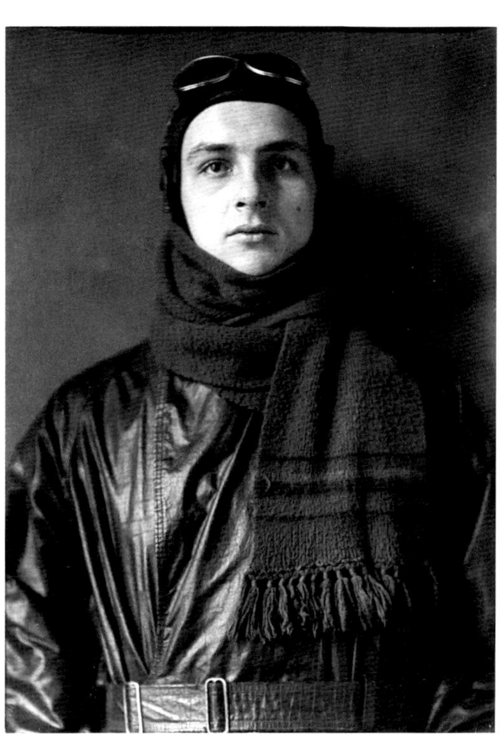

MAURICE TABARD
Louis Chiron, 1929, printed later
© Association des Amis de Maurice Tabard, Paris (cat. 42)

AUGUST SANDER
Young Sport Pilot, 1925
Collection of the International Museum of Photography at
George Eastman House, Rochester, New York; Purchase
© August Sander Archive, Cologne (cat. 30)

JAMES VAN DER ZEE
Swimming Team, Harlem, 1925, printed 1974
Collection of the High Museum of Art, Atlanta;
Purchase, (cat. 31)

AUGUST SANDER
Sport Association, Westerwald, ca. 1924
© August Sander Archive, Cologne (cat. 27)

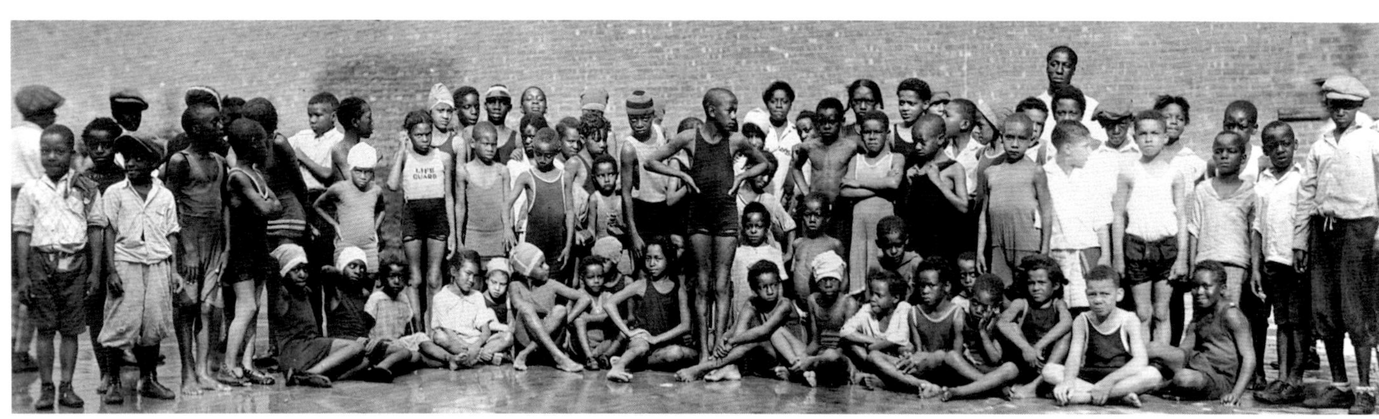

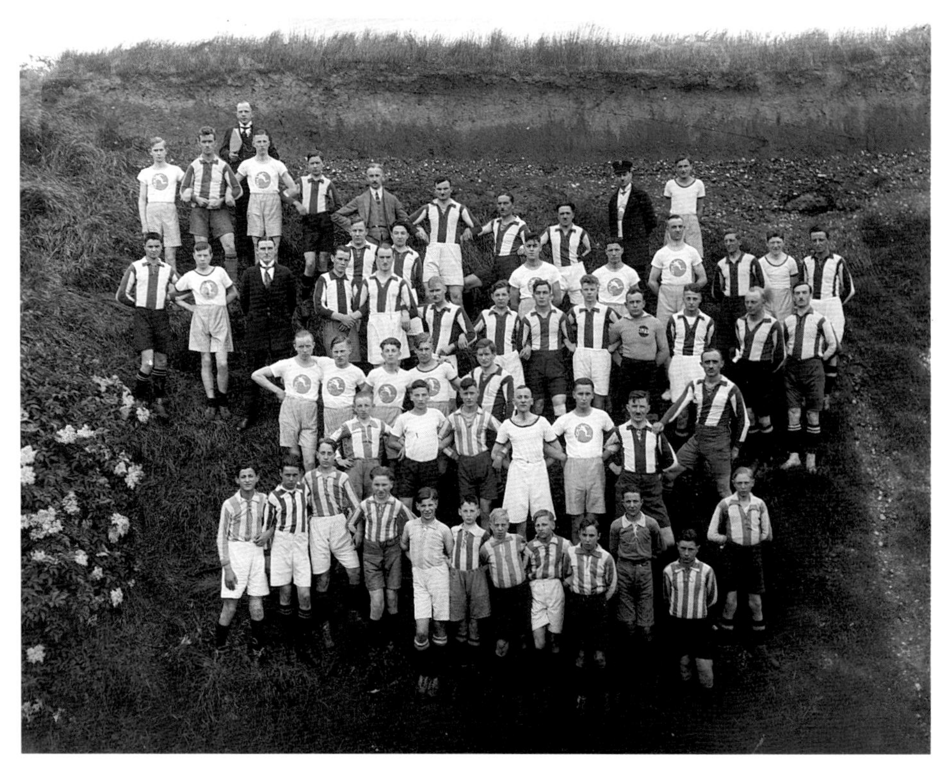

ARTHUR P. BEDOU
Men Playing Croquet under the Great Oak Trees, Mississippi, ca. 1930
Collection of the Schomburg Center for Research in Black Culture,
The New York Public Library, Astor, Lenox and Tilden Foundations (cat. 43)

ANSEL ADAMS
Skiing on Lembert Dome at Tuolomne Meadows, Yosemite National Park, ca. 1930
Collection of Dr. and Mrs. Michael Adams
Courtesy of The Ansel Adams Publishing Rights Trust (cat. 45)

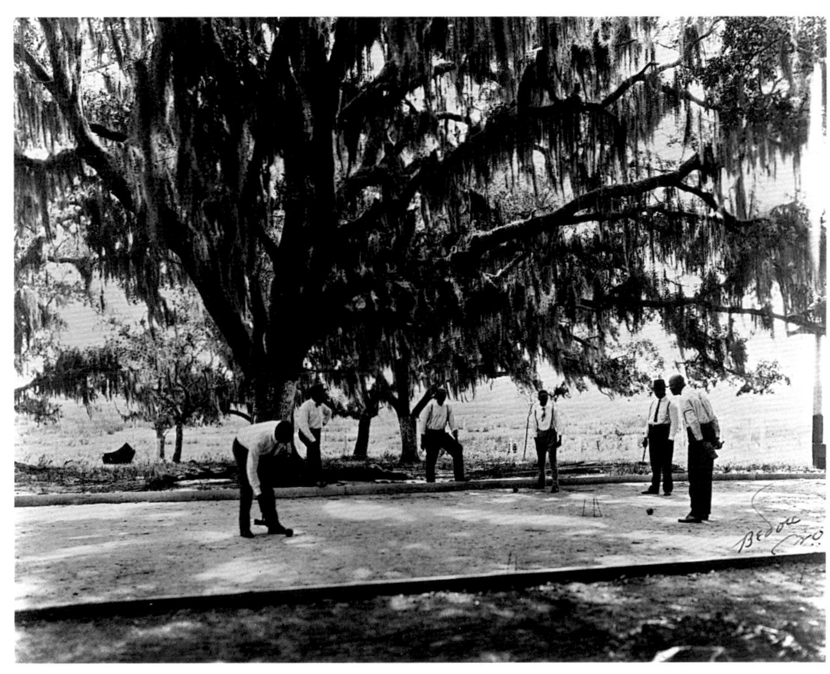

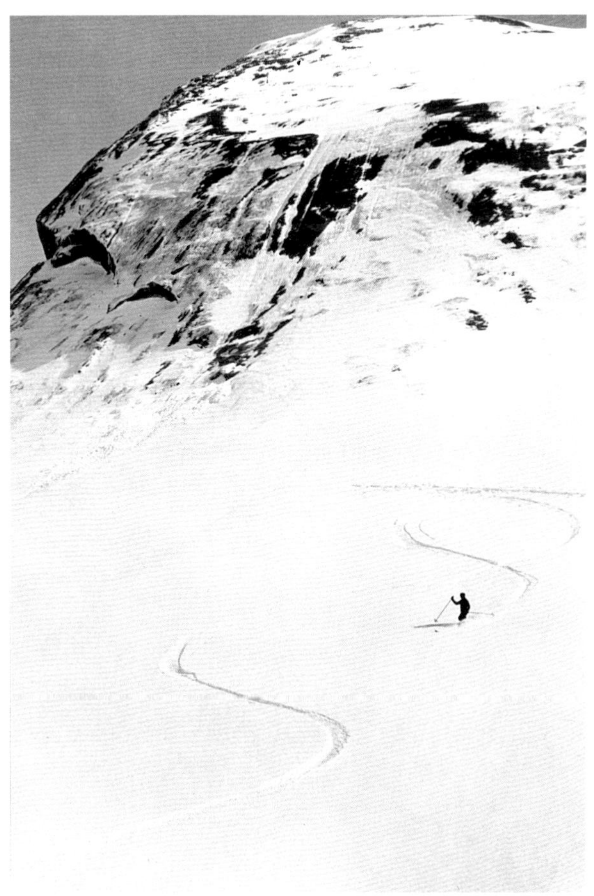

LÁSZLÓ MOHOLY-NAGY
Boxing – Adam Sport Article, 1924
Collection of The J. Paul Getty Museum, Malibu, California (cat. 28)

Sailing, 1926
Collection of the International Museum of Photography at
George Eastman House, Rochester, New York; Purchase (cat. 33)

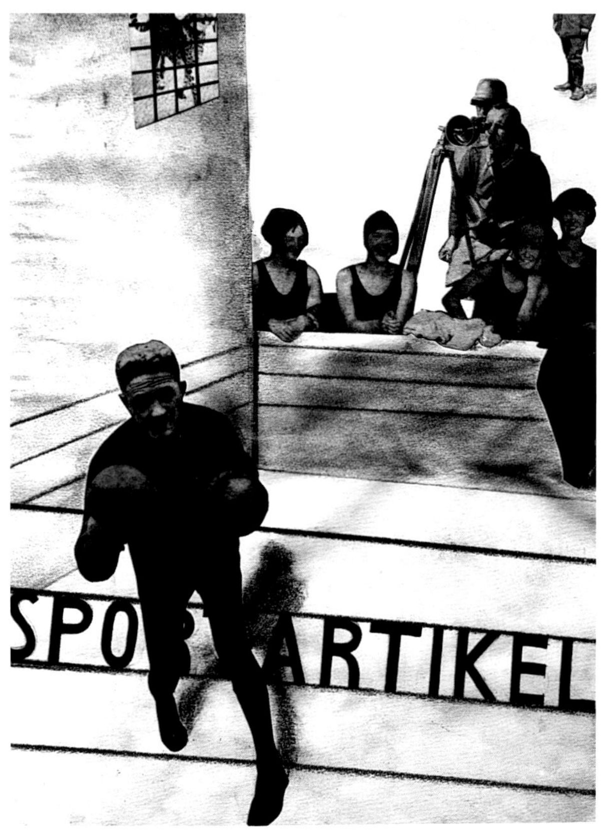

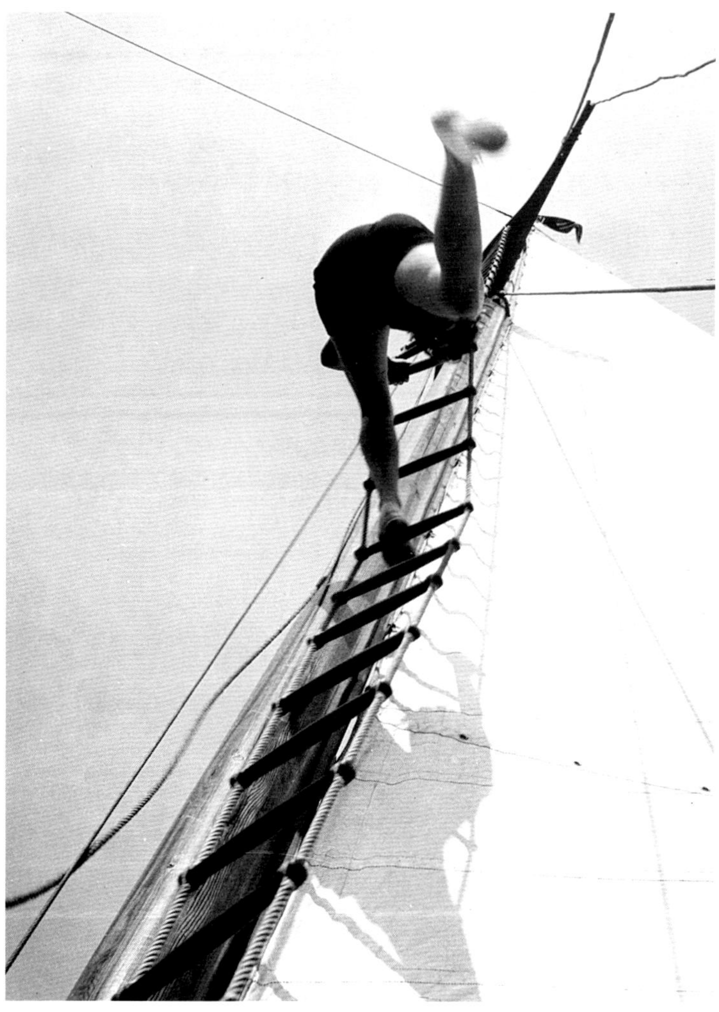

EL LISSITZKY
Runner in the City, ca. 1926
Courtesy Houk Friedman, New York (cat. 32)

WILLI BAUMEISTER
Athlete, 1926
Courtesy Archiv Baumeister, Stuttgart (cat. 35)

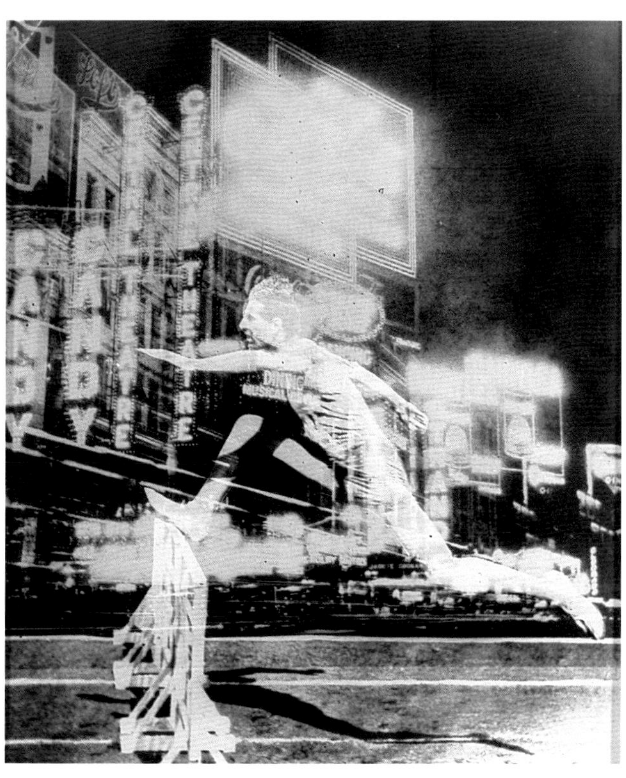

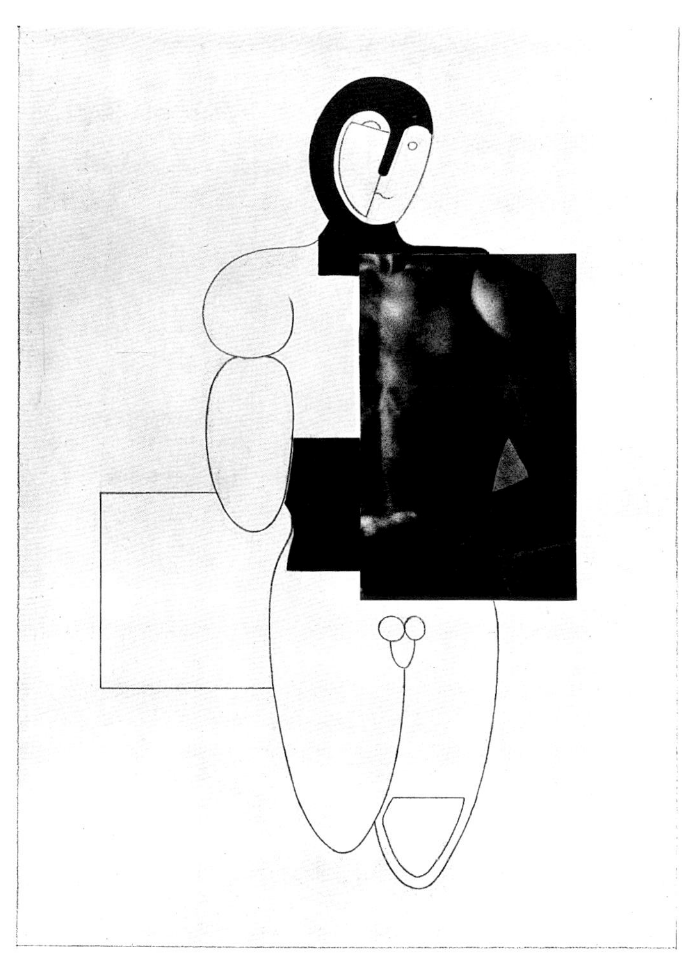

GEORGE HOYNINGEN-HUENE
Johnny Weissmuller, 1930
Courtesy Staley-Wise Gallery, New York (cat. 46)

NICKOLAS MURAY
Babe Ruth (George Herman Ruth), ca. 1927
Collection of The Museum of Modern Art,
New York; Gift of Mrs. Nickolas Muray (cat. 36)

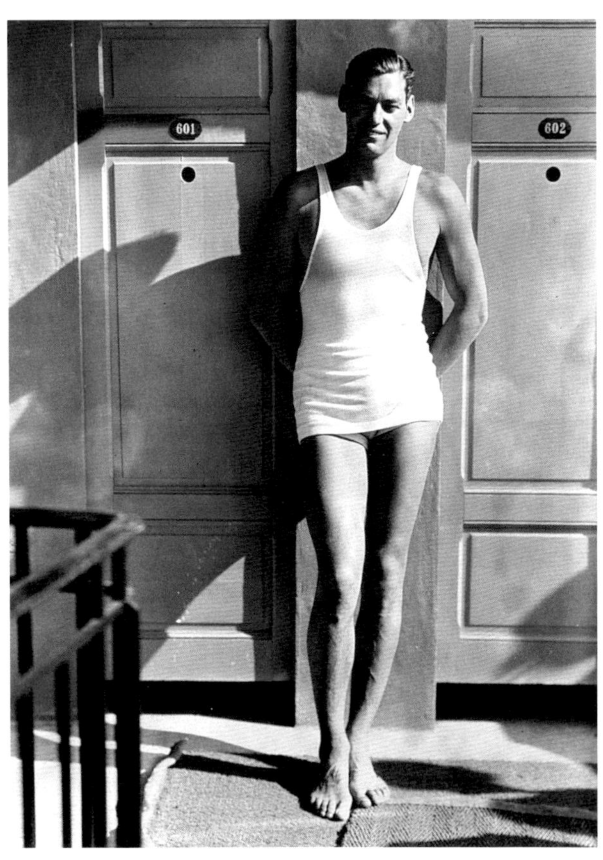

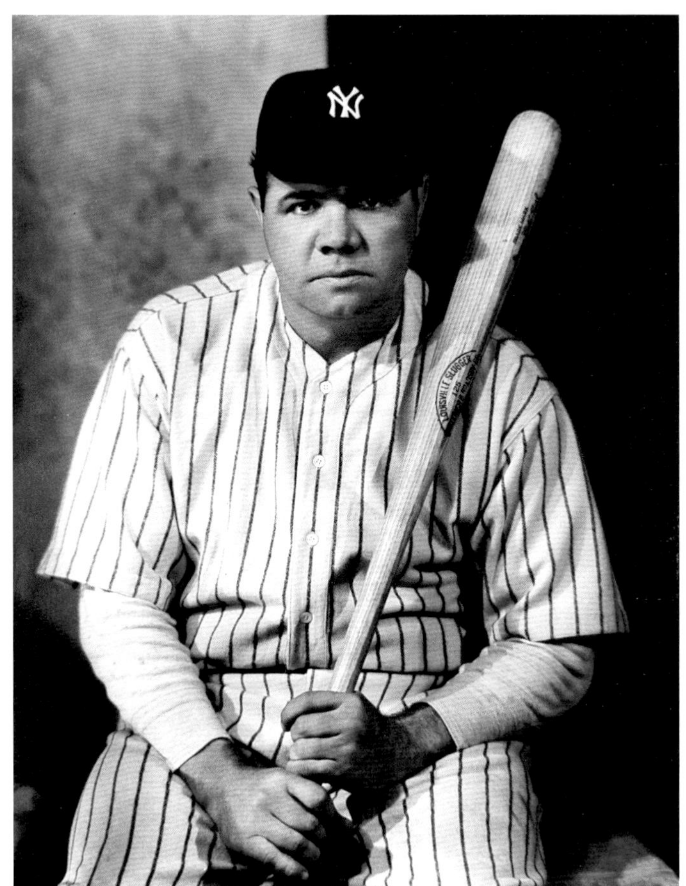

LOTHAR JECK
Orlikon Bike Course in Zurich, 1928, printed later
Courtesy Archiv Rolf Jeck, Basel (cat. 38)

JOHN GUTMANN
Out of the Pool, 1934
Courtesy Fraenkel Gallery, San Francisco
© 1986 John Gutmann (cat. 53)

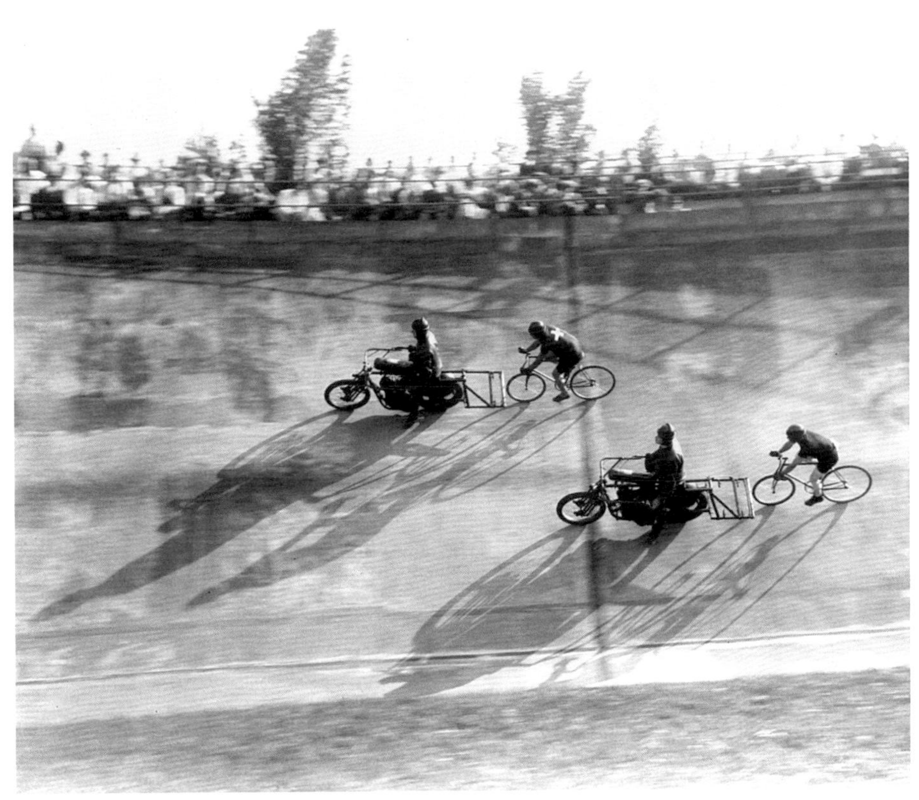

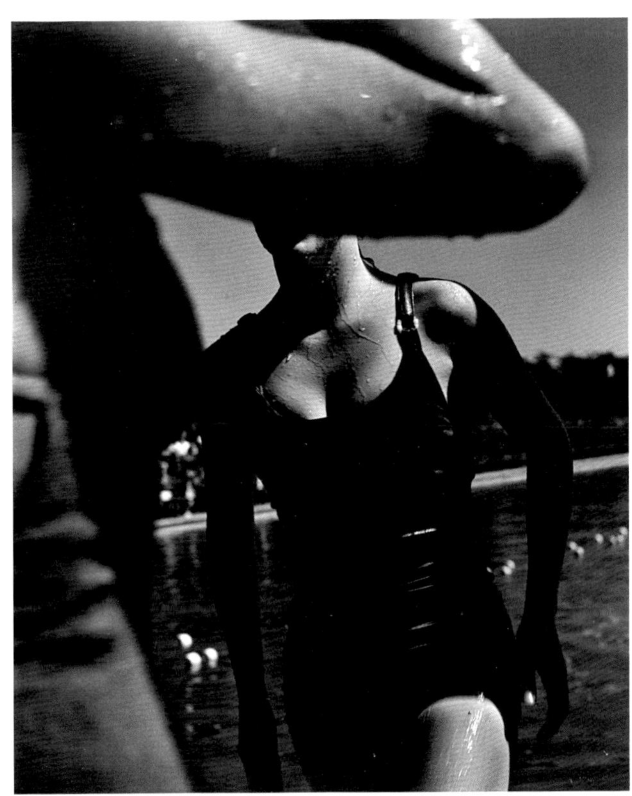

HAROLD E. EDGERTON

Wes Fesler Kicking a Football, 1934
Collection of the International Museum of Photography at George
Eastman House, Rochester, New York; Gift of Dr. Harold E. Edgerton
© The Estate of Harold E. Edgerton (cat. 52)

Densmore Shute Bending the Shaft, 1938
Collection of the International Museum of Photography at George
Eastman House, Rochester, New York; Gift of Dr. Harold E. Edgerton
© The Estate of Harold E. Edgerton (cat. 66)

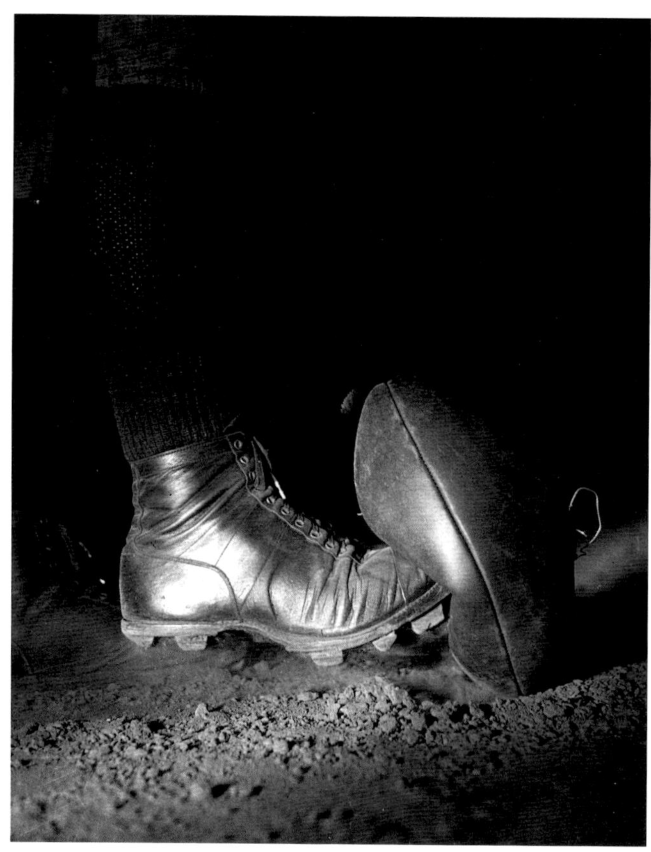

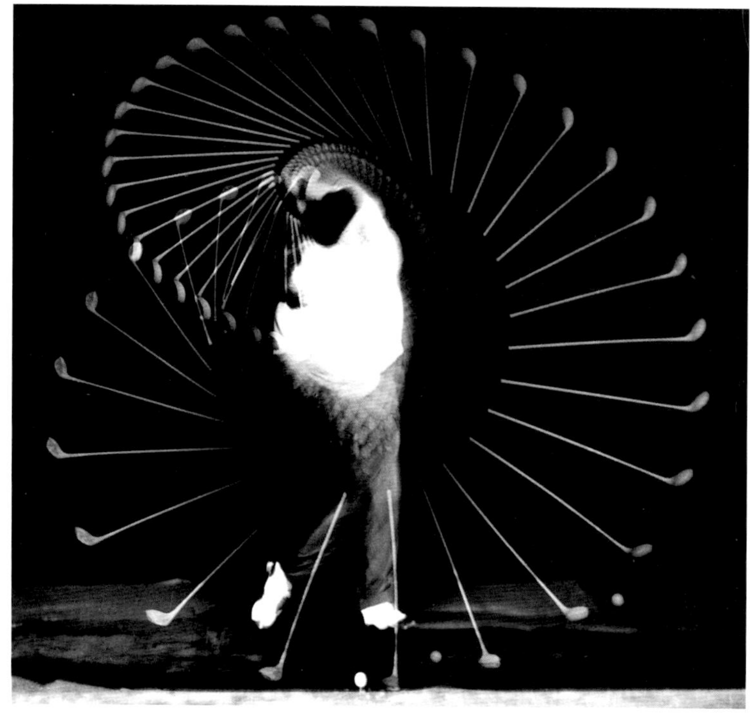

WILLARD VAN DYKE
Boxer's Hands, ca. 1933
Collection of Patricia Stevens Lowinsky (cat. 49)

HAROLD E. EDGERTON
Boxing, 1938
Collection of Patricia Stevens Lowinsky
© The Estate of Harold E. Edgerton (cat. 67)

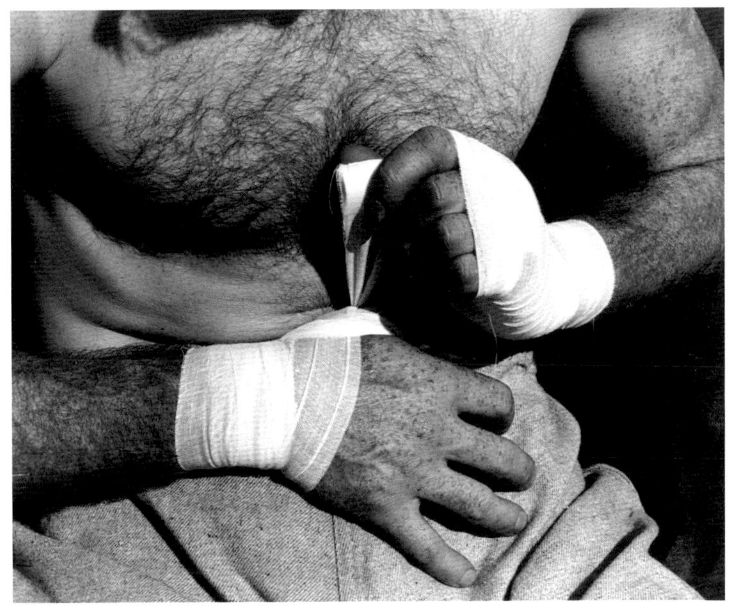

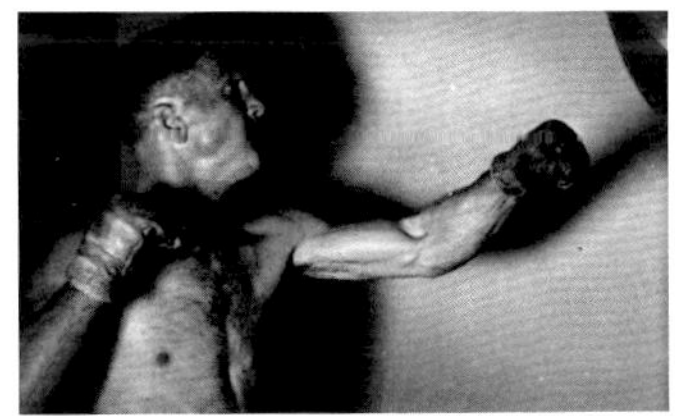 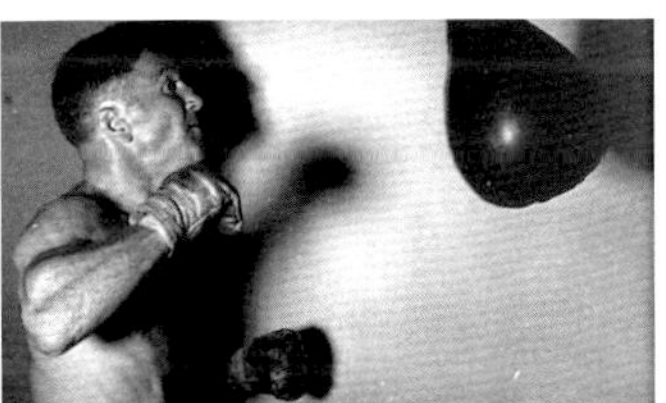 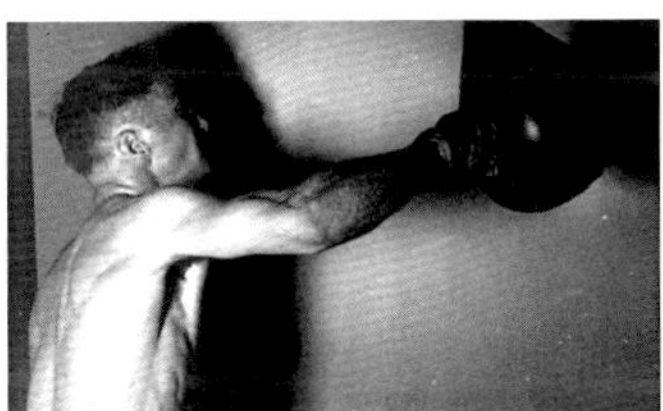 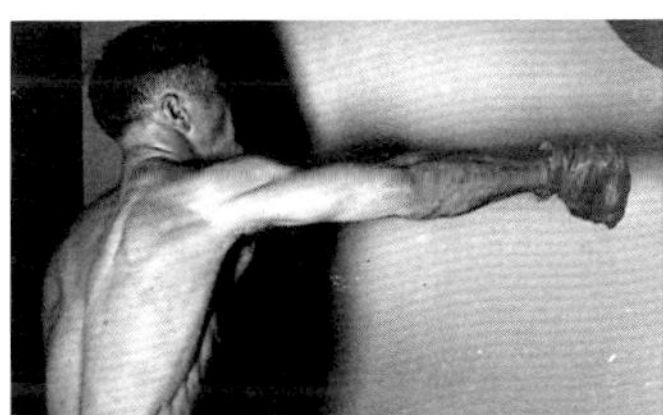

RHEINHOLD SPIRA
Swimmer, ca. 1933
Courtesy Monah L. Gettner/Hyperion Press Ltd., New York (cat. 50)

BILL BRANDT
Tic-tac Men at Ascot Races, 1935
Courtesy Houk Friedman, New York (cat. 57)

MARGARET BOURKE-WHITE
The Yacht Vanitie in a Practice Spin, Newport, 1934
Margaret Bourke-White Papers, George Arents Research Library
for Special Collections at Syracuse University, New York
© The Estate of Margaret Bourke-White (cat. 55)

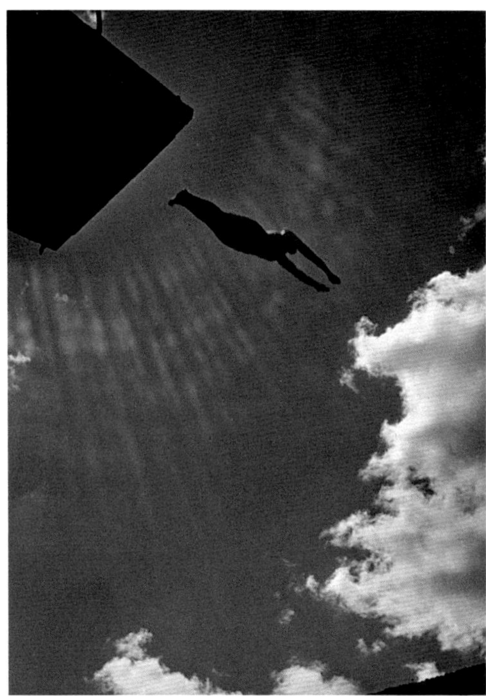

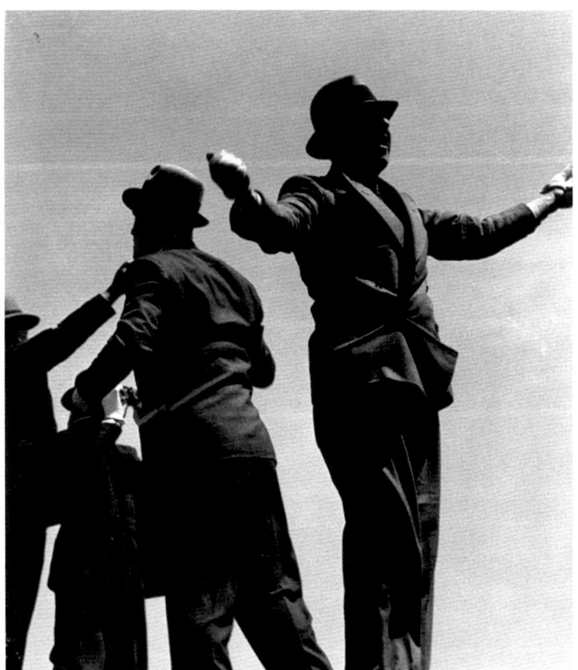

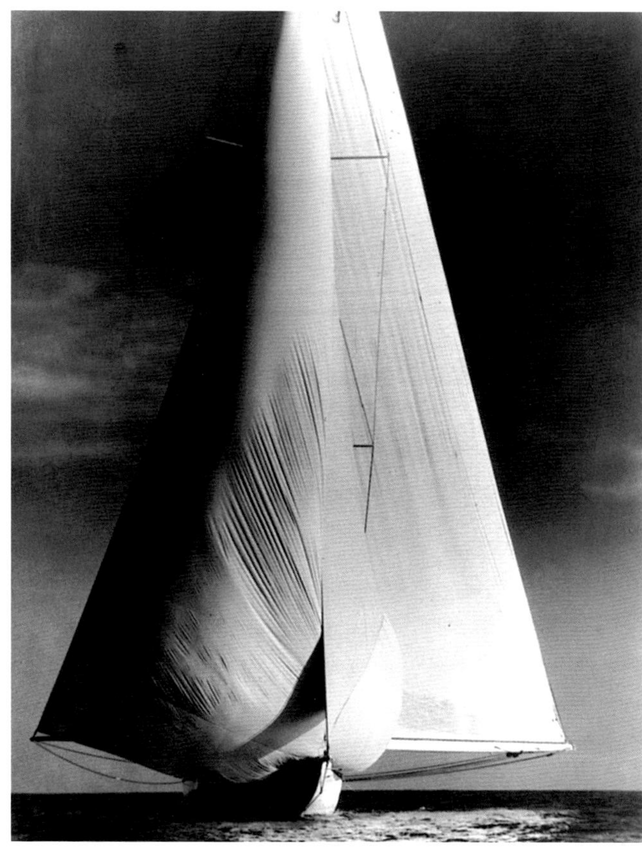

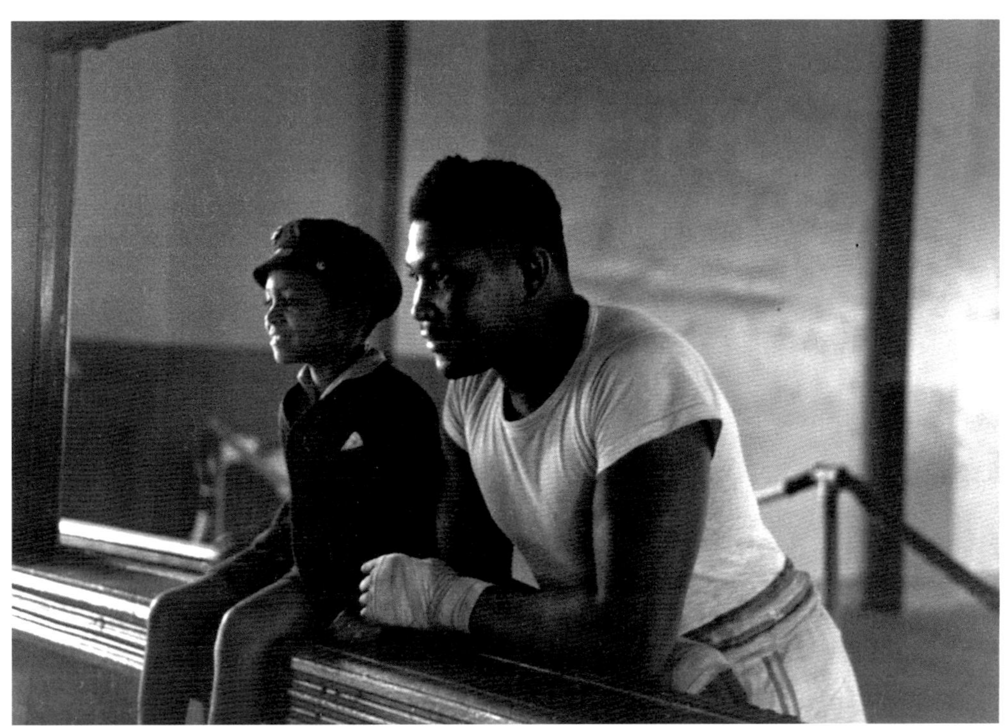

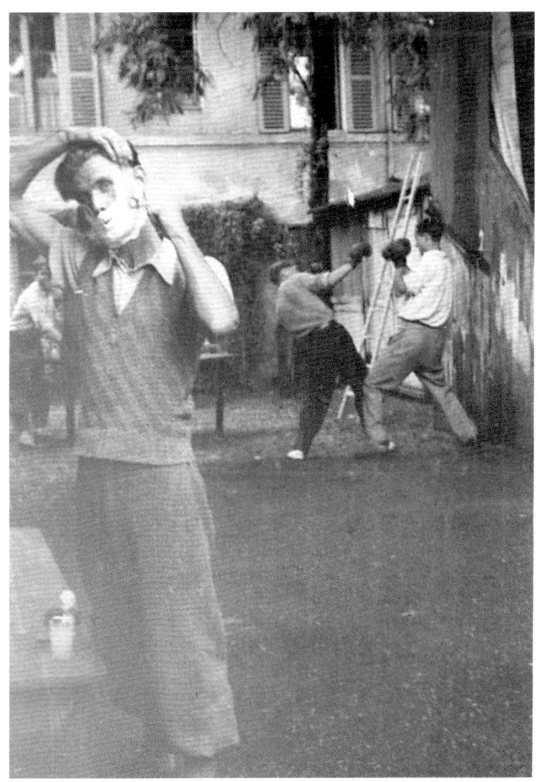

PIET ZWART
Sport, ca. 1935
Collection of the New Orleans Museum of Art; Purchase 80.37 (cat. 60)

LOTHAR JECK
Gymnasts, 1936, printed later
Courtesy Archiv Rolf Jeck, Basel (cat. 61)

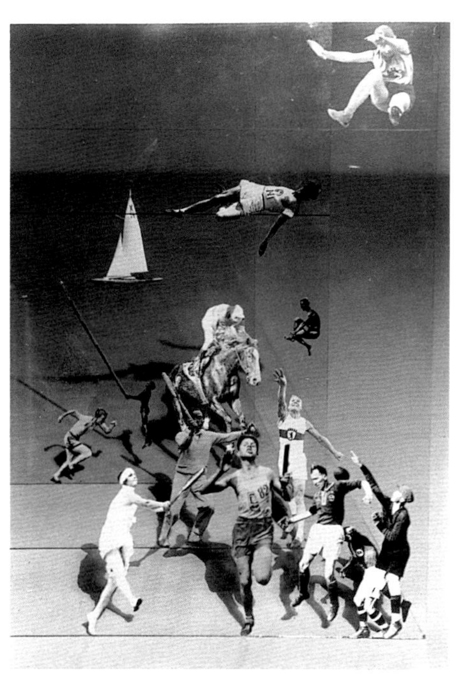

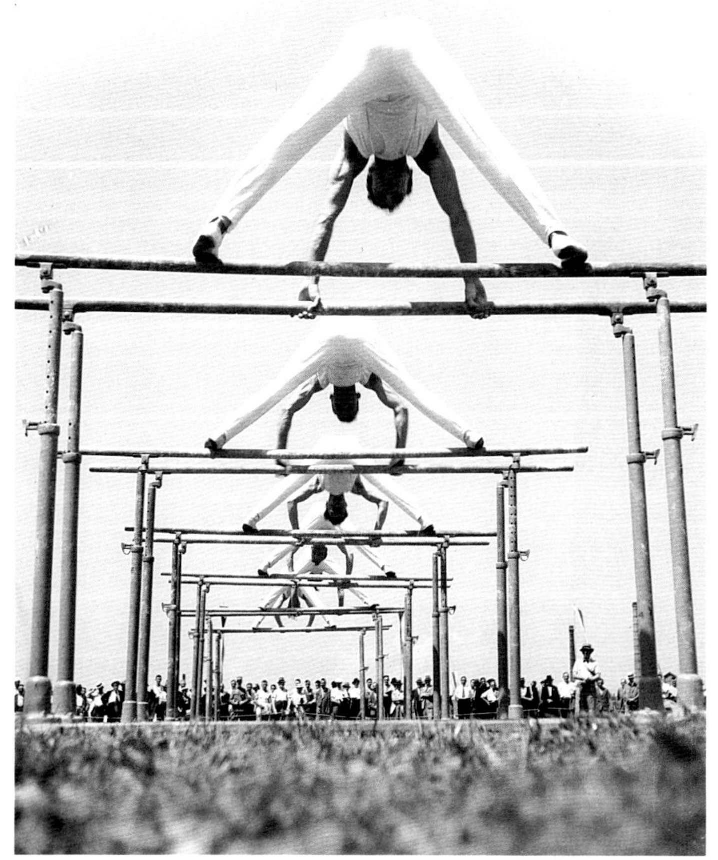

EDWARD QUIGLEY
Tennis Racquet, 1935
Keith de Lellis Collection, New York (cat. 59)

RENÉ-JACQUES
Illustration to Les Olympiques (The Olympics)
by Henry de Montherlant, 1948
Courtesy Ministère de la Culture, Association française
pour la diffusion du patrimoine photographique, Paris (cat. 84)

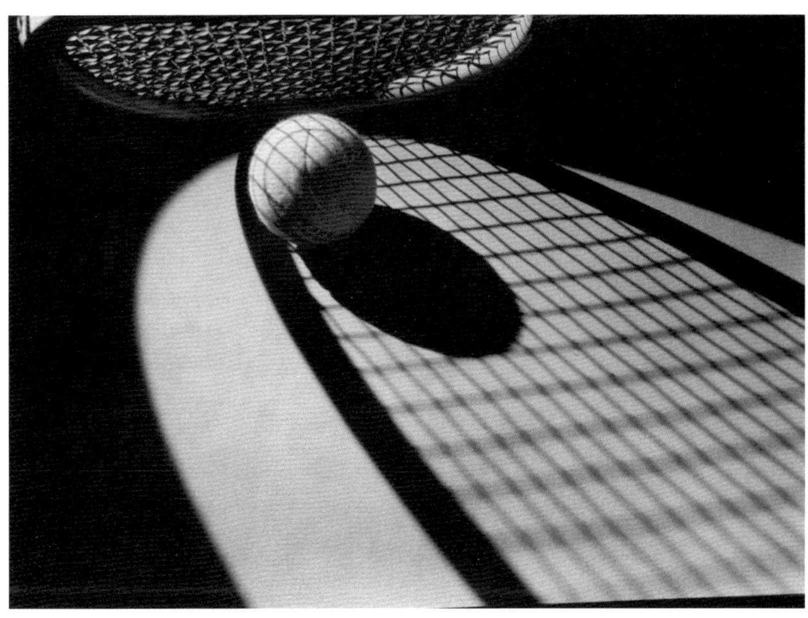

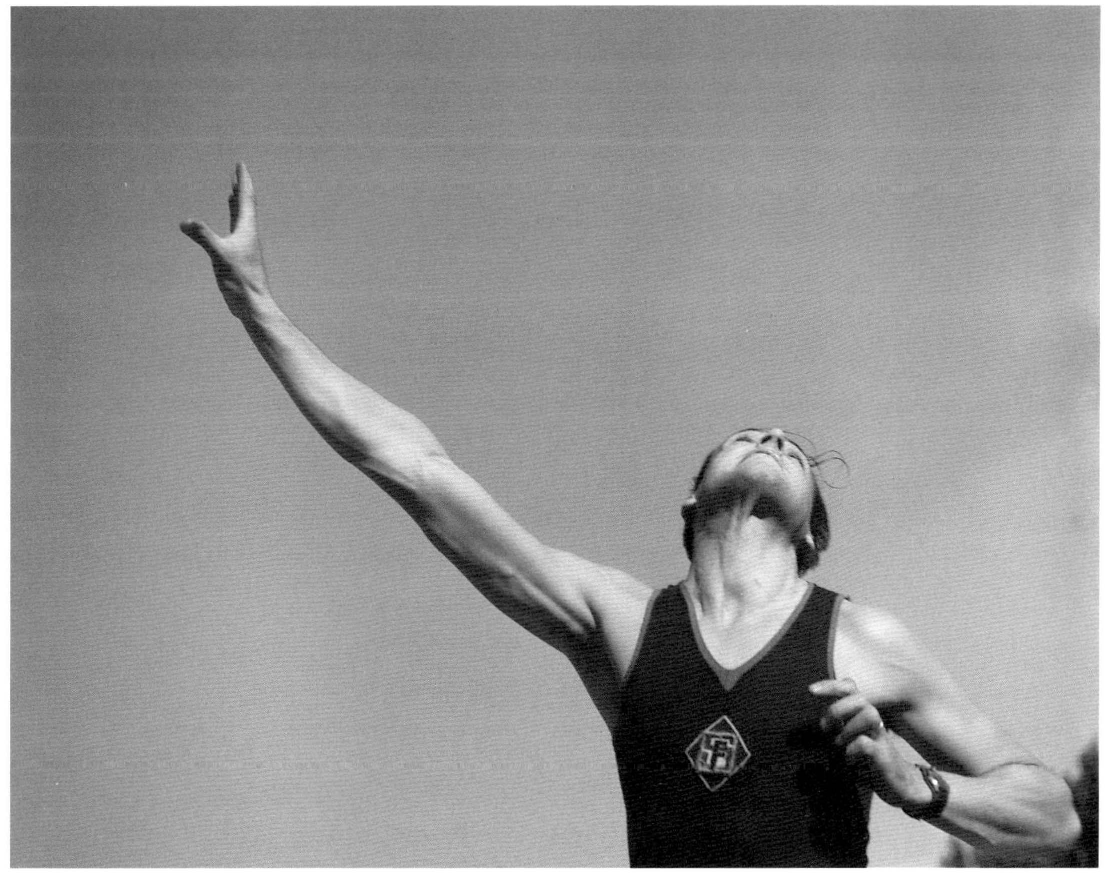

ALEXANDER RODCHENKO
Dynamo Sports Club, 1930, printed later
Courtesy Walker, Ursitti & McGinniss, New York (cat. 48)

GEORGI ZELMA
Champions of Moscow on Red Square, 1938, printed later
Courtesy Walker, Ursitti & McGinniss, New York (cat. 69)

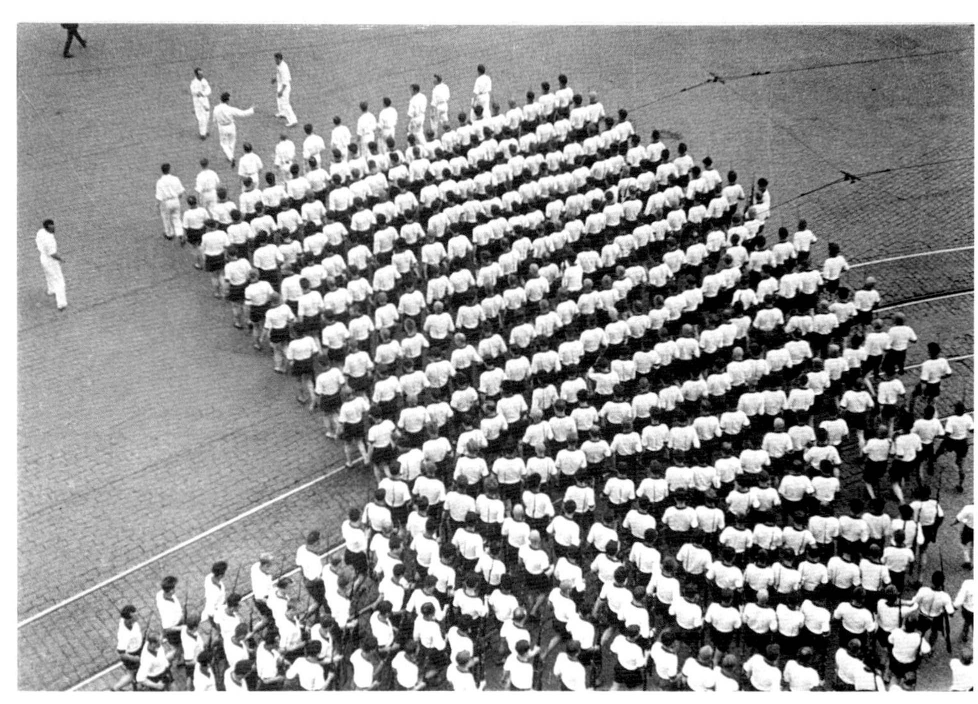

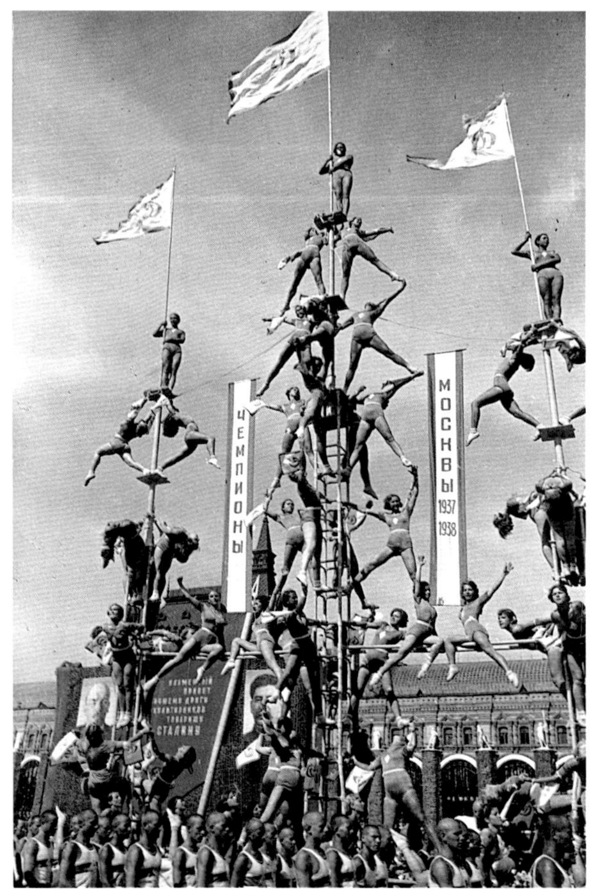

ALEXANDER RODCHENKO
Wheel, Gymnastics Festival, Red Square, Moscow, 1936, printed later
Courtesy Walker, Ursitti & McGinniss, New York (cat. 62)

HENRI CARTIER-BRESSON
Sport Parade, Red Square, Moscow, 1954
Courtesy of the artist
© Henri Cartier-Bresson (cat. 91)

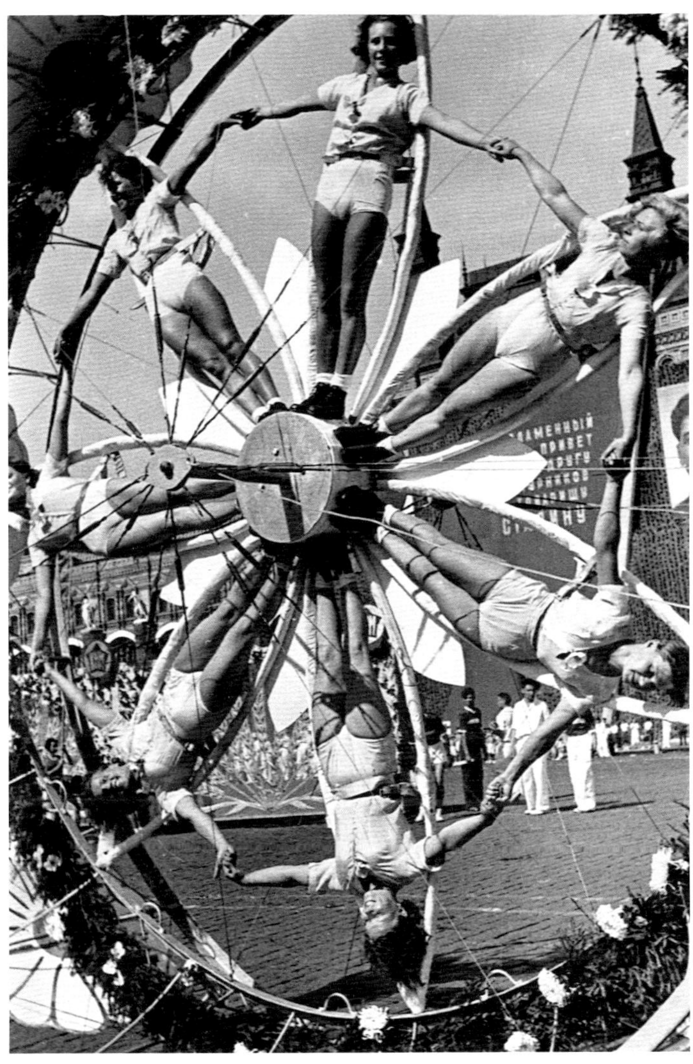

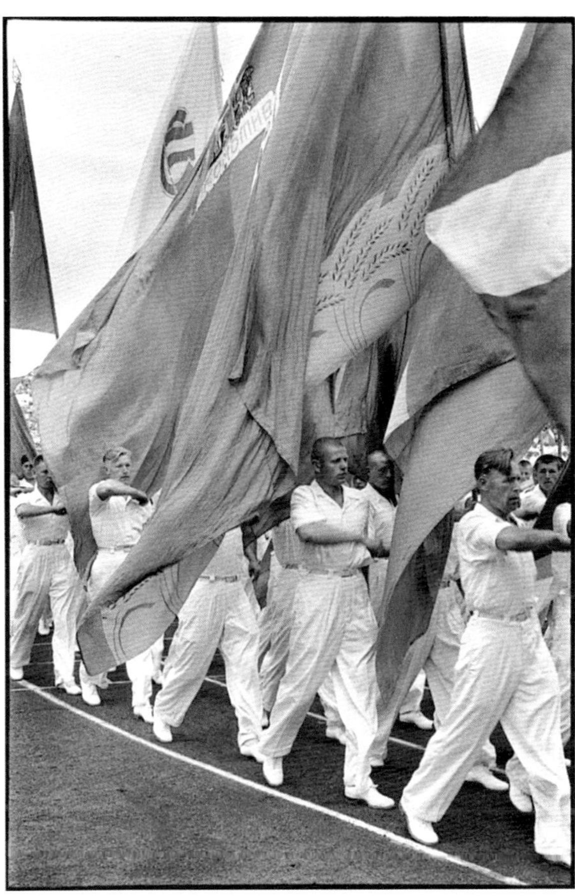

W. EUGENE SMITH
Notre Dame, Kansas, 1937
Collection of the Center for Creative Photography,
The University of Arizona, Tucson
© 1991 The Heirs of W. Eugene Smith (cat. 63)

American Football, 1941
Collection of the Center for Creative Photography,
The University of Arizona, Tucson
© 1991 The Heirs of W. Eugene Smith (cat. 76)

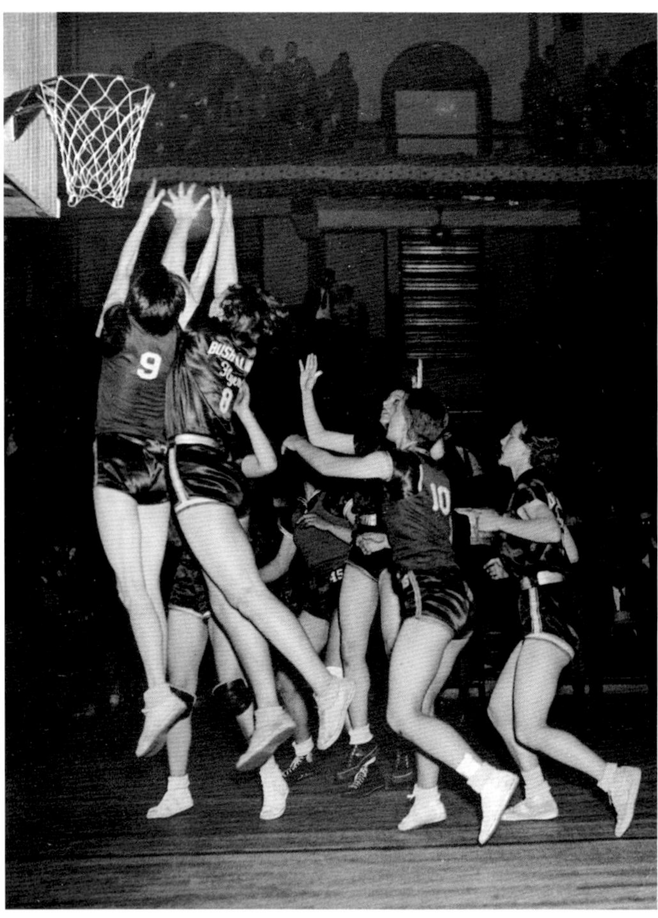

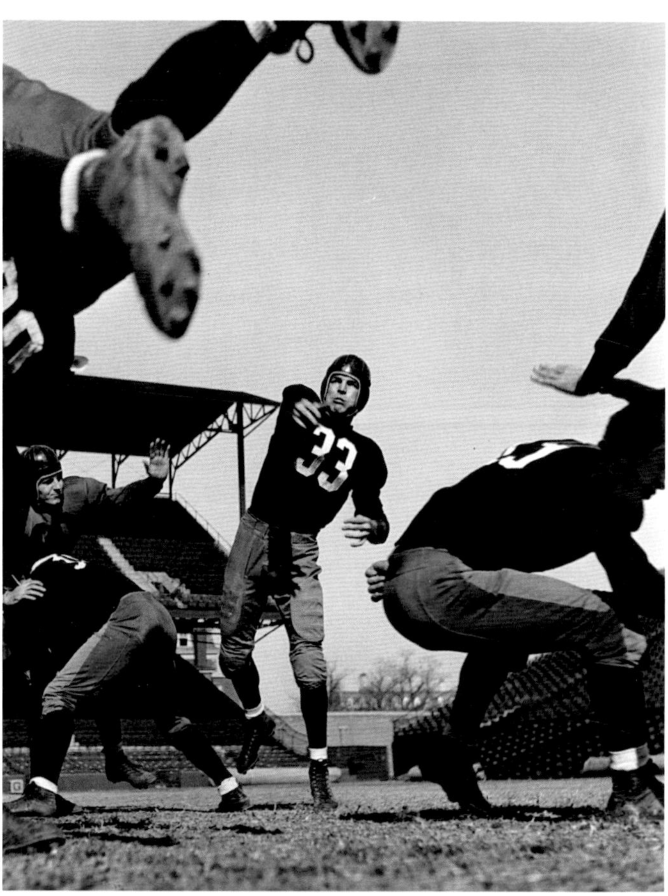

MARION POST WOLCOTT
Sulky Race, Shelbyville County Fair, Kentucky, 1940, printed later
Courtesy Yancey Richardson/Lumina Fine Photography & Art, New York
© The Estate of Marion Post Wolcott (cat. 73)

WILLIAM HEICK
Five Cents a Cue, North Beach, San Francisco, 1947
Courtesy of the artist (cat. 80)

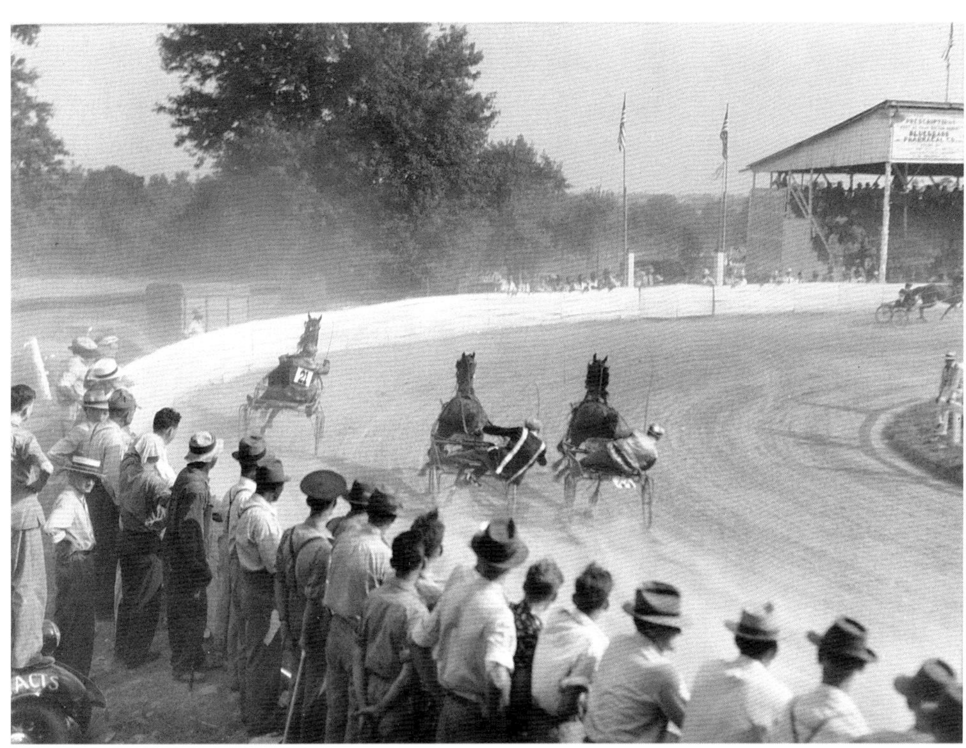

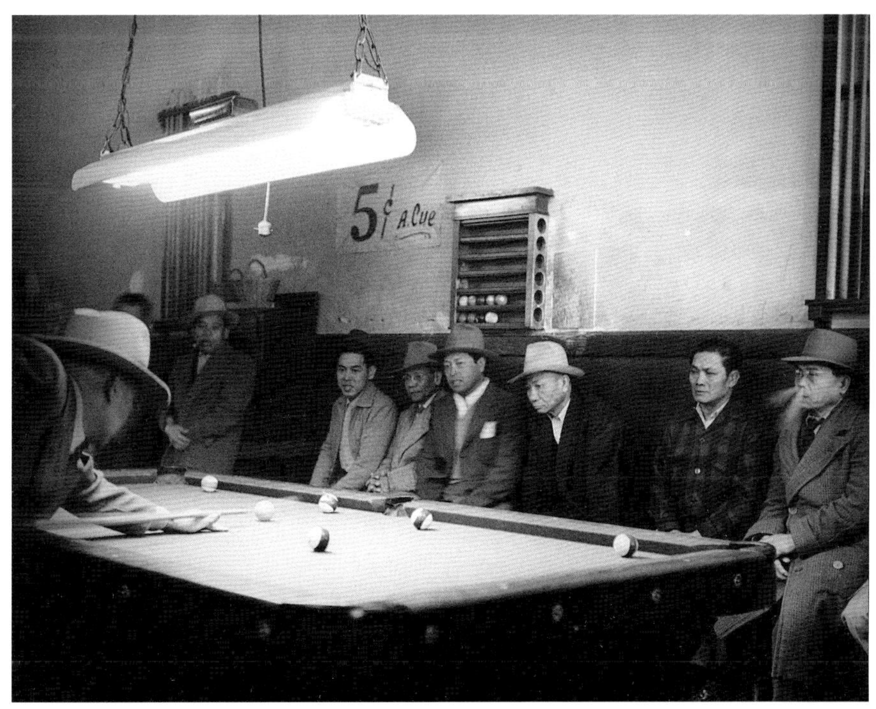

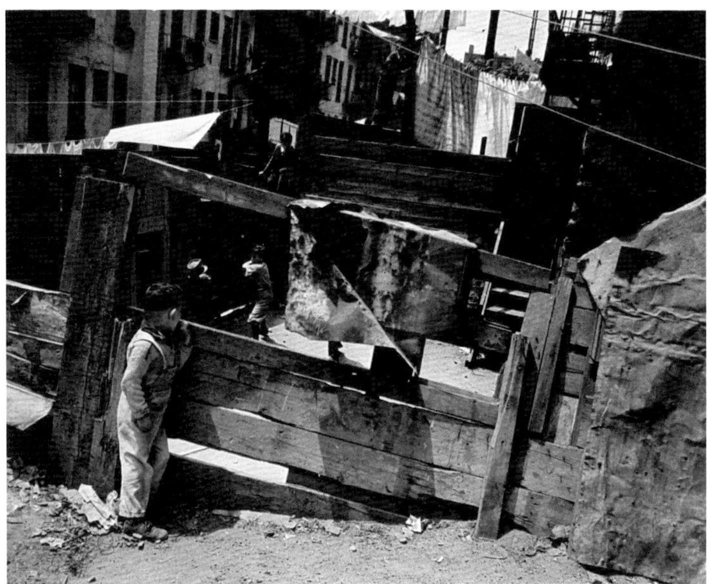

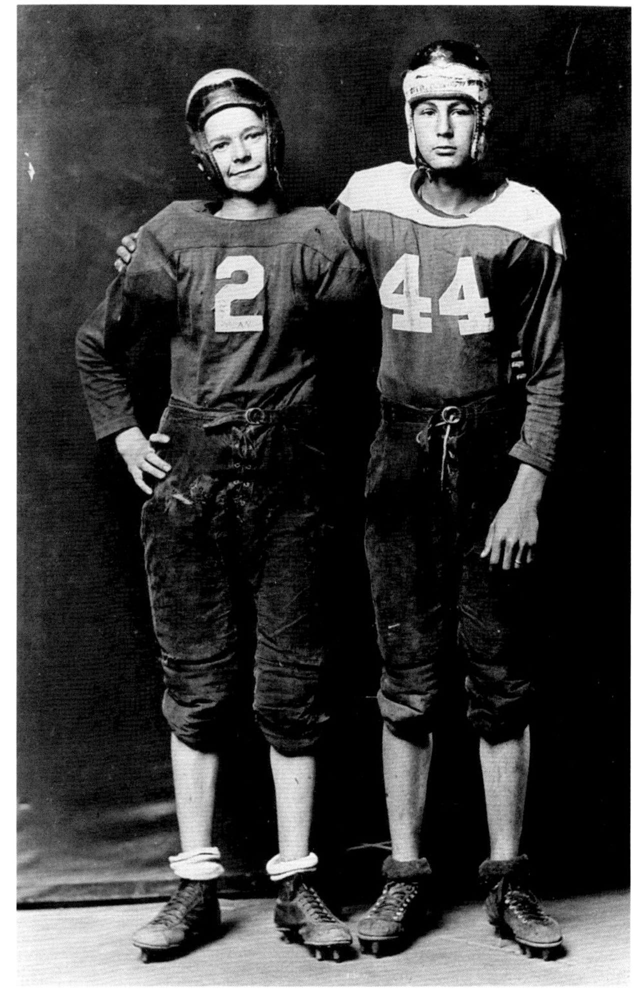

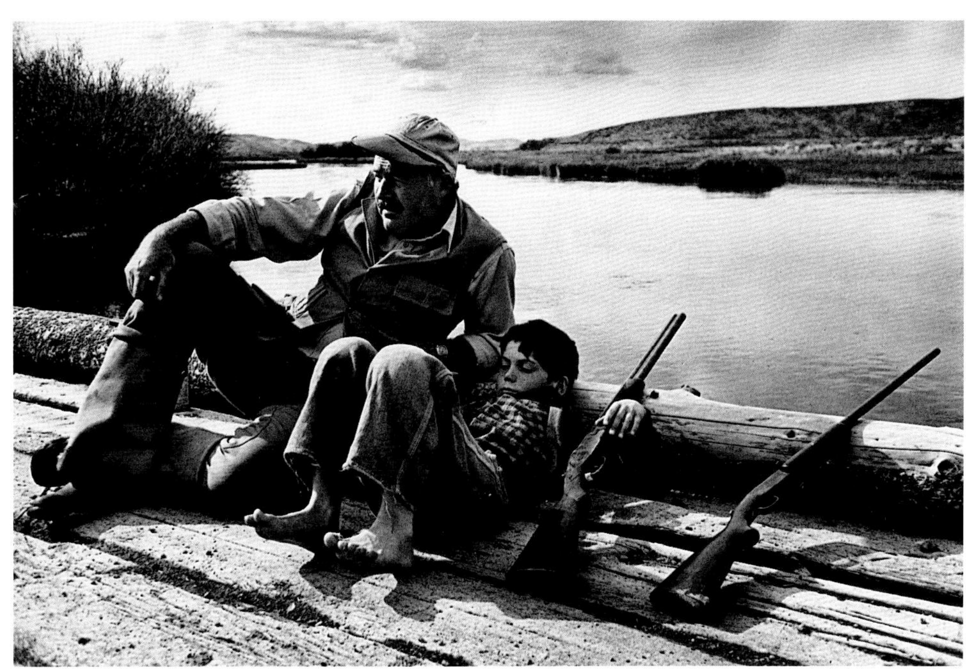

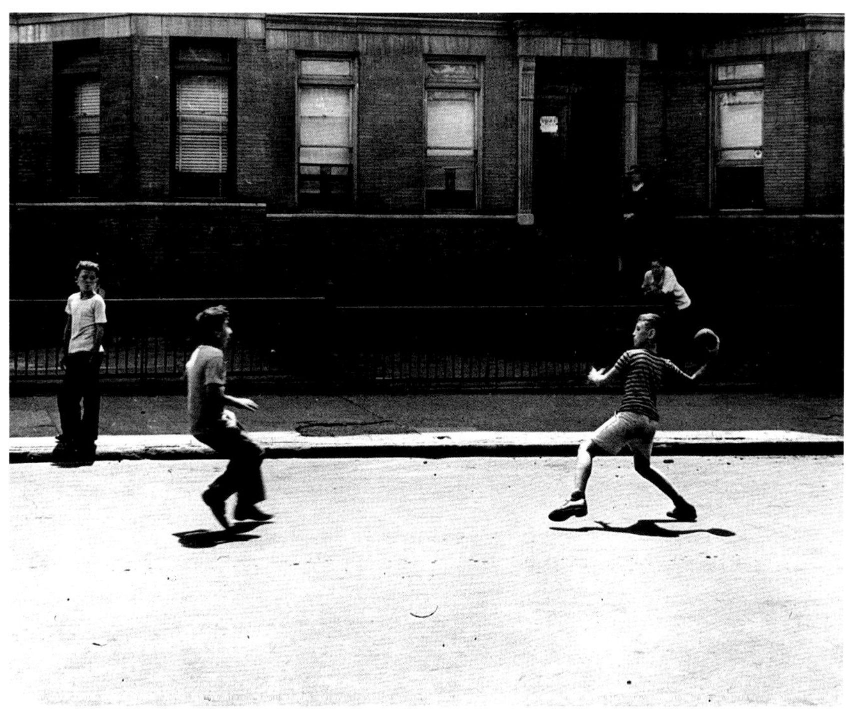

SIDNEY GROSSMAN
Whitey Bimstein, Trainer, from the series "BOXING," 1951
Collection of The Museum of Fine Arts, Houston;
The Target Collection of American Photography,
Museum purchase with funds provided by Target Stores (cat. 88)

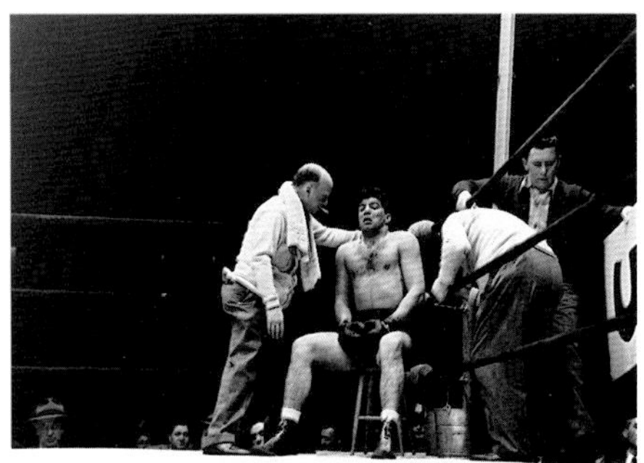
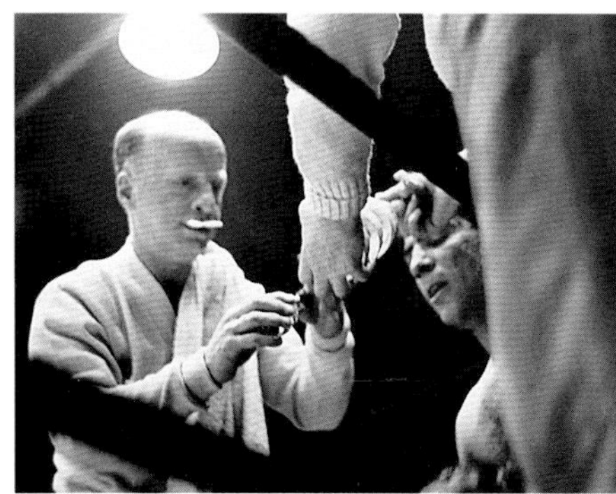
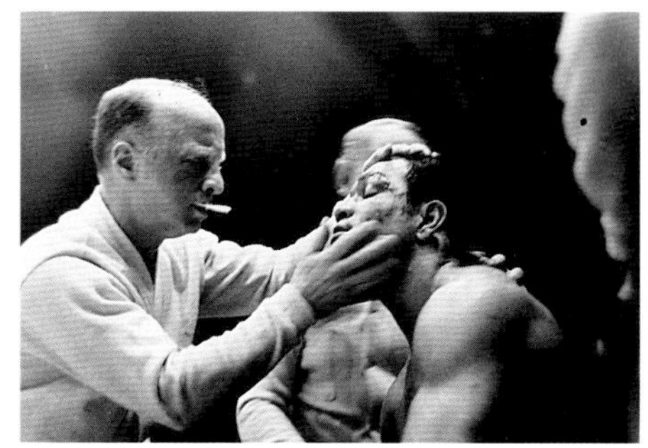
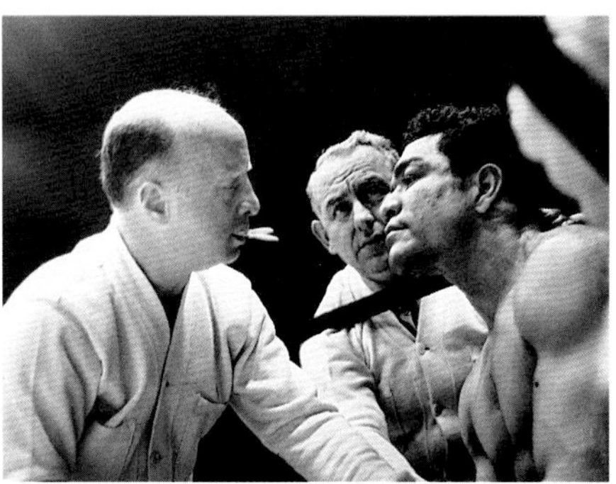
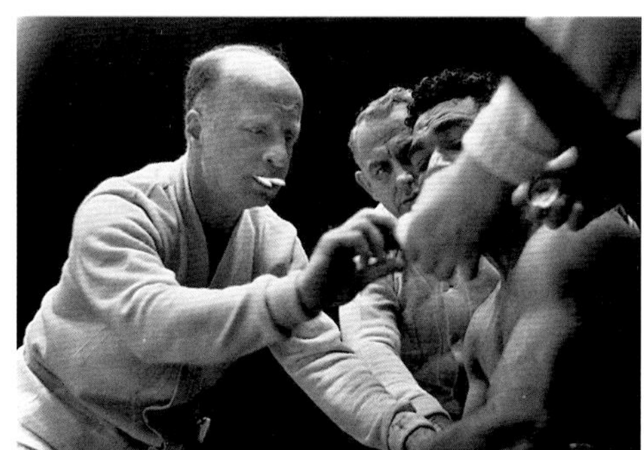
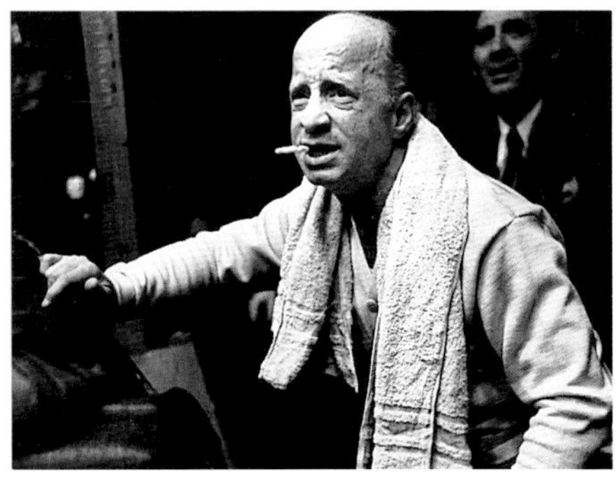
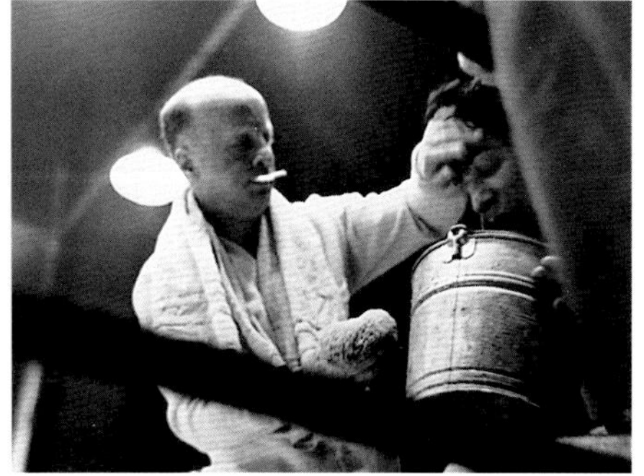
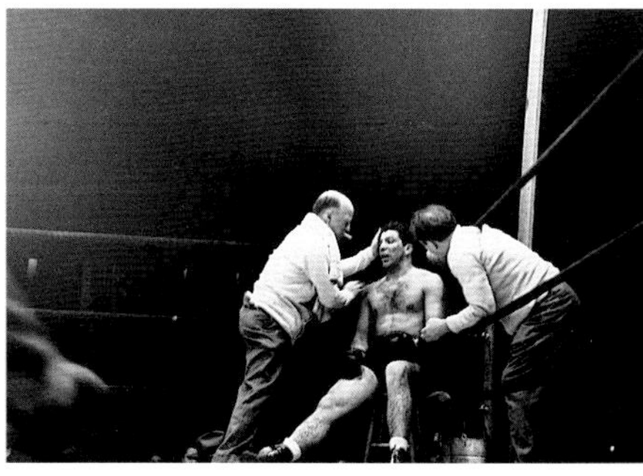
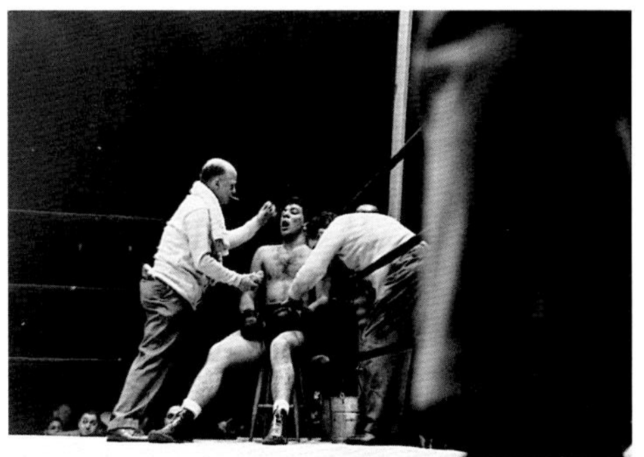
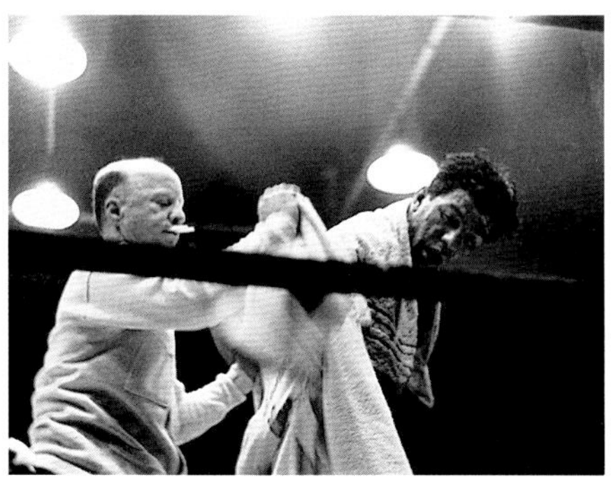

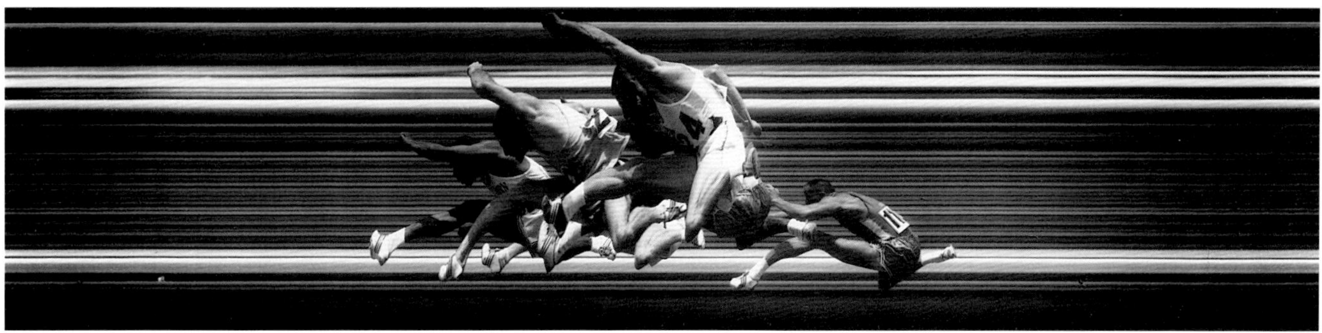

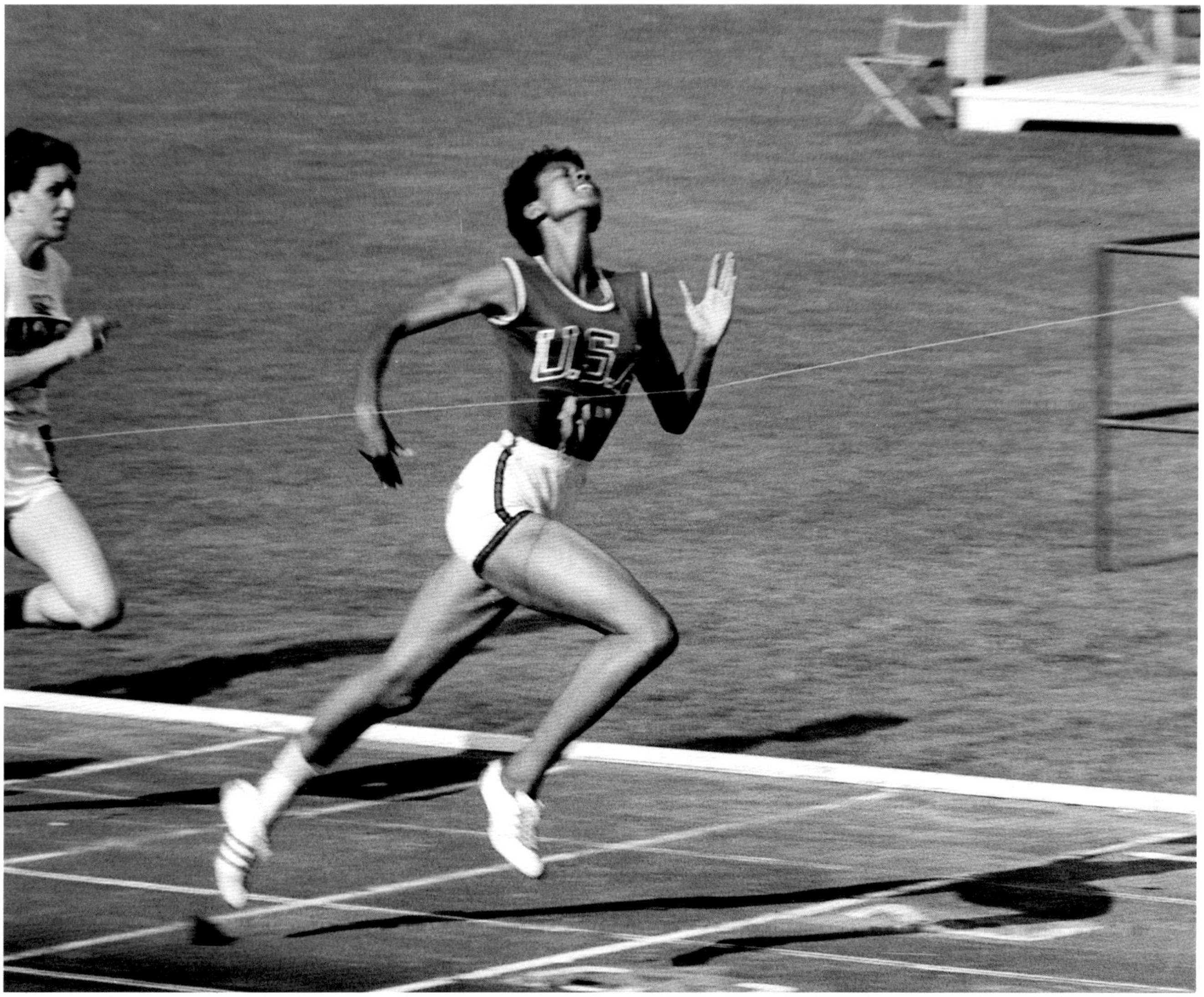

GARRY WINOGRAND
Workout: Floyd Patterson, ca. 1954
Collection of the Center for Creative Photography,
The University of Arizona, Tucson
© The Estate of Garry Winogrand (cat. 89)

ROY DeCARAVA
Ex-Fighter, 1961
Courtesy of the artist and The Witkin Gallery, Inc., New York (cat. 99)

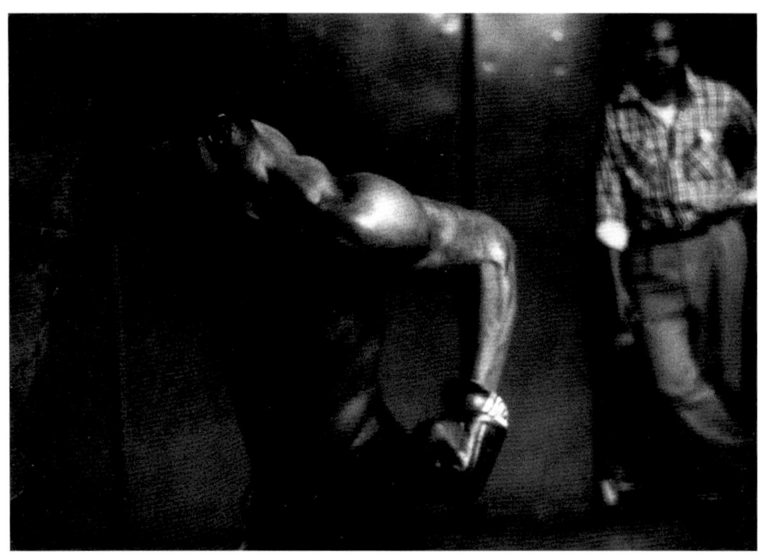

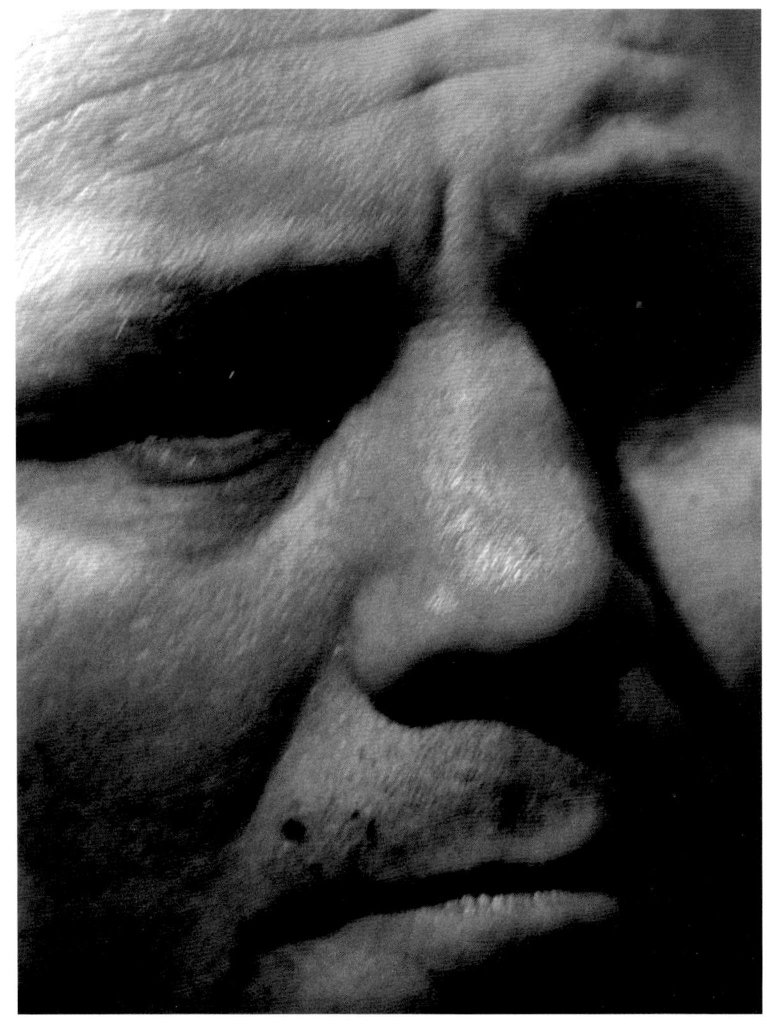

AUSTIN HANSEN
Harlemites Gathered for "Joe Louis Day" Parade, 1946
Collection of the Schomburg Center for Research in Black Culture,
The New York Public Library, Astor, Lenox and Tilden Foundations (cat. 79)

ROBERT DOISNEAU
The Center of the Sporting Club, 1954
Collection of Patricia Stevens Lowinsky (cat. 90)

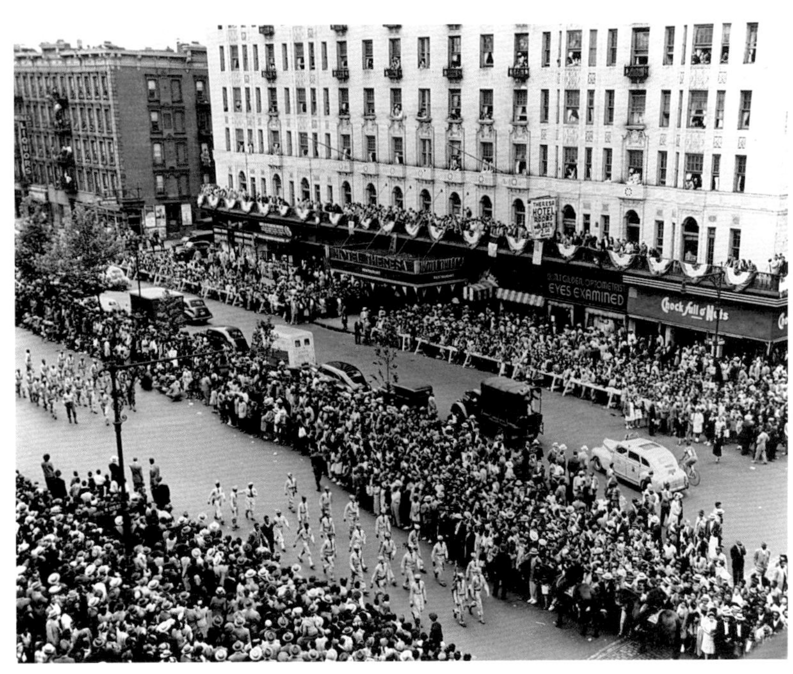

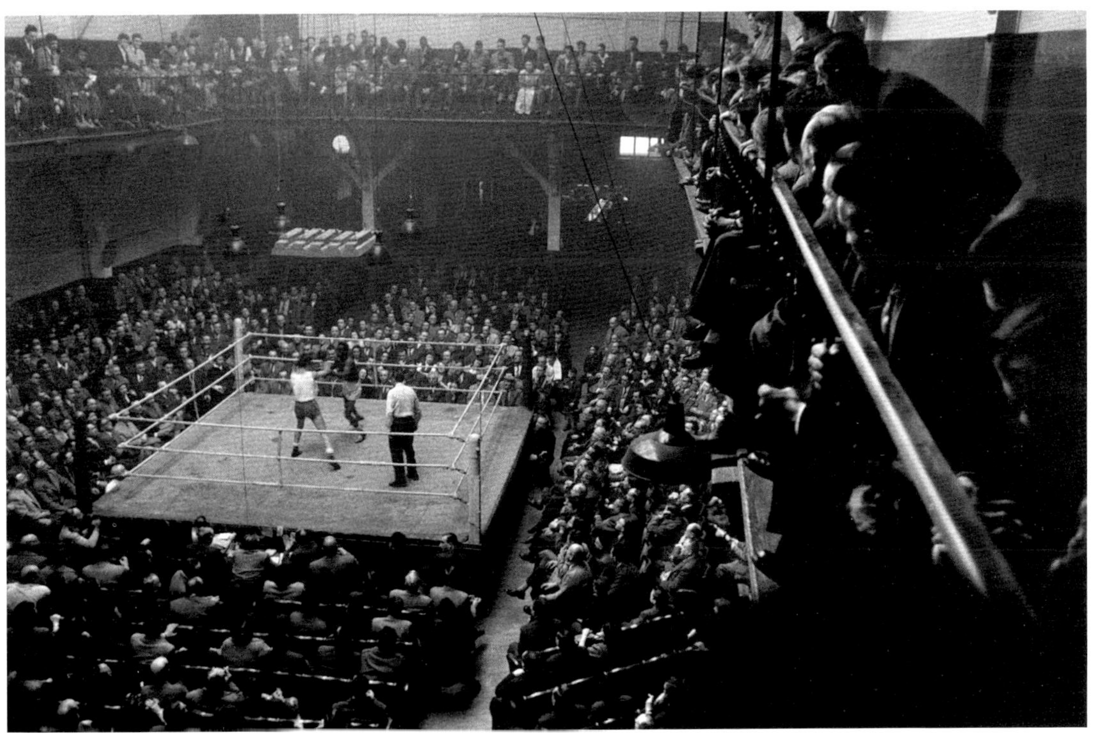

ROBERT S. VAN FLEET
The School's on Fire, November 20, 1965
Collection of the International Center of Photography, New York (cat. 107)

GARRY WINOGRAND
Austin, Texas, 1974, printed 1978
Collection of the High Museum of Art;
Lent by Jay Greenstein and Family
© The Estate of Garry Winogrand (cat. 116)

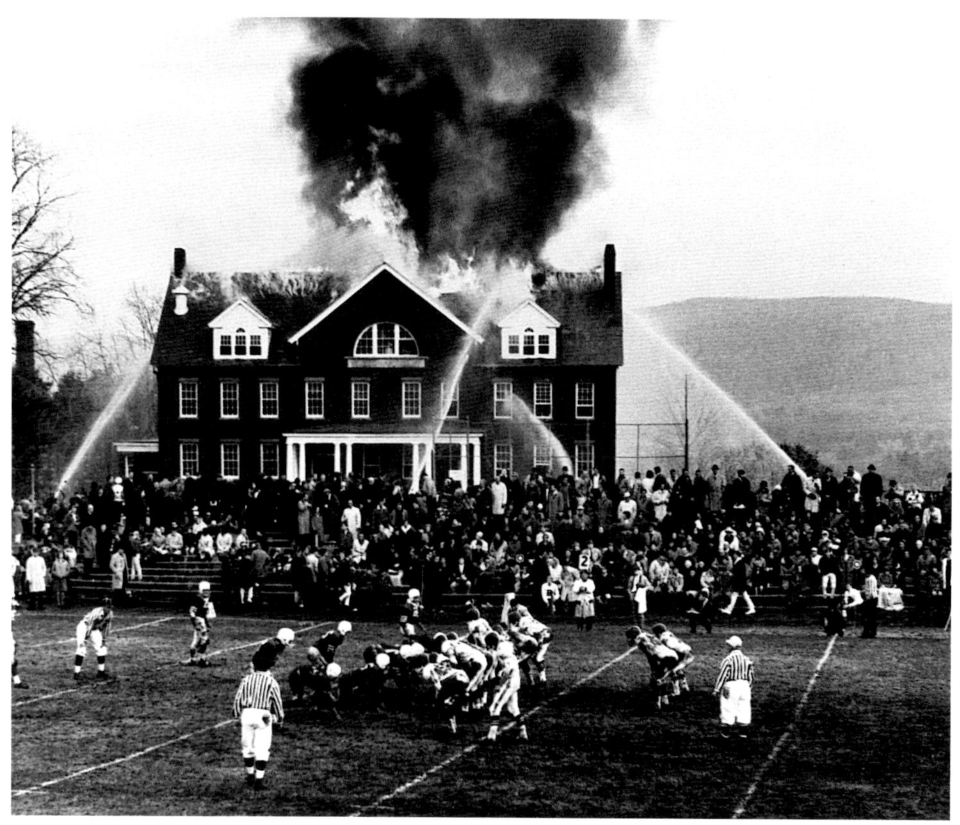

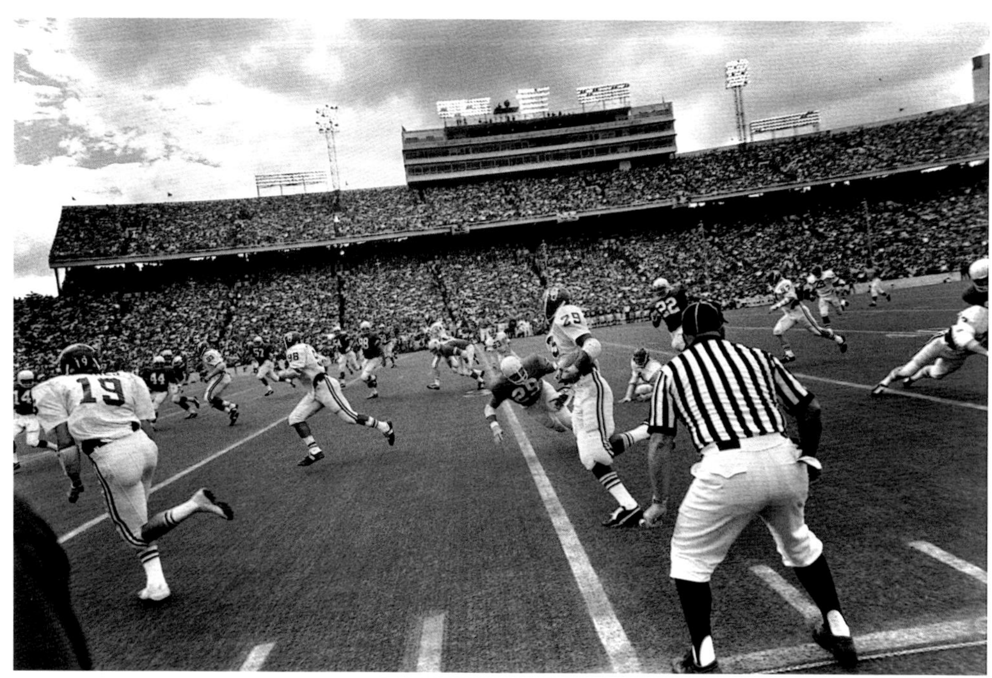

LARRY BURROWS
Tokyo Driving Range, September 11, 1964
Courtesy Laurence Miller Gallery, New York (cat. 105)

GARRY WINOGRAND
Rodeo, Fort Worth, Texas, 1974, printed 1978
Collection of the High Museum of Art, Atlanta;
Lent by Jay Greenstein and Family
© The Estate of Garry Winogrand (cat. 117)

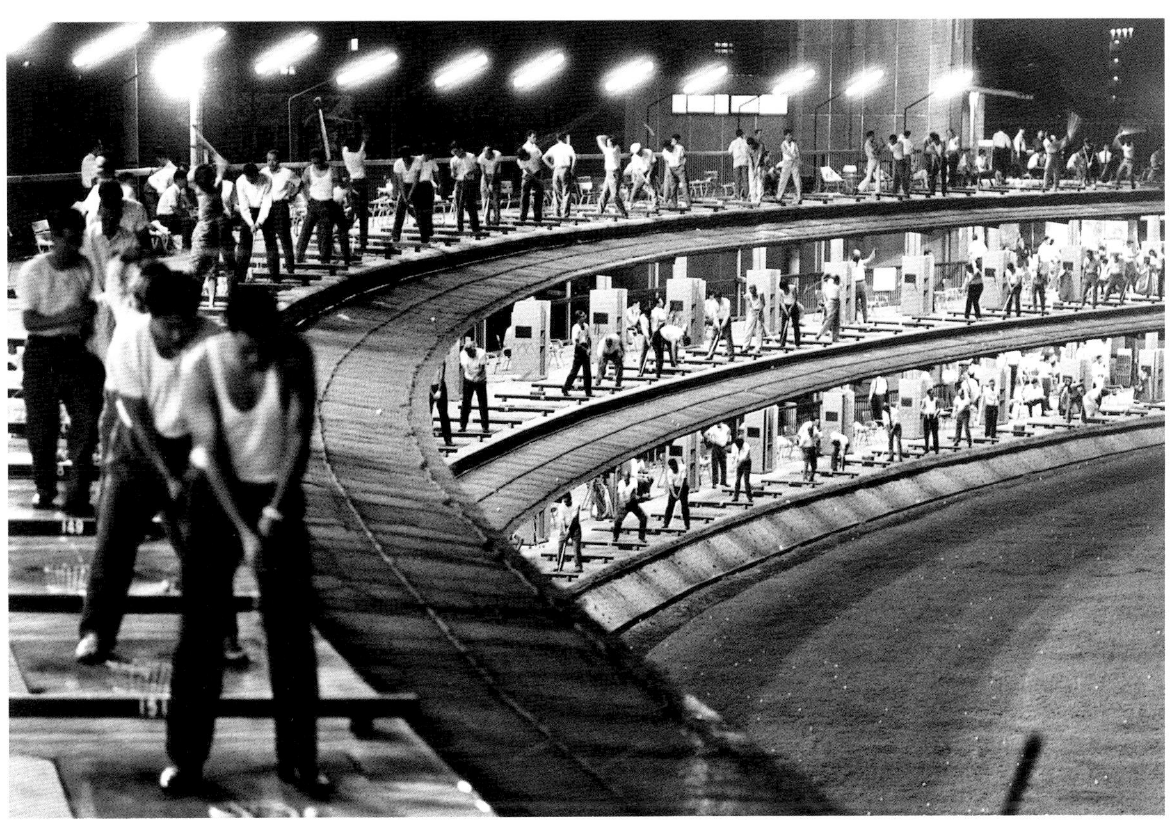

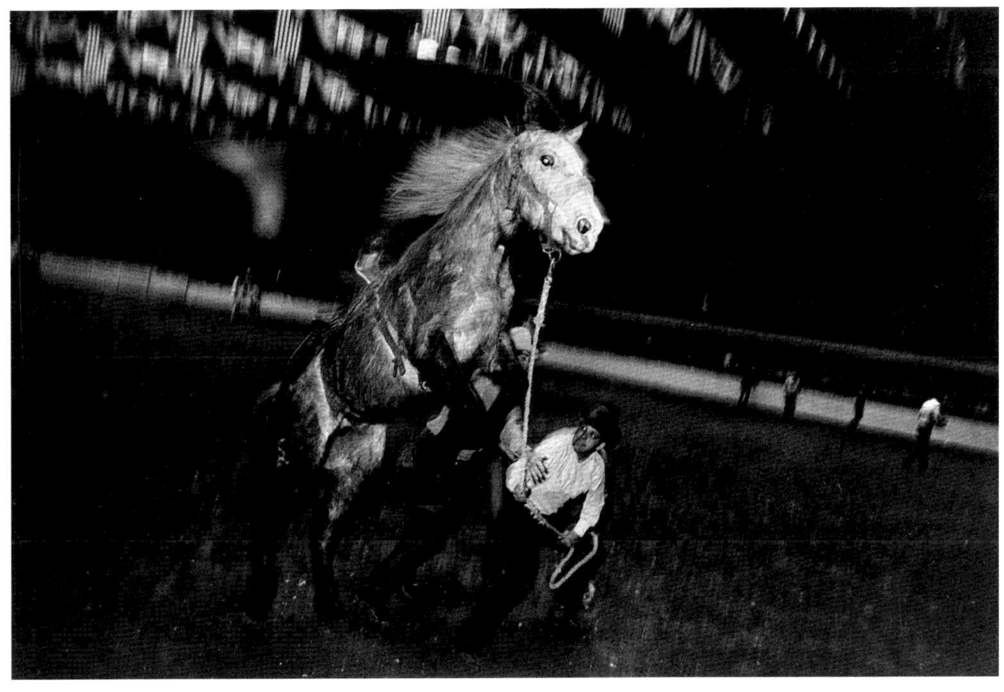

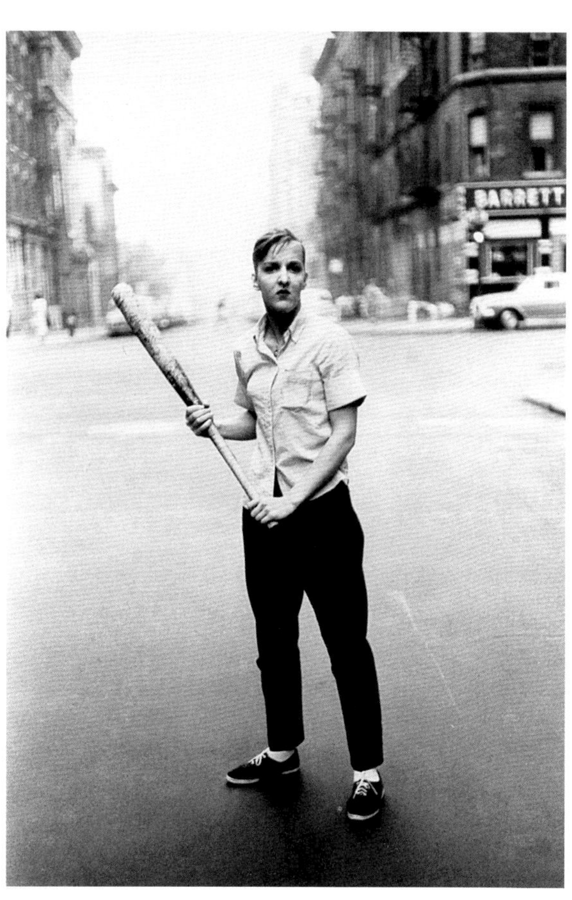

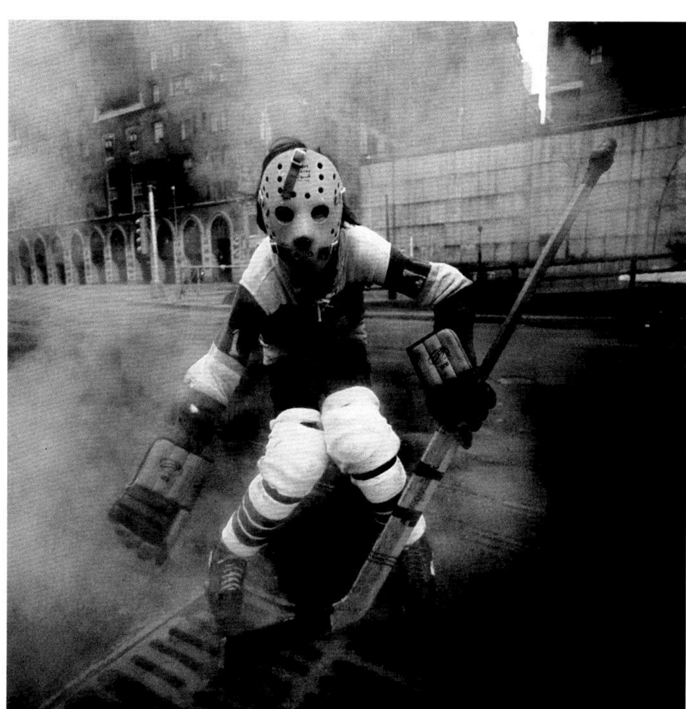

FRANCESCO SCAVULLO
Willie Mays, Old Timer's Day, Portland, Oregon, 1979
Courtesy of the artist and Staley-Wise Gallery,
New York (cat. 130)

JEROME LIEBLING
Handball Players, Miami Beach, 1978
Courtesy of the artist and Howard Greenberg Gallery,
New York (cat. 125)

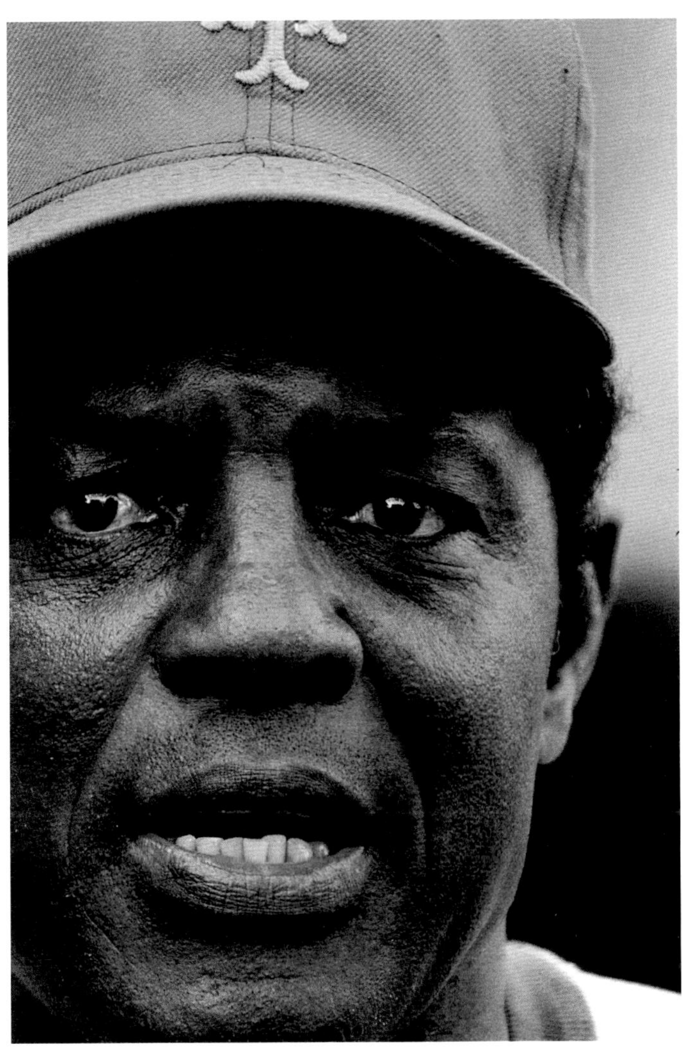

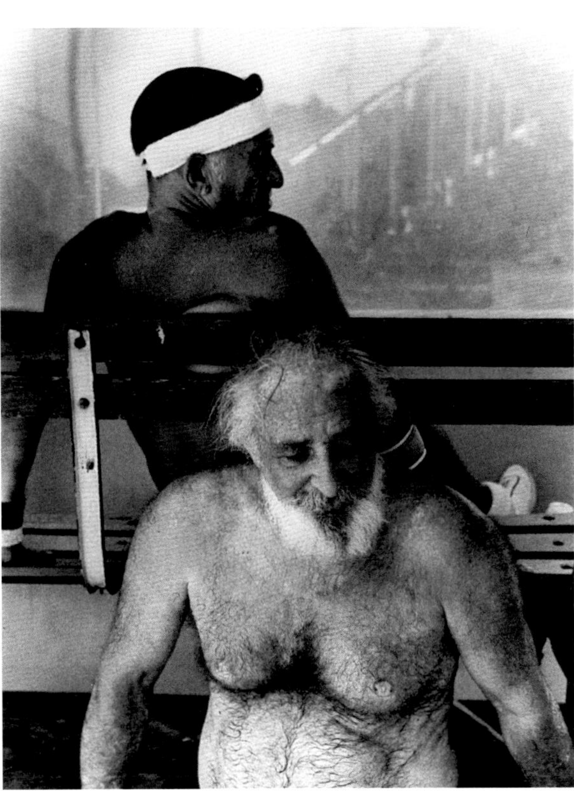

RAY METZGER
Kayak, Frankfurt, 1961
Lucinda Bunnen Collection (cat. 100)

PAUL KWILECKI
Woman Fishing under Trestle, 1979
Courtesy of the artist (cat. 133)

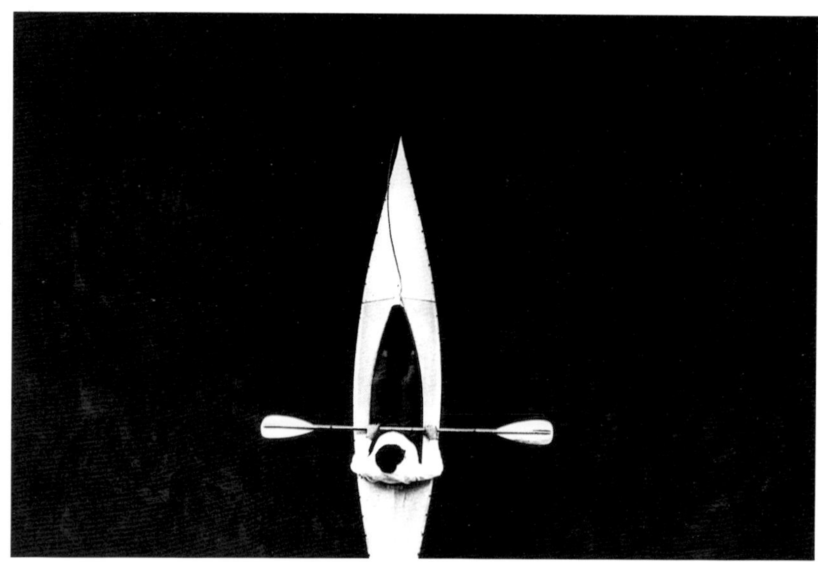

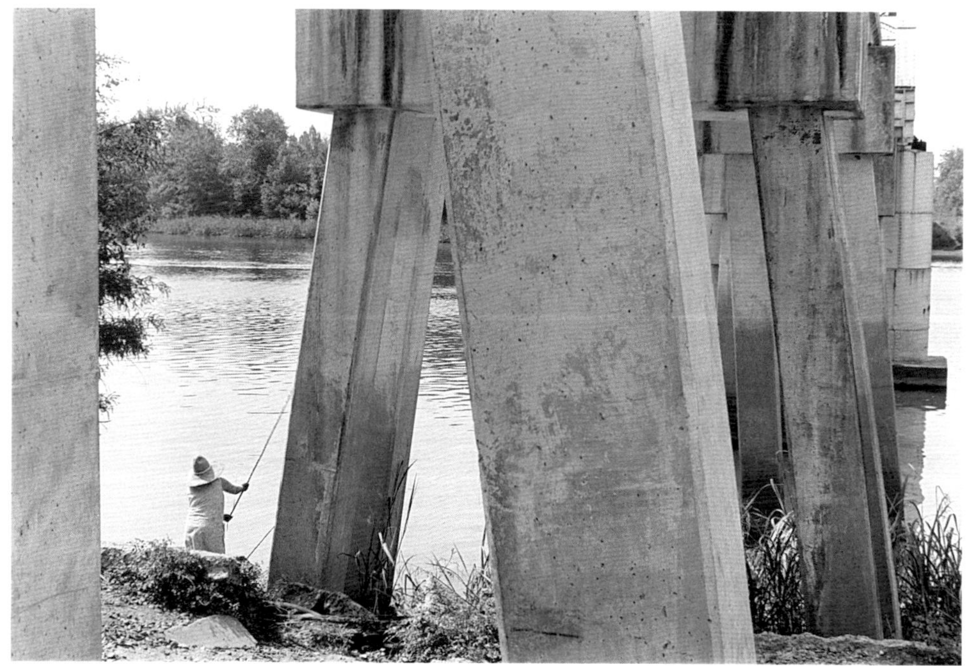

WAYNE LEVIN
Untitled, from "Sea Dream Series," 1983
Courtesy of the artist (cat. 151)

STEPHEN DANKO
Re-Entry, 1978
Collection of the San Francisco Museum
of Modern Art; Purchase (cat. 127)

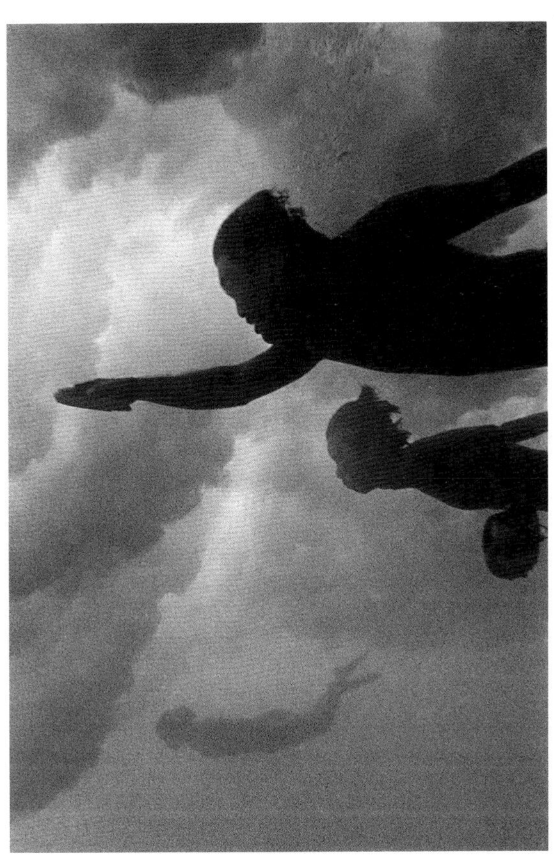

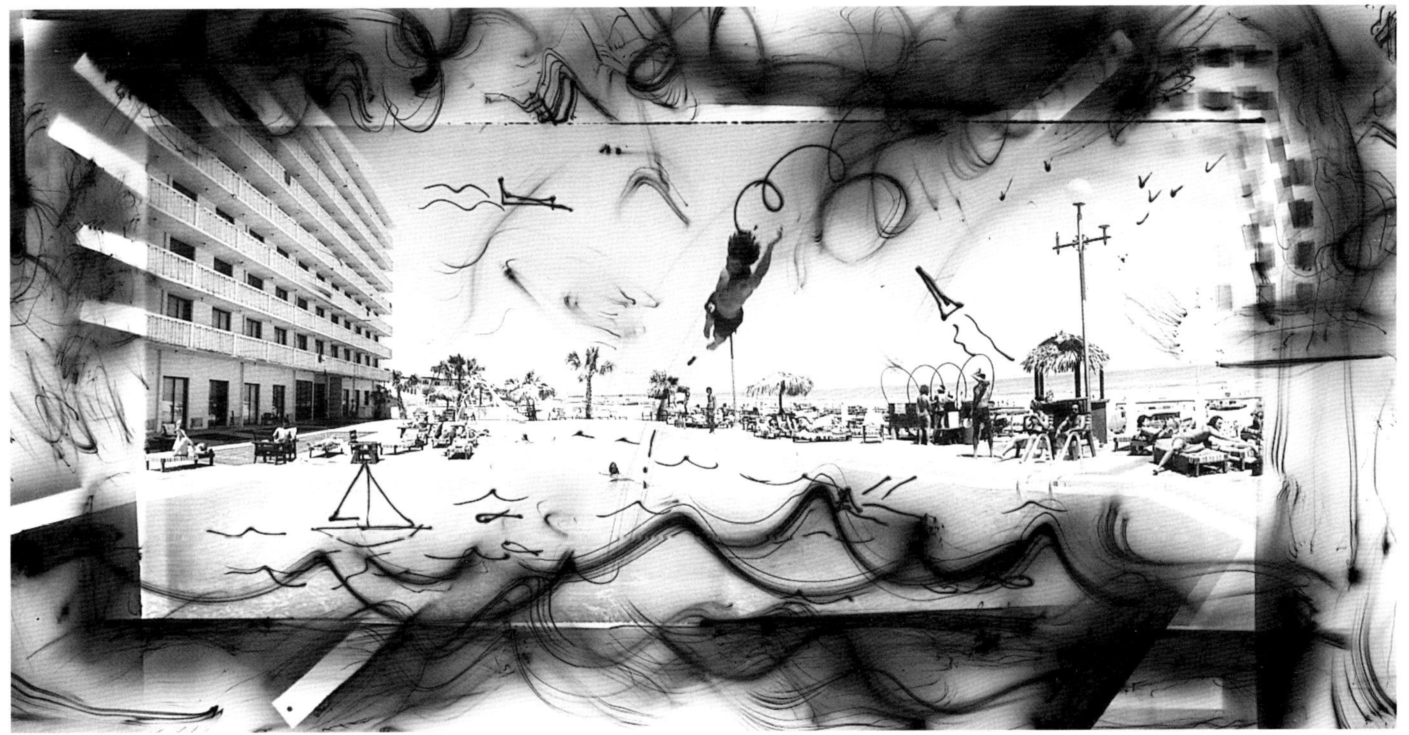

DANNY LYON
Llanito, New Mexico, 1970
Etherton/Stern Gallery, Tucson, Arizona (cat. 110)

HELEN LEVITT
New York, 1982
Courtesy Laurence Miller Gallery, New York (cat. 148)

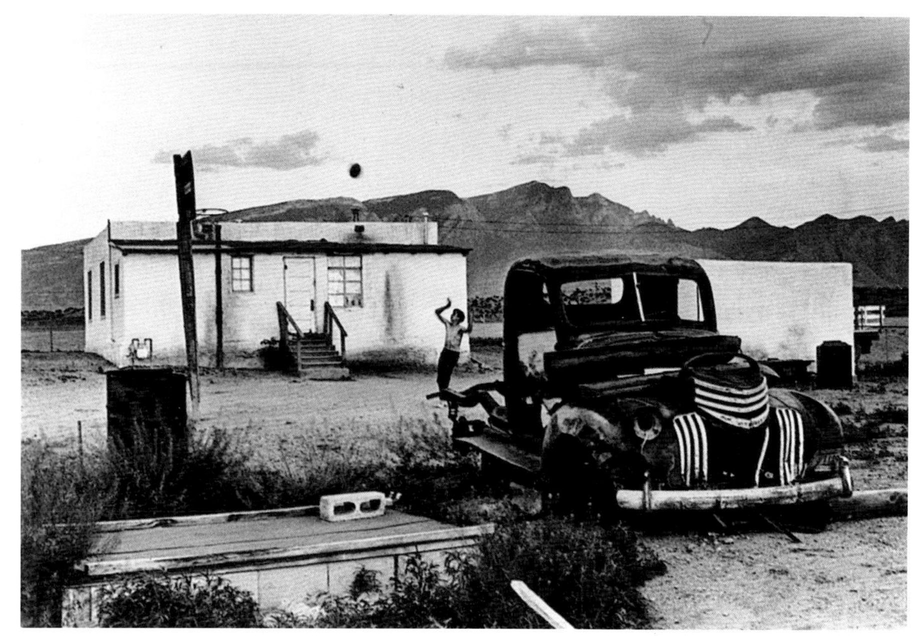

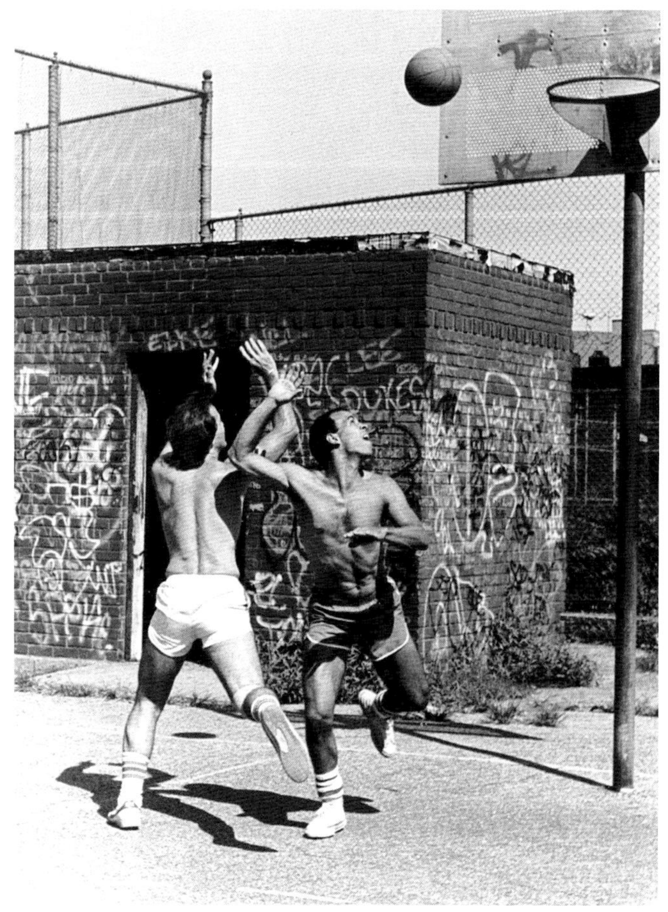

NICHOLAS NIXON
Adams Street, Watertown, MA, 1977
Courtesy of Zabriskie Gallery, New York (cat. 122)

COREEN SIMPSON
Morgan/Grambling Game, Morgan State University Marching Band,
Baltimore, ca. 1979
Collection of the Schomburg Center for Research in Black Culture,
The New York Public Library, Astor, Lenox and Tilden Foundations (cat. 131)

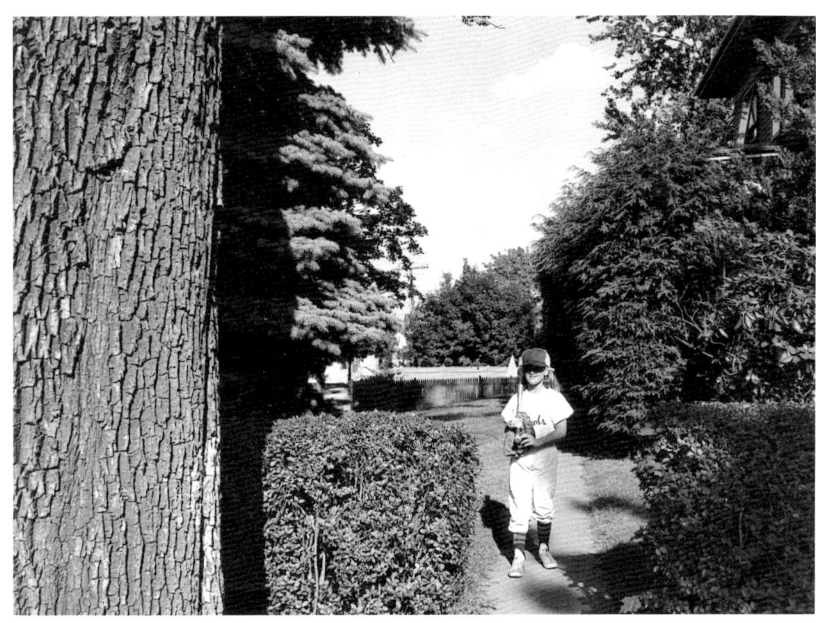

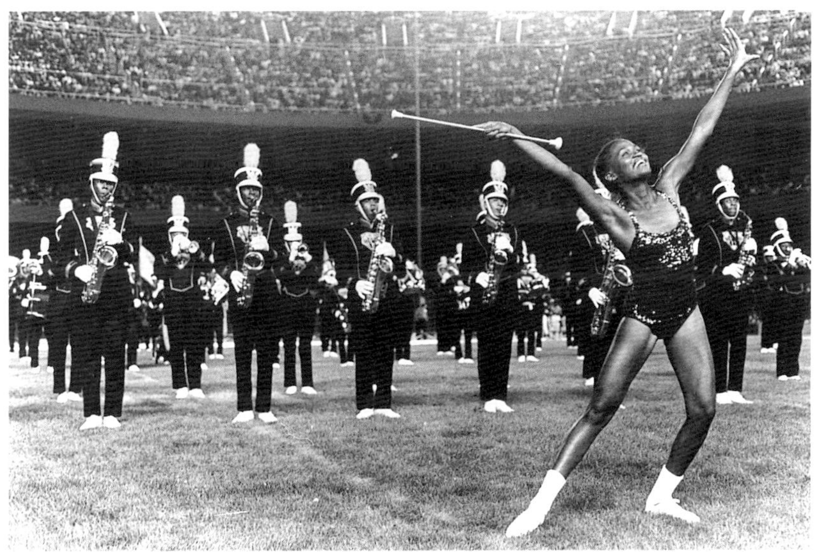

GORDON PARKS
Muhammad Ali after the Henry Cooper Fight,
London, England, 1966
Courtesy of the artist (cat. 108)

MARTINE BARRAT
Neil Ferrara, trainer, and David Brown: 9 years old,
45 pounds, 28 fights, 24 wins, Brooklyn, New York, 1980
Courtesy of the artist (cat. 138)

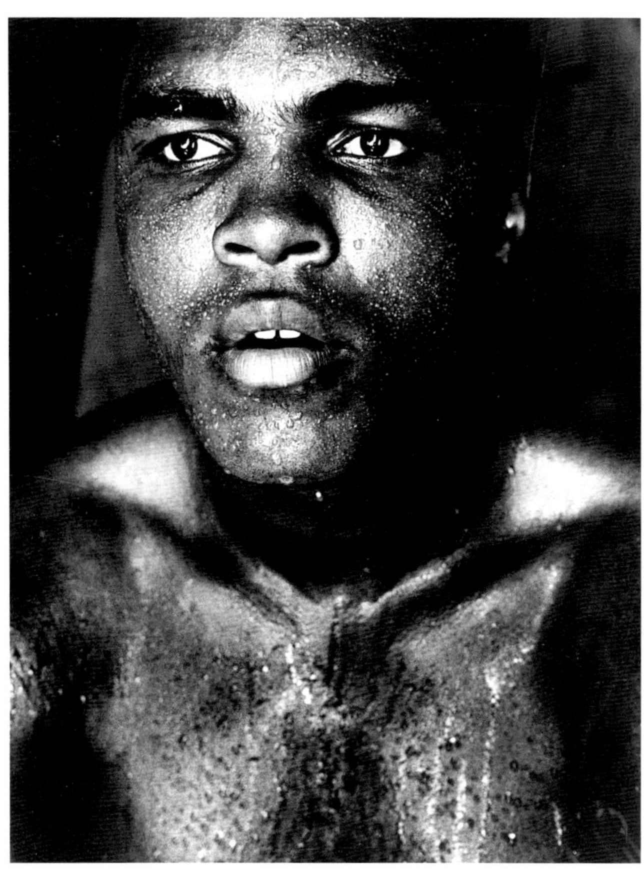

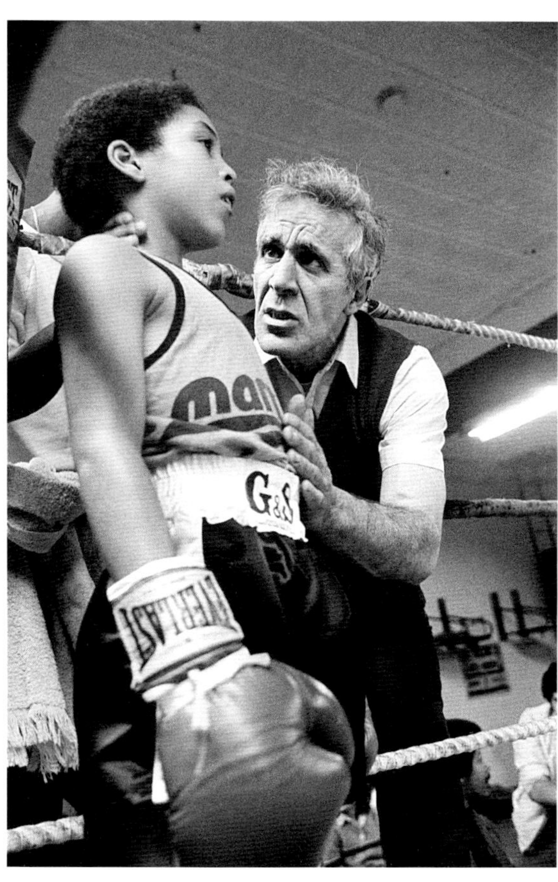

MARTINE BARRAT
*Carlos Villafane, eight years old, and his brother Jimmy
training at the Artemio Colon Gym in Harlem,* 1980
Courtesy of the artist (cat. 137)

JO ANN CALLIS
Loyola Marymount University, 1984 *Olympic Games,
Los Angeles,* 1984
Collection of the Amateur Athletic Foundation of Los Angeles (cat. 159)

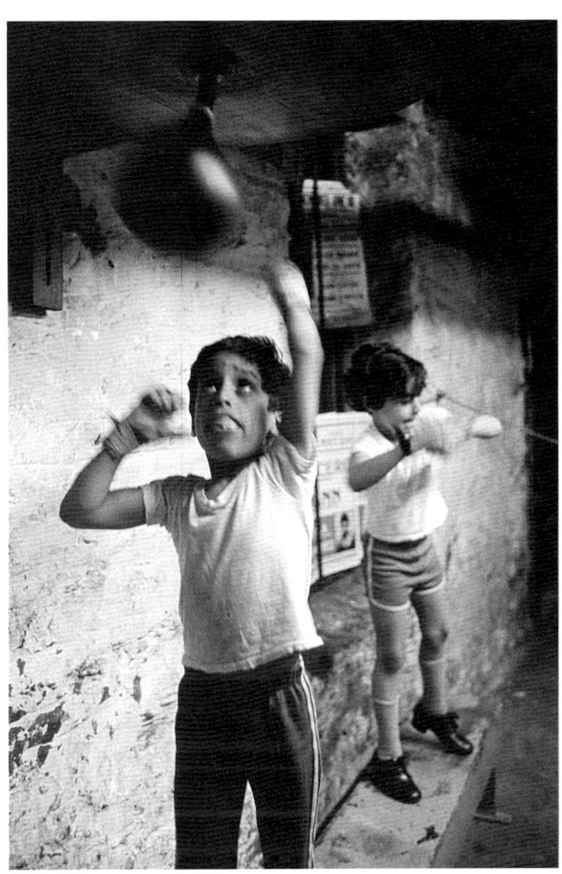

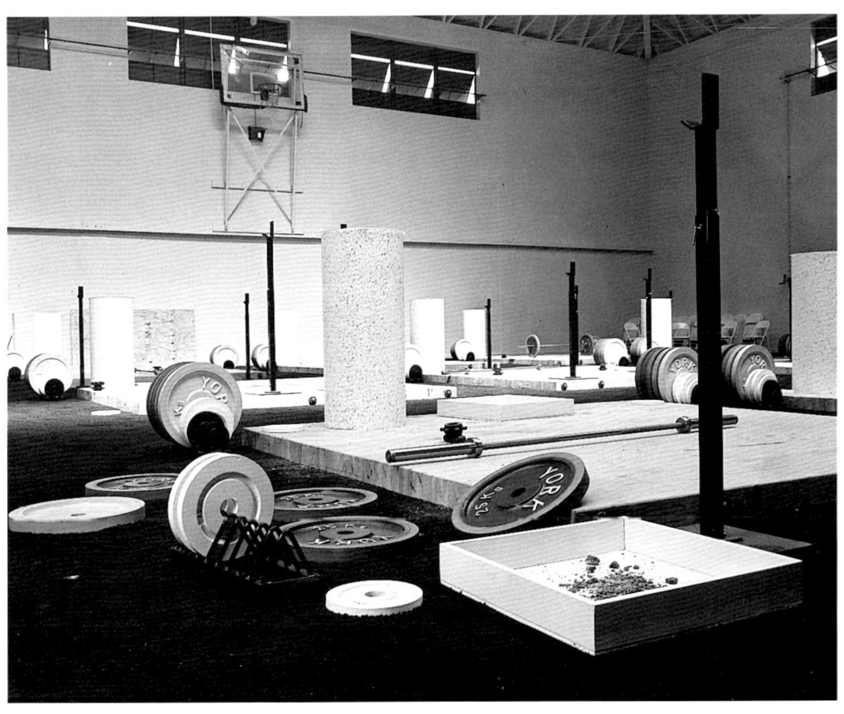

JOHN KENNARD
Busch Stadium, St. Louis, Missouri, 1979
Courtesy of the artist
© 1985 John Kennard (cat. 132)

BALDWIN LEE
Untitled, Monroe, LA, 1986
Courtesy of the artist (cat. 169)

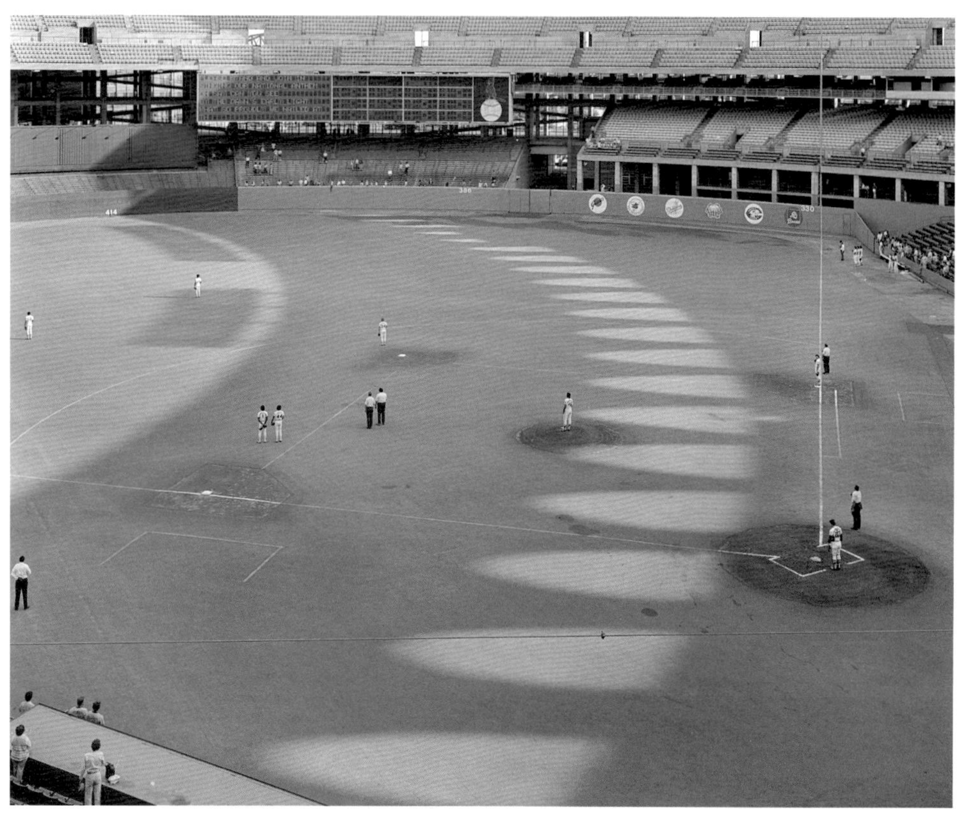

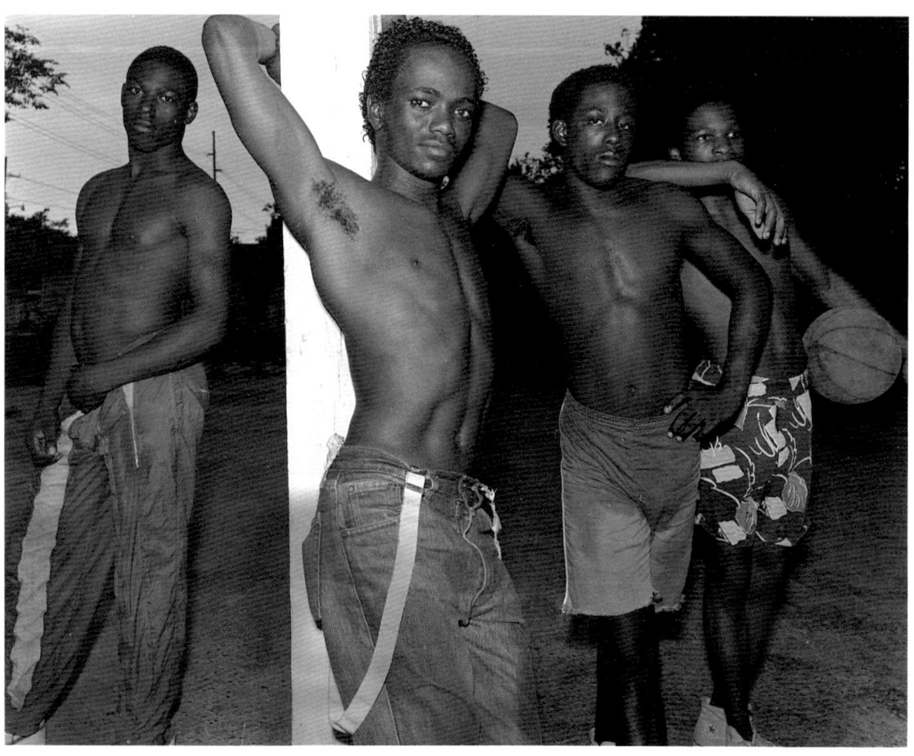

GEOFF WINNINGHAM
Houston Memorial vs. Houston Kashmere,
from the series "Rites of Fall: High School Football in Texas," 1976
Courtesy of the artist (cat. 119)

LARRY FINK
Philly Boxing, January 1990
Courtesy of the artist (cat. 189)

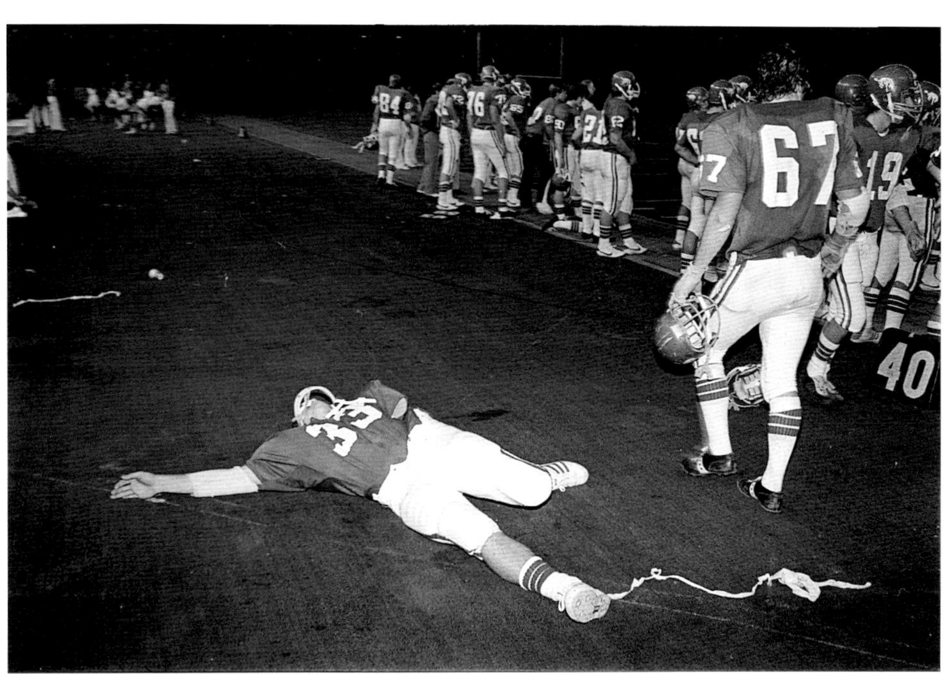

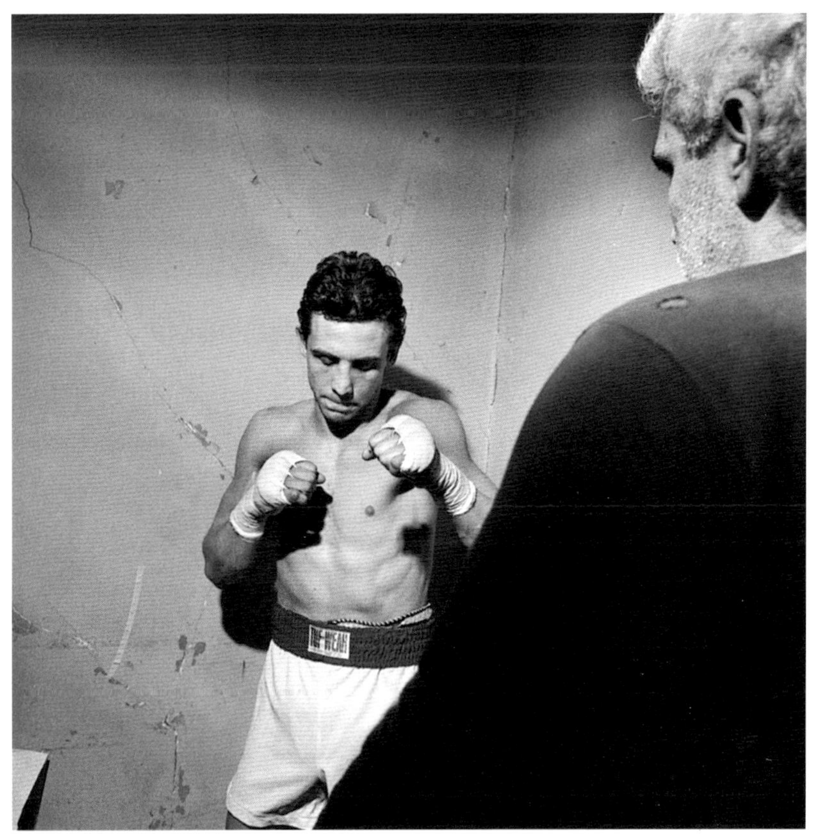

NANCY HOLT
Untitled, from the series "Time Outs," 1985
Courtesy John Weber Gallery, New York (cat. 163)

Untitled, from the series "Time Outs," 1985
Courtesy John Weber Gallery, New York (cat. 164)

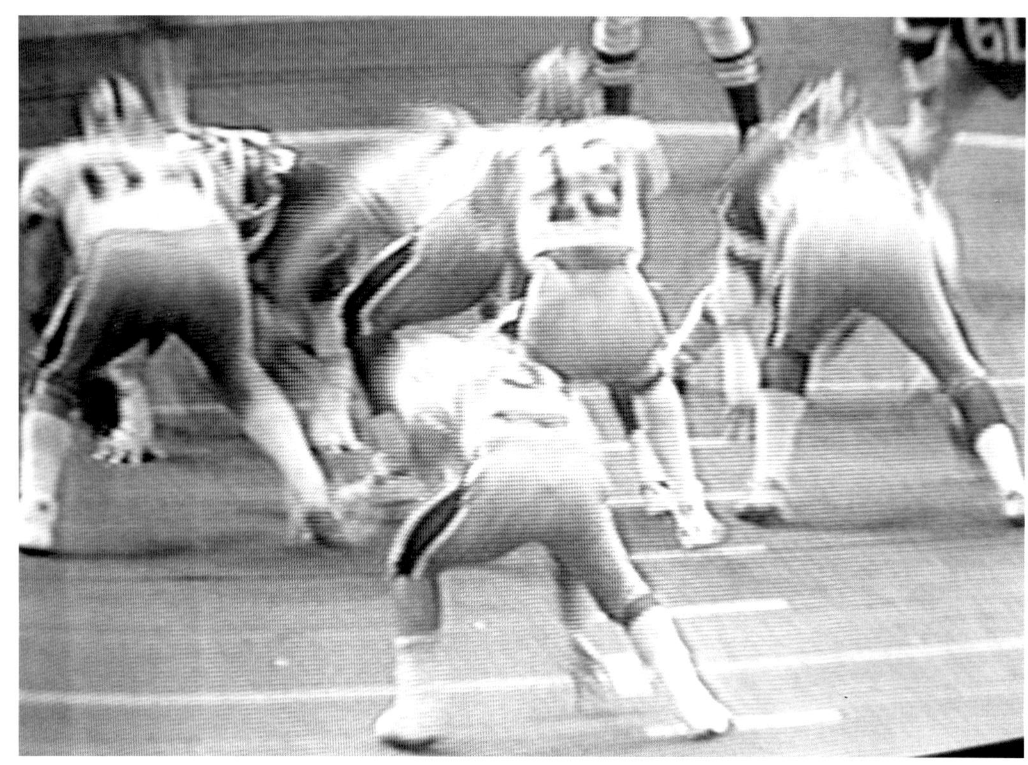

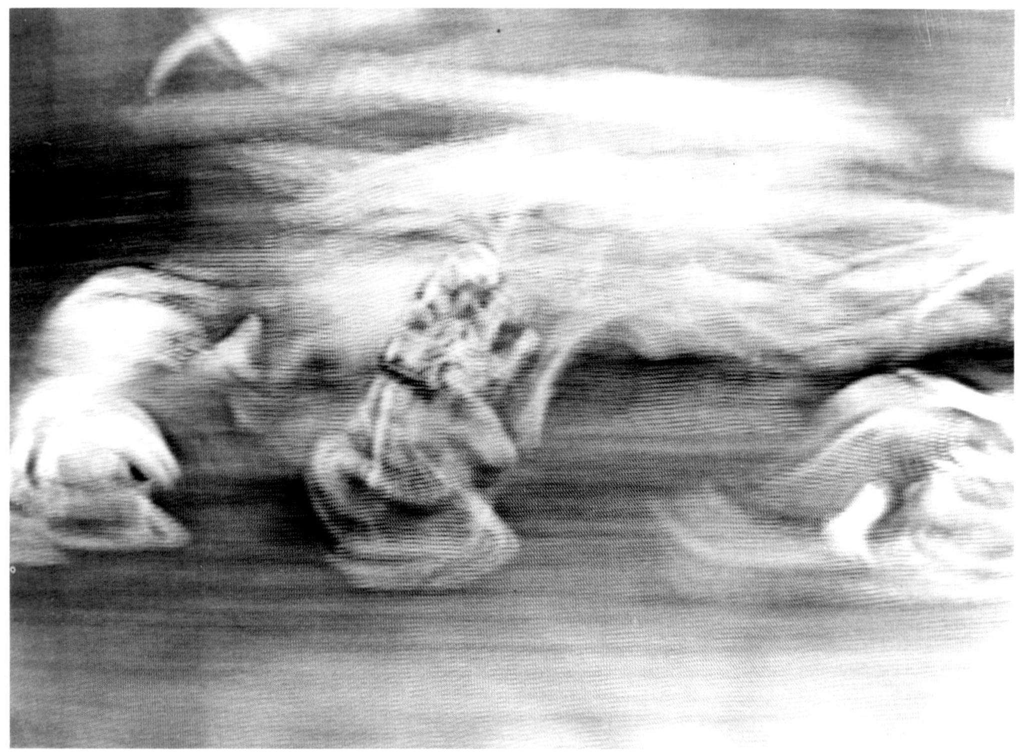

MAURO ALTAMURA
Collision, 1983
Courtesy of the artist and Lieberman & Saul Gallery,
New York (cat. 152)

PAUL BERGER
Camera Text or Picture, No. 15, 1979
Courtesy of the artist (cat. 135)

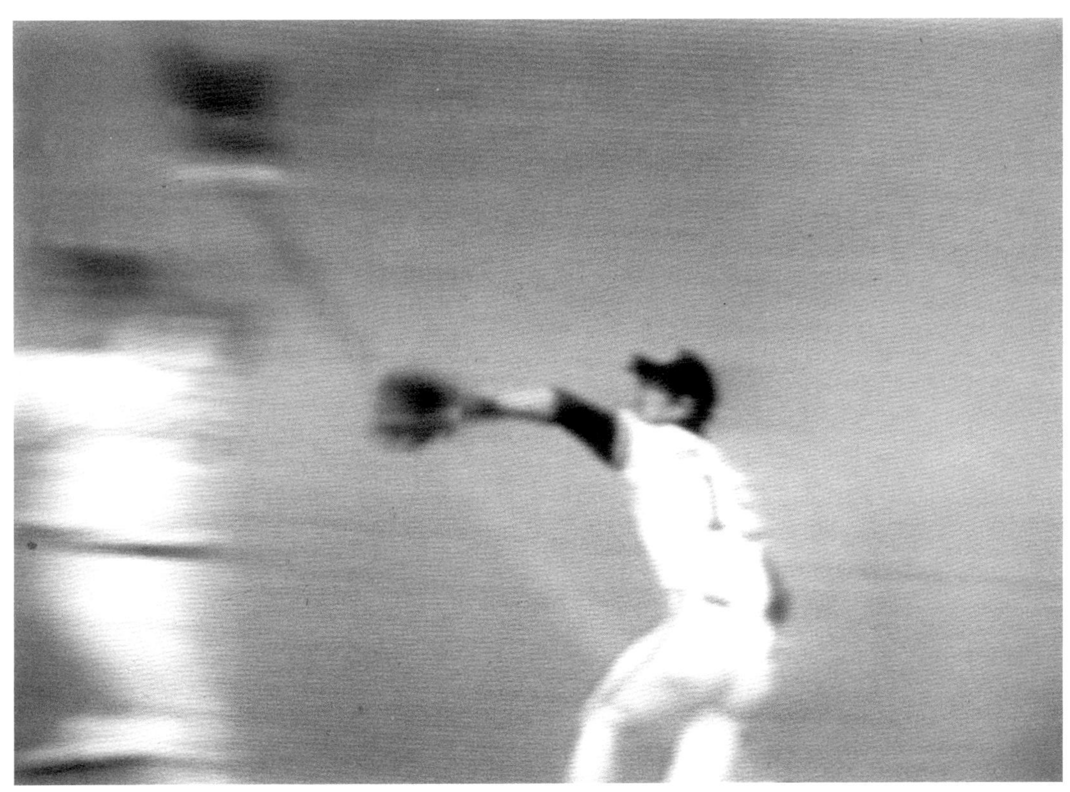

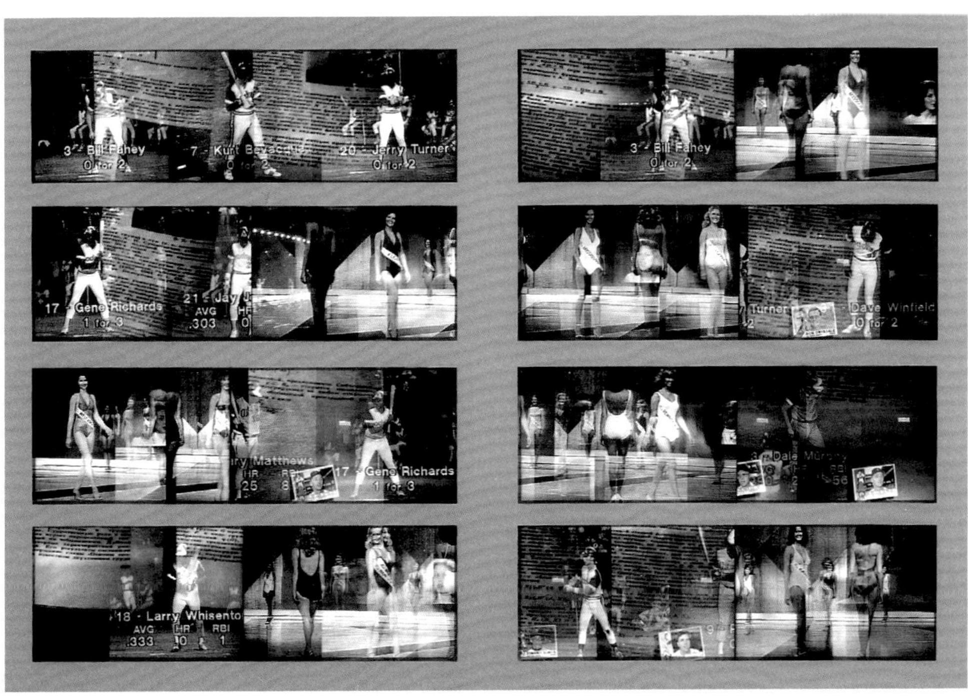

BRUCE WEBER
Andrew Minsker, Lightweight Boxer, Colorado Sports Festival, 1983
Courtesy Fay Gold Gallery, Atlanta (cat. 154)

ROBERT MAPPLETHORPE
Lisa Lyon, 1982
Courtesy Robert Miller Gallery, New York
© 1982 The Estate of Robert Mapplethorpe (cat. 144)

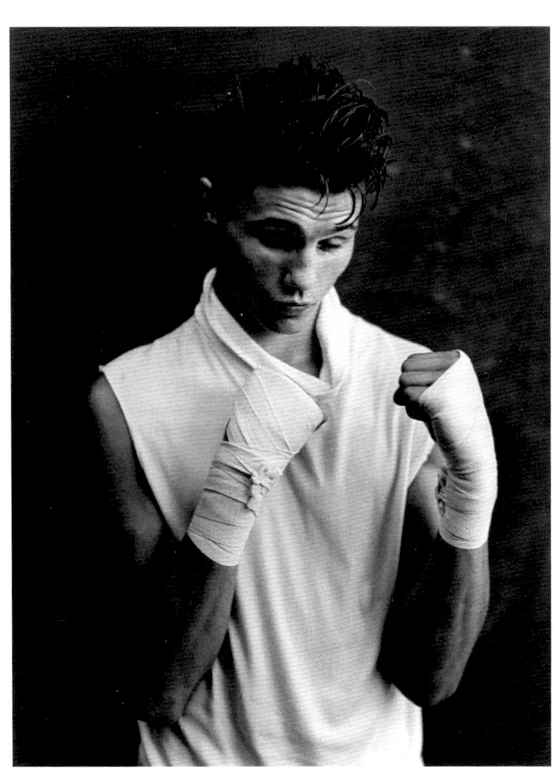

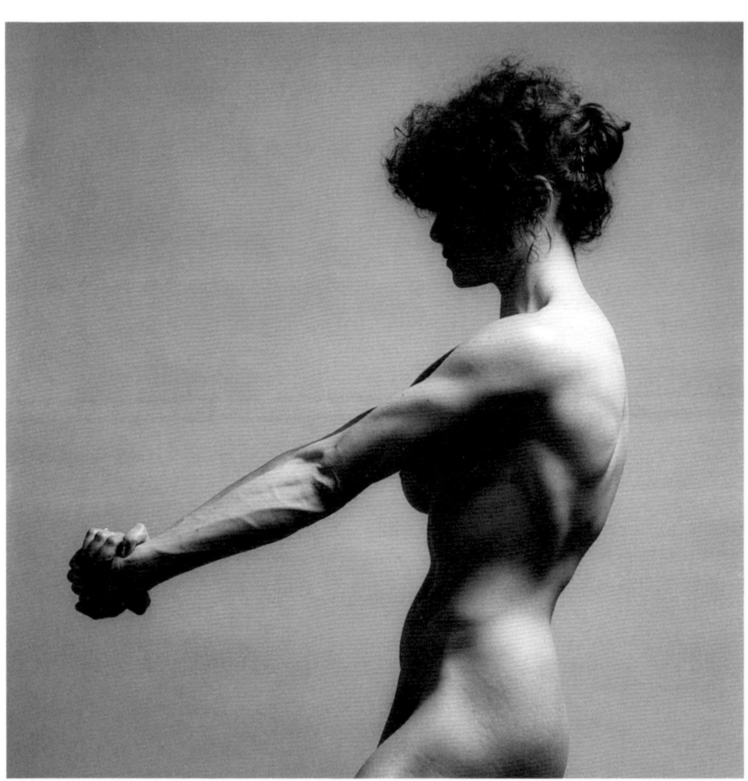

EXHIBITION CHECKLIST

In the listing of dimensions, height precedes width. The measurements indicate the image size; in a few cases, the size of the mount is given, as noted. Centimeter measurements are given in parentheses. When one date is given, it indicates that the photograph is vintage. Nonvintage prints show two dates; the first refers to the negative, and the second to the print. When the print date is unknown, but assumed later, "printed later" appears following the negative date. When known, print edition numbers follow the medium. Foreign titles are given in their original language with English translations following in parentheses. Most untitled works are followed by descriptive phrases in parentheses. Alternative and previous titles are also given in parentheses and are italicized. An asterisk indicates that the work is illustrated in the catalogue.

* **1. EADWEARD MUYBRIDGE**
British, 1830-1904
"Abe Edgington," owned by Leland Stanford; driven by C. Marvin, trotting at 2:24 gait over the Palo Alto track, June 15, 1878
Albumen print
5 3/16 x 8 1/2 in. (13.1 x 21.5 cm.)
Collection of the Division of Prints and Photographs, Library of Congress, Washington, D.C.
(Shown at Atlanta and Houston only)

* **2. WILLIAM HENRY JACKSON**
American, 1843-1942
Trout Fishing at Wagon Wheel Gap, 1883
Albumen print
17 x 21 1/4 in. (43.2 x 53.9 cm.)
Collection of The Colorado Historical Society, Denver

* **3. THOMAS EAKINS**
American, 1844-1916
Marey Wheel Photographs of George Reynolds, 1884
Albumen print
2 7/8 x 3 13/16 in. (7.3 x 9.7 cm.)
Collection of the Hirshhorn Museum and Sculpture Garden, Smithsonian Institution, Washington, D.C.;
Gift of Joseph H. Hirshhorn, 1966
(Shown at Atlanta, Houston, and Santa Clara only)

4. THOMAS EAKINS
American, 1844-1916
Marey Wheel Photographs of George Reynolds, 1884
Albumen print
2 5/16 x 3 7/8 in. (5.9 x 9.8 cm.)
Collection of the Hirshhorn Museum and Sculpture Garden, Smithsonian Institution, Washington, D.C.;
Gift of Joseph H. Hirshhorn, 1966
(Shown at Wilmington and Buffalo only)

* **5. ALICE AUSTEN**
American, 1866-1952
Untitled (tennis scene), ca. 1884
Gelatin silver print
4 5/8 x 7 3/4 in. (11.8 x 19.7 cm.)
Alice Austen Collection, Staten Island Historical Society, New York
(Shown at Atlanta only)

* **6. EADWEARD MUYBRIDGE**
British, 1830-1904
Untitled (man throwing a discus), from "Animal Locomotion," plate 307, 1887
Collotype
10 3/8 x 10 11/16 in. (26.3 x 27.1 cm.)
Collection of The Metropolitan Museum of Art, New York;
Gift of The Philadelphia Commercial Museum, 1938

7. EADWEARD MUYBRIDGE
British, 1830-1904
Untitled (two men boxing), from "Animal Locomotion," plate 338, 1887
Collotype
9 x 12 3/4 in. (22.9 x 32.4 cm.)
Collection of The Metropolitan Museum of Art, New York;
Gift of The Philadelphia Commercial Museum, 1938

* **8. EADWEARD MUYBRIDGE**
British, 1830-1904
Untitled (woman playing tennis), from "Animal Locomotion," plate 297, 1887
Collotype
8 15/16 x 13 in. (22.7 x 32.9 cm.)
Collection of The Metropolitan Museum of Art, New York;
Gift of The Philadelphia Commercial Museum, 1938

* **9. GOODWIN & COMPANY**
American, active New York, 1886-1890
Old Judge Tobacco Insert Cards
a. *Burns, Chicago*, 1887
b. *Clarke, Chicago*, 1888
c. *Daly, Chicago*, 1887
d. *Darling, Chicago*, 1887
Four albumen prints mounted on cardboard
Each approximately 6 1/2 x 4 1/4 in. (16.5 x 10.8 cm.)
Collection of The Metropolitan Museum of Art, New York;
Gift of Jefferson R. Burdick, 1962

* **10. ANDERSON COMPANY**
American, active New York, 1893-1899
Boxing Cards, 1889
a. *Double Counter*
b. *Cross Counter*
c. *Cross Buttock*
d. *Knockdown*
Four albumen prints
Each 6 3/8 x 4 3/16 in. (16.2 x 12.2 cm.)
Collection of the Division of Prints and Photographs, Library of Congress, Washington, D.C.
(Shown at Atlanta and Houston only)

* **11. ATTRIBUTED TO CARLETON E. WATKINS**
American, 1829-1916
Hotel del Monte, Swimming Tanks, ca. 1889
Albumen print
4 3/4 x 7 3/4 in. (12.1 x 19.7 cm.)
Collection of Wm. B. Becker

* **12. KUHNS FAMILY**
American, active 1879-1908
Girl with a Bicycle, ca. mid-1890s
Tintype
2 5/8 x 3 3/8 in. (6.6 x 8.3 cm.)
Collection of the Atlanta Historical Society, Inc.

13. ANONYMOUS
American, dates unknown
Untitled (swimming party), August 1893
Albumen print
2 3/8 in. diameter (6.1 cm. diameter)
Collection of the International Museum of Photography at George Eastman House, Rochester, New York;
Museum collection

14. JOSEPH BYRON
American, born England, 1844-1923
Skating, Van Cortland Park, New York City, 1897
Gelatin silver print
7 11/16 x 9 1/2 in. (19.5 x 24.1 cm.)
The Byron Collection, Museum of the City of New York

* **15. FRANCES BENJAMIN JOHNSTON**
American, 1864-1952
A Football Team, from an album of 159 photographs documenting The Hampton Institute, Hampton, Virginia, 1899-1900
Platinum print
7 5/8 x 9 1/2 in. (19.4 x 24.1 cm.)
Collection of The Museum of Modern Art, New York;
Gift of Lincoln Kirstein

16. ANONYMOUS
American, dates unknown
The University of Georgia Football Team, 1902
Gelatin silver print
8 3/4 x 12 1/2 in. (22.2 x 31.7 cm.)
Collection of the Hargrett Rare Book and Manuscript Library, University of Georgia, Athens
(Shown at Atlanta only)

* **17. ALFRED STIEGLITZ**
American, 1864-1946
Going to the Start, 1904, from *Camera Work*, no.12 (October 1905), plate III
Photogravure
8 11/16 x 7 1/2 in. (22.1 x 19 cm.)
Collection of The Metropolitan Museum of Art, New York;
Gift of J. B. Neumann, 1958

18. ANONYMOUS
American, dates unknown
Coaching in Central Park, May 1, 1910
Gelatin silver print
6 1/2 x 8 1/2 in. (16.5 x 21.6 cm.)
Bagoe Collection, The New-York Historical Society
(Shown at Atlanta only)

* **19. HARRY P. FISCHER**
American, 1879-1949
YMCA, Marietta, Ohio, ca. 1910, printed later
Gelatin silver print
7 1/2 x 9 9/16 in. (19.1 x 24.3 cm.)
Harry P. Fischer Collection, Dawes Memorial Library, Marietta College, Marietta, Ohio

* **20. ANONYMOUS**
American, dates unknown
Fulton Bag and Cotton Mill Team,
Atlanta, 1910
Gelatin silver print
3 1/2 x 5 1/2 in. (8.8 x 13.9 cm.)
Collection of Michael W. Griffith,
Lilburn, Georgia
(Shown at Atlanta only)

* **21. LEWIS W. HINE**
American, 1874-1940
Pin Boys in a Subway Bowling Alley,
New York City, 1910
Gelatin silver print
5 1/10 x 7 1/10 in. (13 x 18 cm.)
Collection of the International
Museum of Photography at George
Eastman House, Rochester, New York;
Gift of Photo League, New York:
Ex-collection Lewis Wickes Hines

22. ALFRED STIEGLITZ
American, 1864-1946
The Pool – Deal, 1910, from *Camera Work,*
no. 36 (October 1911), plate XI
Photogravure
4 15/16 x 6 1/4 in. (12.6 x 15.9 cm.)
Collection of The Minneapolis
Institute of Arts, The William Hood
Dunwoody Fund

* **23. JACQUES-HENRI LARTIGUE**
French, 1894-1986
The Day of the Races at Auteuil, 1910,
printed 1984
Gelatin silver print
3 3/8 x 4 1/2 in. (8.6 x 11.4 cm.)
Collection of the High Museum
of Art, Atlanta; Purchase
© Association des Amis de
Jacques-Henri Lartigue

* **24. JACQUES-HENRI LARTIGUE**
French, 1894-1986
Grand Prix of the Automobile Club
of Paris, 1912
Sepia-toned gelatin silver print
6 7/10 x 9 1/10 in. (17 x 23.1 cm.)
Collection of the International
Museum of Photography at
George Eastman House, Rochester,
New York; Purchase
© Association des Amis de
Jacques-Henri Lartigue

* **25. ANDRÉ KERTÉSZ**
American, born Hungary, 1894-1985
Underwater Swimmer, Esztergom,
Hungary, 1917, printed 1973
Gelatin silver print
7 x 9 11/16 in. (17.8 x 24.6 cm.)
Collection of the High Museum of Art,
Atlanta; Purchase with funds from a
Friend of the Museum

* **26. ANDRÉ KERTÉSZ**
American, born Hungary, 1894-1985
Swimming, Duna Haraszti,
September 14, 1919, printed 1973
Gelatin silver print
9 11/16 x 7 3/4 in. (24.6 x 19.7 cm.)
Collection of the High Museum of Art,
Atlanta; Purchase with funds from a
Friend of the Museum

* **27. AUGUST SANDER**
German, 1876-1964
Sport Association, Westerwald, ca. 1924
Gelatin silver print
8 1/2 x 10 9/10 in. (21.7 x 27.7 cm.)
© August Sander Archive, Cologne

* **28. LÁSZLÓ MOHOLY-NAGY**
American, born Hungary, 1895-1946
Boxing – Adam Sport Article, 1924
Gelatin silver print (photomontage)
11 1/32 x 8 1/4 in. (28 x 20.9 cm.)
Collection of The J. Paul Getty
Museum, Malibu, California
(Shown at Atlanta only)

* **29. ARTHUR GAY**
American, 1895-1981
Untitled, from the portfolio
"Bodybuilders," 1925, printed later
Gelatin silver print
19 x 15 3/8 in. (48.3 x 39 cm.)
Courtesy Lewis Lehr, New York

* **30. AUGUST SANDER**
German, 1876-1964
Young Sport Pilot, 1925
Gelatin silver print
8 x 5 3/4 in. (20.3 x 14.6 cm.)
Collection of the International
Museum of Photography at
George Eastman House,
Rochester, New York; Purchase
© August Sander Archive, Cologne

* **31. JAMES VAN DER ZEE**
American, 1886-1983
Swimming Team, Harlem, 1925,
printed 1974
Gelatin silver print, edition 69 of 75
2 5/8 x 9 5/16 in. (6.7 x 23.7 cm.)
Collection of the High Museum of Art,
Atlanta; Purchase

* **32. EL LISSITZKY**
Russian, 1890-1941
Runner in the City, ca. 1926
Gelatin silver print (photomontage)
8 1/8 x 7 in. (20.6 x 17.8 cm.)
Courtesy Houk Friedman, New York

* **33. LÁSZLÓ MOHOLY-NAGY**
American, born Hungary, 1895-1946
Sailing, 1926
Gelatin silver print
18 1/2 x 10 3/4 in. (47 x 27.3 cm.)
Collection of the International Museum
of Photography at George Eastman
House, Rochester, New York; Purchase

34. JAMES VAN DER ZEE
American, 1887-1983
Alphi Phi Alpha Basketball Team, 1926
Gelatin silver print
9 2/5 x 7 in. (23.3 x 17.9 cm.)
Collection of The Metropolitan
Museum of Art, New York; Gift of
The James Van Der Zee Institute, 1970

* **35. WILLI BAUMEISTER**
German, 1889-1955
Athlete, 1926
Gelatin silver print, pencil drawing,
and ink collage
14 13/16 x 9 3/16 in. (37.6 x 23.4 cm.)
Courtesy Archiv Baumeister, Stuttgart

* **36. NICKOLAS MURAY**
American, born Hungary, 1892-1965
Babe Ruth (George Herman Ruth),
ca. 1927
Gelatin silver print
13 3/8 x 10 7/16 in. (34 x 26.5 cm.)
Collection of The Museum
of Modern Art, New York;
Gift of Mrs. Nickolas Muray

* **37. AUGUST SANDER**
German, 1876-1964
The Boxer Heinz Heese, 1928
Gelatin silver print
10 2/5 x 7 7/8 in. (25.9 x 20 cm.)
Collection of The Metropolitan
Museum of Art, New York;
Warner Communications Inc.
Purchase Fund, 1978
© August Sander Archive, Cologne

* **38. LOTHAR JECK**
Swiss, 1898-1983
Orlikon Bike Course in Zurich, 1928,
printed later
Gelatin silver print
19 5/8 x 23 1/8 in. (49.8 x 58.7 cm.)
Courtesy Archiv Rolf Jeck, Basel

* **39. GUSTAV KLUCIS**
Russian, 1895-1938
Untitled, 1928
Printing on postcard (photomontage)
6 x 4 1/4 in. (15.2 x 10.8 cm.)
Signed as part of image: *Klucis.*
Text in Russian: *Our physical culture*
greetings to the worker sportsman from all
over the world/Spartakiada/Moscow/1928.
Collection of W. Michael Sheehe,
New York

* **40. GUSTAV KLUCIS**
Russian, 1895-1938
Untitled, 1928
Printing on postcard (photomontage)
6 x 4 1/4 in. (15.2 x 10.8 cm.)
Signed as part of image: *Klucis.*
Text in Russian: *Every sportsman must be*
a sharpshooter/Moscow 1928/Spartakiada.
Text in German: *Every worker-sportsman*
must be a soldier of the Revolution.
Collection of W. Michael Sheehe,
New York

* **41. GUSTAV KLUCIS**
Russian, 1895-1938
Untitled, 1928
Printing on postcard (photomontage)
6 x 4 1/4 in. (15.2 x 10.8 cm.)
Signed as part of image: *Klucis.*
Text in Russian: *Spartakiada/Moscow/*
1928.
Collection of W. Michael Sheehe,
New York

* **42. MAURICE TABARD**
French, 1897-1984
Louis Chiron, 1929, printed later
Gelatin silver print
11 3/16 x 8 5/16 in. (28.3 x 21.1 cm.)
© Association des Amis de
Maurice Tabard, Paris

* **43. ARTHUR P. BEDOU**
American, 1886-1966
Men Playing Croquet under the
Great Oak Trees, Mississippi, ca. 1930
Gelatin silver print
8 x 10 in. (20.3 x 25.4)
Collection of the Schomburg Center
for Research in Black Culture,
The New York Public Library,
Astor, Lenox and Tilden Foundations

44. ANSEL ADAMS
American, 1902-1984
High Country Climb, Yosemite
National Park, ca. 1930
Gelatin silver print
8 x 10 in. (20.3 x 25.4 cm.)
Collection of Dr. and
Mrs. Michael Adams

* **45. ANSEL ADAMS**
American, 1902-1984
Skiing on Lembert Dome at Tuolomne
Meadows, Yosemite National Park, ca. 1930
9 x 6 1/8 in. (22.9 x 15.6 cm.)
Gelatin silver print
Collection of Dr. and
Mrs. Michael Adams
Courtesy The Ansel Adams Publishing
Rights Trust. All Rights Reserved

* **46. GEORGE HOYNINGEN-HUENE**
American, born Russia, 1900-1968
Johnny Weissmuller, 1930
Gelatin silver print
9 7/8 x 7 1/2 in. (25.1 x 19.1 cm.)
Courtesy Staley-Wise Gallery,
New York

47. JACQUES-HENRI LARTIGUE
French, 1894-1986
Biarritz, 1930, printed later
Gelatin silver print
14 x 6 3/4 in. (35.6 x 17.1 cm.)
Courtesy Monah L. Gettner/
Hyperion Press Ltd., New York

*** 48. ALEXANDER RODCHENKO**
Russian, 1891-1956
Dynamo Sports Club, 1930, printed later
Gelatin silver print
11 1/4 x 16 1/2 in. (28.6 x 41.9 cm.)
Courtesy Walker, Ursitti & McGinniss,
New York

*** 49. WILLARD VAN DYKE**
American, 1906-1986
Boxer's Hands, ca. 1933
Gelatin silver print
7 1/2 x 9 1/2 in. (19 x 24.1 cm.)
Collection of Patricia Stevens Lowinsky

*** 50. RHEINHOLD SPIRA**
Czechoslovakian, dates unknown
Swimmer, ca. 1933
Gelatin silver print
11 1/2 x 9 in. (29.2 x 22.9 cm.)
Courtesy Monah L. Gettner/
Hyperion Press Ltd., New York

51. BRASSAÏ (Gyula Halász)
French, born Romania, 1899-1984
Girl Playing Snooker, Montmartre, 1933,
printed 1973
Gelatin silver print
11 7/8 x 9 3/16 (30.2 x 23.3 cm.)
Collection of the High Museum of Art,
Atlanta; Purchase with funds from a
Friend of the Museum

*** 52. HAROLD E. EDGERTON**
American, 1903-1990
Wes Fesler Kicking a Football, 1934
Gelatin silver print
13 13/16 x 10 15/16 in. (35.1 x 27.7 cm.)
Collection of the International
Museum of Photography at George
Eastman House, Rochester, New York;
Gift of Dr. Harold E. Edgerton
© The Estate of Harold E. Edgerton

*** 53. JOHN GUTMANN**
American, born Poland, 1905
Out of the Pool, 1934
Gelatin silver print
14 x 11 in. (35.6 x 27.9 cm.)
Courtesy Fraenkel Gallery,
San Francisco
© 1986 John Gutmann

54. JOHN GUTMANN
American, born Poland, 1905
Lunch Hour, San Francisco, 1934
Gelatin silver print
14 x 11 in. (35.6 x 27.9 cm.)
Courtesy Fraenkel Gallery,
San Francisco

*** 55. MARGARET BOURKE-WHITE**
American, 1904-1971
*The Yacht Vanitie in a Practice Spin,
Newport*, 1934
Gelatin silver print
13 5/8 x 10 5/8 in. (34.6 x 27 cm.)
Margaret Bourke-White Papers,
George Arents Research Library
for Special Collections at
Syracuse University, New York
© The Estate of Margaret
Bourke-White

56. WILLIAM M. RITTASE
American, 1894-1968
Divers, ca. 1935
Gelatin silver print
7 1/2 x 9 1/4 in. (19.1 x 23.5 cm.)
Courtesy Howard Greenberg Gallery,
New York

*** 57. BILL BRANDT**
British, born Germany, 1904-1983
Tic-tac Men at Ascot Races, 1935
Gelatin silver print
7 7/8 x 6 3/4 in. (20 x 17.2 cm.)
Courtesy Houk Friedman, New York

58. EDWARD QUIGLEY
American, 1898-1977
Football Helmet, 1935
Gelatin silver print
4 1/2 x 5 3/4 in. (11.4 x 14.6 cm.)
Keith de Lellis Collection, New York

*** 59. EDWARD QUIGLEY**
American, 1898-1977
Tennis Racquet, 1935
Gelatin silver print
5 x 7 in. (12.7 x 17.7 cm.)
Keith de Lellis Collection, New York

*** 60. PIET ZWART**
Dutch, 1885-1977
Sport, ca. 1935
Gelatin silver print (photomontage)
6 5/8 x 4 3/4 in. (16.8 x 12.1 cm.)
Collection of the New Orleans
Museum of Art; Purchase 80.37

*** 61. LOTHAR JECK**
Swiss, 1898-1983
Gymnasts, 1936, printed later
Gelatin silver print
23 1/8 x 19 5/8 in. (58.7 x 49.8 cm.)
Courtesy Archiv Rolf Jeck, Basel

*** 62. ALEXANDER RODCHENKO**
Russian, 1891-1956
*Wheel, Gymnastics Festival, Red Square,
Moscow*, 1936, printed later
Gelatin silver print
15 1/2 x 10 1/2 in. (39.4 x 26.7 cm.)
Courtesy Walker, Ursitti & McGinniss,
New York

*** 63. W. EUGENE SMITH**
American, 1918-1978
Notre Dame, Kansas, 1937
12 7/8 x 9 3/4 in. (32.7 x 24.8 cm.)
Gelatin silver print
Collection of the Center
for Creative Photography,
The University of Arizona, Tucson
© 1991 The Heirs of W. Eugene
Smith. All Rights Reserved

64. MARGARET BOURKE-WHITE
American, 1904-1971
Churchill Downs, 1937, printed later
Gelatin silver print
13 3/4 x 15 in. (34.9 x 38.1 cm.)
Courtesy The Estate of Margaret
Bourke-White and *LIFE*
© Time Warner Inc.

*** 65. ROBERT CAPA**
American, born Hungary, 1913-1954
*A boxer and his son at Stillman's Gym,
New York*, 1937
Gelatin silver print
10 5/8 x 16 in. (26.9 x 40.6 cm.)
© 1991 The Estate of Robert Capa/
International Center of Photography,
New York

*** 66. HAROLD E. EDGERTON**
American, 1903-1990
Densmore Shute Bending the Shaft, 1938
Gelatin silver print
10 15/16 x 12 1/16 in. (27.7 x 30.7 cm.)
Collection of the International
Museum of Photography at George
Eastman House, Rochester, New York;
Gift of Dr. Harold E. Edgerton
© The Estate of Harold E. Edgerton

*** 67. HAROLD E. EDGERTON**
American, 1903-1990
Boxing, 1938
Four gelatin silver prints
Each 4 1/2 x 7 1/2 in. (11.4 x 19.1 cm.)
Collection of Patricia Stevens Lowinsky
© The Estate of Harold E. Edgerton

68. JOHN W. MOSLEY
American, 1907-1969
*Willie Reddish and His Manager,
Philadelphia*, 1938
Gelatin silver print
9 1/2 x 7 1/8 in. (24.1 x 18.1 cm.)
Blockson Afro-American Collection,
Temple University, Philadelphia

*** 69. GEORGI ZELMA**
Russian, 1906-1984
Champions of Moscow on Red Square, 1938,
printed later
Gelatin silver print
11 1/4 x 8 in. (28.6 x 20.3 cm.)
Courtesy Walker, Ursitti & McGinniss,
New York

*** 70. JOSEF BREITENBACH**
American, born Germany, 1896-1984
Man Shaving with Boxers, 1939
Gelatin silver print
9 1/4 x 7 in. (23.4 x 17.8 cm.)
Collection of Patricia Stevens Lowinsky
© 1988 The Estate of Josef
Breitenbach

*** 71. MAX YAVNO**
American, 1911-1985
Backyard Baseball, ca. 1939
Gelatin silver print
10 1/4 x 13 in. (26 x 33 cm.)
The Museum of Contemporary
Art, Los Angeles: The Max Yavno
Collection

*** 72. MIKE DISFARMER**
American, 1884-1959
Cleon McAnear and Bill Barnett, ca. 1940
Gelatin silver print
18 1/2 x 12 in. (47 x 30.5 cm.)
The Arkansas Arts Center Foundation
Collection, Little Rock

*** 73. MARION POST WOLCOTT**
American, 1910-1990
*Sulky Race, Shelbyville County Fair,
Kentucky*, 1940, printed later
Gelatin silver print
11 x 14 in. (27.9 x 35.6 cm.)
Courtesy Yancey Richardson/
Lumina Fine Photography & Art,
New York
© The Estate of Marion Post Wolcott

*** 74. JOSEPH COSTA**
American, born 1904
HAROLD E. EDGERTON
American, 1903-1990
Joe Louis and Arturo Godoy, 1940
Gelatin silver print
13 3/4 x 11 in. (34.9 x 27.9 cm.)
Collection of the International
Museum of Photography at
George Eastman House,
Rochester, New York;
Gift of Dr. Harold E. Edgerton
© The Estate of Harold E. Edgerton

*** 75. ROBERT CAPA**
American, born Hungary, 1913-1954
*Ernest Hemingway and His Son Gregory,
Sun Valley, Idaho*, 1941
Gelatin silver print
10 3/4 x 15 7/8 in. (27.3 x 40.3 cm.)
© 1991 The Estate of Robert Capa/
International Center of Photography,
New York

*** 76. W. EUGENE SMITH**
American, 1918-1978
American Football, 1941
Gelatin silver print
14 x 11 in. (35.6 x 27.9 cm.)
Collection of the Center
for Creative Photography,
The University of Arizona, Tucson
© 1991 The Heirs of W. Eugene
Smith. All Rights Reserved

*** 77. ARTHUR LEIPZIG**
American, born 1918
*Association Football, Brooklyn,
New York*, 1943
Gelatin silver print
7 1/2 x 9 1/2 in. (19.1 x 24.1 cm.)
Courtesy of the artist and Howard
Greenberg Gallery, New York

78. GJON MILI
American, born Albania, 1904-1984
Carol Lynne, 1945
Gelatin silver print
19 x 14 3/4 in. (48.3 x 37.5 cm.)
Courtesy The Estate of Gjon Mili
and *LIFE*
© Time Warner Inc.

* **79. AUSTIN HANSEN**
American, born Virgin Islands, 1910
*Harlemites Gathered for "Joe Louis Day"
Parade*, 1946
Gelatin silver print
11 x 14 in. (27.9 x 35.6 cm.)
Collection of the Schomburg Center
for Research in Black Culture,
The New York Public Library,
Astor, Lenox and Tilden Foundations

* **80. WILLIAM HEICK**
American, born 1917
*Five Cents a Cue, North Beach,
San Francisco*, 1947
Gelatin silver print
8 x 10 in. (20.3 x 25.4 cm.)
Courtesy of the artist

81. ARTHUR LEIPZIG
American, born 1918
East River, New York City, 1948
Gelatin silver print
10 1/2 x 13 1/2 in. (26.7 x 34.3 cm.)
Courtesy of the artist and Howard
Greenberg Gallery, New York

82. IRVING PENN
American, born 1917
Joe Louis, New York, February 15, 1948
Gelatin silver print
10 1/4 x 8 1/4 in. (26 x 21 cm.)
Collection of Patricia Stevens
Lowinsky

83. NAT FEIN
American, born 1914
Three Is Out, 1948
Gelatin silver print
10 x 12 1/2 in. (25.4 x 31.8 cm.)
Collection of the National Baseball
Hall of Fame & Museum, Inc.,
Cooperstown, New York

* **84. RENÉ-JACQUES**
French, born Cambodia
(Kampuchea), 1908
*Illustration to Les Olympiques (The Olympics)
by Henry de Montherlant*, 1948
Gelatin silver print
11 13/16 x 15 3/4 in. (30 x 40 cm.)
Courtesy Ministère de la Culture,
Association française pour la diffusion
du patrimoine photographique, Paris

85. RENÉ-JACQUES
French, born Cambodia
(Kampuchea), 1908
*Illustration to Les Olympiques (The Olympics)
by Henry de Montherlant*, 1948
Gelatin silver print
11 13/16 x 15 3/4 in. (30 x 40 cm.)
Courtesy Ministère de la Culture,
Association française pour la diffusion
du patrimoine photographique, Paris

86. RALPH BARTHOLOMEW
American, 1907-1985
Teens Bowling, ca. 1948-1956
Gelatin silver print
14 x 11 in. (35.6 x 27.9 cm.)
Keith de Lellis Collection, New York

87. HAROLD E. EDGERTON
American, 1903-1990
A Tennis Serve by Gussie Moran, 1949
Gelatin silver print
13 4/5 x 10 9/10 in. (35.1 x 27.7 cm.)
Collection of the International
Museum of Photography at George
Eastman House, Rochester, New York;
Gift of Dr. Harold E. Edgerton
© The Estate of Harold E. Edgerton

* **88. SIDNEY GROSSMAN**
American, 1913-1955
Whitey Bimstein, Trainer, from
the series "BOXING," 1951
Ten gelatin silver prints
Average 10 x 13 1/2 in. (25.4 x 34.3 cm.)
Collection of The Museum of Fine
Arts, Houston; The Target Collection
of American Photography, Museum
purchase with funds provided by
Target Stores
(Shown at Atlanta, Houston, and
Santa Clara only)

* **89. GARRY WINOGRAND**
American, 1928-1984
Workout: Floyd Patterson, ca. 1954
Gelatin silver print
9 3/5 x 13 1/2 in. (24.3 x 34.3 cm.)
Collection of the Center for
Creative Photography,
The University of Arizona, Tucson
© 1991 The Estate of Garry
Winogrand. All Rights Reserved

* **90. ROBERT DOISNEAU**
French, born 1912
The Center of the Sporting Club, 1954
Gelatin silver print
9 x 14 in. (22.9 x 35.6 cm.)
Collection of Patricia Stevens Lowinsky

* **91. HENRI CARTIER-BRESSON**
French, born 1908
Sport Parade, Red Square, Moscow, 1954
Gelatin silver print
14 x 11 in. (35.6 x 27.9 cm.)
Courtesy of the artist
© Henri Cartier-Bresson

92. LARRY SILVER
American, born 1934
Man with dumb bells, from the series
"Muscle Beach, Santa Monica,
California," 1954, printed 1990
Gelatin silver print
11 5/8 x 13 3/8 in. (29.5 x 33.9 cm.)
High Museum of Art, Atlanta;
Gift of Gloria Silver
(Shown at Atlanta only)

93. LARRY SILVER
American, born 1934
Spectators watching bodybuilding competition,
from the series "Muscle Beach,
Santa Monica, California," 1954,
printed 1984
Gelatin silver print
11 1/8 x 16 3/4 in. (28.2 x 42.5 cm.)
High Museum of Art, Atlanta;
Gift of Gloria Silver

94. ROBERT FRANK
American, born Switzerland, 1924
Detroit Rodeo, from the series "The
Americans," 1955, printed before 1976
Gelatin silver print
8 9/16 x 12 7/8 in. (21.8 x 32.7 cm.)
Collection of The Museum of Modern
Art, New York; Gift of Paul A. Katz
and Arthur Penn

* **95. AARON SISKIND**
American, 1903-1991
Pleasures and Terrors of Levitation # 25, 1956
Gelatin silver print
11 1/8 x 10 1/2 in. (28.3 x 26.7 cm.)
Collection of the High Museum of Art,
Atlanta; Gift of Mr. and Mrs. Robert B.
Menschel

* **96. GEORGE SILK**
American, born New Zealand, 1916
*The Hurdlers, U.S. Olympic Trials,
Palo Alto, CA*, 1959, printed later
Gelatin silver print
4 3/8 x 19 in. (11.1 x 48.3 cm.)
Courtesy of the artist and *LIFE*
© Time Warner Inc.

* **97. MARK KAUFFMAN**
American, born 1922
*Wilma Rudolph at Finish of Women's
100-Meter Dash, Rome Olympics*,
1960, printed later
Gelatin silver print
15 x 19 in. (38.1 x 48.3 cm.)
Courtesy of the artist and *LIFE*
© Time Warner Inc.

98. CHARLES HOFF
American, 1905-1970
*Ingemar Johansson Defeated by Floyd
Patterson, New York, June 20*, 1960
Gelatin silver print
7 1/2 x 9 1/2 in. (19.1 x 24.1 cm.)
Courtesy Howard Greenberg Gallery,
New York

* **99. ROY DeCARAVA**
American, born 1919
Ex-Fighter, 1961
Gelatin silver print
17 x 14 in. (43.2 x 35.6 cm.)
Courtesy of the artist and
The Witkin Gallery, Inc., New York

* **100. RAY METZGER**
American, born 1931
Kayak, Frankfurt, 1961
Gelatin silver print
8 x 10 in. (20.3 x 25.4 cm.)
Lucinda Bunnen Collection
(Shown at Atlanta only)

* **101. JOHN G. ZIMMERMAN**
American, born 1928
*Toronto Maple Leafs Goalie Johnny Bower
Kicks Away a Goal-bound Puck*, 1962,
printed later
Ektacolor print
20 x 30 in. (50.8 x 76.2 cm.)
Courtesy of the artist and *Sports Illustrated*

* **102. DIANE ARBUS**
American, 1923-1971
*Teenager with a baseball bat,
New York City*, 1962
Gelatin silver print
14 x 11 in. (35.6 x 27.9 cm.)
Courtesy Robert Miller Gallery,
New York
© The Estate of Diane Arbus, 1978

* **103. RICHARD AVEDON**
American, born 1923
*Lew Alcindor, 61st Street and Amsterdam
Avenue, New York City, May 2*, 1963
Gelatin silver print, edition 1 of 8
19 1/2 x 15 5/8 in. (49.5 x 39.7 cm.)
Collection of the Center
for Creative Photography,
The University of Arizona, Tucson
© 1963 by Richard Avedon. All Rights
Reserved

104. HAROLD E. EDGERTON
American, 1903-1990
Pole Vaulter, 1964
Dye transfer print
14 x 11 in. (35.6 x 27.9 cm.)
Courtesy Brent Sikkema Fine Art,
New York
© The Estate of Harold E. Edgerton

* **105. LARRY BURROWS**
British, 1926-1971
Tokyo Driving Range, September 11, 1964
Gelatin silver print
12 x 18 in. (30.5 x 45.7 cm.)
Courtesy Laurence Miller Gallery,
New York

* **106. NEIL LEIFER**
American, born 1942
Ali vs. Liston II, Lewiston, Maine, 1965,
printed later
Ektacolor print
27 x 31 1/2 in. (68.6 x 80)
Courtesy of the artist and *Sports Illustrated*

* **107. ROBERT S. VAN FLEET**
American, born 1918
The School's on Fire, November 20, 1965
Gelatin silver print
13 1/4 x 16 1/4 in. (33.6 x 41.2 cm.)
Collection of the International
Center of Photography, New York

*** 108. GORDON PARKS**
American, born 1912
*Muhammad Ali after the Henry Cooper
Fight, London, England, 1966*
Gelatin silver print
16 x 20 in. (40.6 x 50.8 cm.)
Courtesy of the artist

109. DIANE ARBUS
American, 1923-1971
Charles Atlas at his Palm Beach Home,
from *Sunday Times Magazine,* London,
October 19, 1969
Gelatin silver print
20 x 16 in. (50.8 x 40.6 cm.)
Courtesy Robert Miller Gallery,
New York
© The Estate of Diane Arbus

*** 110. DANNY LYON**
American, born 1942
Llanito, New Mexico, 1970
Gelatin silver print
11 x 14 in. (27.9 x 35.6 cm.)
Etherton/Stern Gallery,
Tucson, Arizona

111. TOD PAPAGEORGE
American, born 1940
Shea Stadium, 1970
Gelatin silver print
8 1/8 x 12 1/16 in. (20.6 x 30.7 cm.)
Collection of The Museum of
Modern Art, New York;
Gift of the photographer

112. GARRY WINOGRAND
American, 1928-1984
*Muhammad Ali – Oscar Bonavena Press
Conference, New York, 1970*
Gelatin silver print
10 5/8 x 15 7/8 in. (27 x 40.3 cm.)
Collection of The Museum of
Modern Art, New York; Purchase

113. HELEN LEVITT
American, born 1918
New York, 1972
Dye transfer print
11 x 14 in. (27.9 x 35.6 cm.)
Courtesy Laurence Miller Gallery,
New York

114. WALTER IOOSS, JR.
American, born 1941
*Three-Quarter Century Softball,
St. Petersburg, FL, April 1973,*
printed later
Ektacolor print
30 x 20 in. (76.2 x 50.8 cm.)
Courtesy of the artist and
Sports Illustrated

115. RALPH MORSE
American, born 1918
HENRY GROSINSKY
American, born 1934
Hank Aaron's 715th Homerun,
April 8, 1974, printed later
Ektacolor print
14 3/4 x 19 in. (37.5 x 48.3 cm.)
Courtesy of the artists and *LIFE*
© Time Warner Inc.

*** 116. GARRY WINOGRAND**
American, 1928-1984
Austin, Texas, 1974, printed 1978
Gelatin silver print
11 x 13 7/8 in. (27.9 x 35.2 cm.)
Collection of the High Museum of Art;
Lent by Jay Greenstein and Family
© 1991 The Estate of Garry
Winogrand. All Rights Reserved

*** 117. GARRY WINOGRAND**
American, 1928-1984
Rodeo, Fort Worth, Texas, 1974,
printed 1978
Gelatin silver print
11 x 13 7/8 in. (27.9 x 35.2 cm.)
Collection of the High Museum of Art;
Lent by Jay Greenstein and Family
© 1991 The Estate of Garry
Winogrand. All Rights Reserved

*** 118. HOWARDENA PINDELL**
American, born 1943
Untitled (Video Drawing: Baseball), 1974,
printed 1979
Ektacolor print
5 x 7 in. (12.7 x 17.8 cm.)
Courtesy of the artist

*** 119. GEOFF WINNINGHAM**
American, born 1943
Houston Memorial vs. Houston Kashmere,
from the series "Rites of Fall: High
School Football in Texas," 1976
Gelatin silver print
11 1/2 x 17 in. (29.2 x 43.2 cm.)
Courtesy of the artist

120. GEOFF WINNINGHAM
American, born 1943
Arp vs. East Bernard, College Station, Texas,
from the series "Rites of Fall: High
School Football in Texas," 1977
Gelatin silver print
11 1/2 x 17 in. (29.2 x 43.2 cm.)
Courtesy of the artist

*** 121. ARTHUR TRESS**
American, born 1940
Hockey Player, New York City, 1976
Gelatin silver print
10 x 10 in. (25.4 x 25.4 cm.)
Lucinda Bunnen Collection

*** 122. NICHOLAS NIXON**
American, born 1947
Adams Street, Watertown, MA, 1977
Gelatin silver print, edition 14 of 50
8 x 10 in. (20.3 x 25.4 cm.)
Courtesy Zabriskie Gallery, New York

123. FRANK GOHLKE
American, born 1942
Tennis Court on the Outskirts of St. Paul, 1977
Gelatin silver print
16 x 20 in. (40.6 x 50.8 cm.)
Courtesy Bonni Benrubi Fine
Art Photographs, New York

*** 124. ZDENĚK LHOTÁK**
Czechoslovakian, born 1949
Untitled, from the series "Sparta,"
1978-1988
Gelatin silver print
22 1/2 x 18 1/2 in. (57.2 x 47 cm.)
Courtesy of the artist and
The Witkin Gallery, Inc., New York

*** 125. JEROME LIEBLING**
American, born 1924
Handball Players, Miami Beach, 1978
Gelatin silver print
11 3/4 x 9 in. (29.8 x 22.8 cm.)
Courtesy of the artist and Howard
Greenberg Gallery, New York

126. CHUCK ROGERS
American, contemporary
The Battle of Atlanta, 1978
Cibachrome print
20 x 30 in. (50.8 x 76.2 cm.)
Courtesy of the artist

*** 127. STEPHEN DANKO**
American, born 1946
Re-Entry, 1978
Gelatin silver print with light drawing,
photograms, and grease resist
39 13/16 x 77 1/2 in. (101.2 x 196.9 cm.)
Collection of the San Francisco
Museum of Modern Art; Purchase

*** 128. STEPHEN SHORE**
American, born 1947
*Ft. Lauderdale Yankee Stadium,
Ft. Lauderdale, Florida (Graig Nettles), 1978*
Ektacolor print
12 x 15 5/16 in. (30.4 x 38.8 cm.)
Courtesy Pace/MacGill Gallery,
New York

129. JOEL MEYEROWITZ
American, born 1938
St. Louis and the Arch, Top of the Ninth,
May 1978
Ektacolor print
14 1/2 x 18 1/2 in. (36.8 x 47.9 cm.)
Courtesy James Danzinger Gallery,
New York

*** 130. FRANCESCO SCAVULLO**
American, born 1929
*Willie Mays, Old Timer's Day,
Portland, Oregon, 1979*
Gelatin silver print
20 x 16 in. (50.8 x 40.6 cm.)
Courtesy of the artist and
Staley-Wise Gallery, New York

*** 131. COREEN SIMPSON**
American, born 1942
*Morgan/Grambling Game,
Morgan State University Marching Band,
Baltimore, ca. 1979*
Gelatin silver print
8 x 10 in. (20.3 x 25.4 cm.)
Collection of the Schomburg Center
for Research in Black Culture,
The New York Public Library,
Astor, Lenox and Tilden Foundations

*** 132. JOHN KENNARD**
American, born 1951
Busch Stadium, St. Louis, Missouri, 1979
Gelatin silver print
24 x 30 in. (61 x 76.2 cm.)
Courtesy of the artist
© 1985 John Kennard

*** 133. PAUL KWILECKI**
American, born 1928
Woman Fishing under Trestle, 1979
Gelatin silver print
8 1/8 x 12 1/8 in. (20.6 x 30.9 cm.)
Courtesy of the artist

*** 134. JERRY GORDON**
American, born 1949
The Breakers Hotel, Palm Beach, Florida, 1979
Cibachrome print
17 5/8 x 11 1/2 in. (44.8 x 29.2 cm.)
Collection of the High Museum of Art,
Atlanta; Gift of Lucinda Bunnen

*** 135. PAUL BERGER**
American, born 1948
Camera Text or Picture, No. 15, 1979
Gelatin silver print
19 x 24 in. (48.3 x 61 cm.)
Courtesy of the artist

136. MARK KLETT
American, born 1952
*Grand Opening of the Hailey Rodeo,
Hailey, Idaho, 7/4/79, 1979*
Gelatin silver print
16 x 20 in. (40.6 x 50.8 cm.)
Courtesy Etherton/Stern Gallery,
Tucson, Arizona

*** 137. MARTINE BARRAT**
French, born 1937
*Carlos Villafane, eight years old,
and his brother Jimmy training at the
Artemio Colon Gym in Harlem, 1980*
Gelatin silver print
20 x 16 in. (50.8 x 40.6 cm.)
Courtesy of the artist

* **138. MARTINE BARRAT**
French, born 1937
Neil Ferrara, trainer, and David Brown:
9 years old, 45 pounds, 28 fights, 24 wins,
Brooklyn, New York, 1980
Gelatin silver print
20 x 16 in. (50.8 x 40.6 cm.)
Courtesy of the artist

* **139. CHRISTOPHER JAMES**
American, born 1947
Running Track/Cambridge #7, 1980
Gelatin silver print with hand-tinting
and enameling
5 1/2 x 9 in. (14 x 22.9 cm.)
Courtesy of the artist and
The Witkin Gallery, Inc., New York

* **140. MIKE MANDEL**
American, born 1950
Randy Moffitt and Garry Lavelle, Right-
and Left-Handed Pitching Motions, 1980
Ektacolor print
16 x 15 1/2 in. (40.6 x 39.4 cm.)
Courtesy of the artist

* **141. JIM DOW**
American, born 1942
Veterans Stadium, Philadelphia, 1980
Three ektacolor prints
Overall 10 x 24 in. (25.4 x 61 cm.)
Courtesy Janet Borden, Inc., New York

142. ANTHONY BARBOZA
American, born 1944
Marvin Hagler, 1981
Gelatin silver print
20 x 16 in. (50.8 x 40.6 cm.)
Courtesy of the artist

143. JIM DOW
American, born 1942
Texas Stadium, Irving, Texas, 1981
Three ektacolor plus prints
Overall 10 x 24 in. (25.4 x 61 cm.)
Courtesy Janet Borden, Inc., New York

* **144. ROBERT MAPPLETHORPE**
American, 1946-1989
Lisa Lyon, 1982
Gelatin silver print
20 x 16 in. (50.8 x 40.6 cm.)
Courtesy Robert Miller Gallery,
New York
© 1982 The Estate of Robert
Mapplethorpe

* **145. DAVID HOCKNEY**
British, born 1937
The Skater, New York,
December 1982, #13, 1982
Kodacolor collage on
silkscreened board
26 x 19 1/2 in. (66 x 49.5 cm.)
Courtesy of the artist

146. BILL BAMBERGER
American, born 1956
John Sutcliffe, Polo South Game,
Bahama, NorthCarolina, 1982
Gelatin silver print
15 x 15 in. (38.1 x 38.1 cm.)
Courtesy of the artist

147. JOE DEAL
American, born 1947
Synchronized Swimming, from the
series "Beach Cities," 1982
Gelatin silver print
14 x 14 in. (35.6 x 35.6 cm.)
Courtesy of the artist

* **148. HELEN LEVITT**
American, born 1918
New York, 1982
Gelatin silver print
14 x 11 in. (35.6 x 27.9 cm.)
Courtesy Laurence Miller Gallery,
New York

149. STEPHEN FRAILEY
American, born 1957
Untitled (Goggles and
Sports Announcers), 1982
Ektacolor print
10 x 10 in. (25.4 x 25.4 cm.)
Courtesy of the artist

* **150. JOEL STERNFELD**
American, born 1944
Atlanta, Georgia, 1983
Ektacolor print
16 x 20 in. (40.6 x 59 cm.)
Courtesy Pace/MacGill Gallery,
New York

* **151. WAYNE LEVIN**
American, born 1945
Untitled, from "Sea Dream Series," 1983
Gelatin silver print
18 x 13 in. (45.7 x 33 cm.)
Courtesy of the artist

* **152. MAURO ALTAMURA**
American, born 1954
Collision, 1983
Gelatin silver print
30 x 40 in. (76.2 x 101.6 cm.)
Courtesy of the artist and
Lieberman & Saul Gallery, New York

153. MARK KLETT
American, born 1952
Tubers on the Salt River, Late Summer,
106°, 9/10/83, 1983
Gelatin silver print
16 x 20 in. (40.6 x 50.8 cm.)
Courtesy Etherton/Stern Gallery,
Tucson, Arizona

* **154. BRUCE WEBER**
American, born 1946
Andrew Minsker, Lightweight Boxer,
Colorado Sports Festival, 1983
Gelatin silver print, edition 10 of 15
17 x 14 in. (43.1 x 35.6 cm.)
Courtesy Fay Gold Gallery, Atlanta

155. MARTINE BARRAT
French, born 1937
Kid Chocolate, Havana, Cuba, 1984
Gelatin silver print
20 x 16 in. (50.8 x 40.6 cm.)
Courtesy of the artist

156. SUE ROSSOFF
American, born 1954
Stretch, 1984
Gelatin silver print
20 x 24 in. (50.8 x 61 cm.)
Courtesy Etherton/Stern Gallery,
Tucson, Arizona

157. LEE FRIEDLANDER
American, born 1934
Golden State Warriors vs. the Washington
Bullets, Oakland Coliseum, February 1984
Gelatin silver print
14 x 11 in. (35.6 x 27.9 cm.)
Courtesy Laurence Miller Gallery,
New York

* **158. JACK CARNELL**
American, born 1952
Photographers, Track and Field,
Summer Olympics, Los Angeles, 1984
Ektacolor print
12 x 17 7/8 in. (30.4 x 45.3 cm.)
Courtesy of the artist

* **159. JO ANN CALLIS**
American, born 1940
Loyola Marymount University,
1984 Olympic Games, Los Angeles, 1984
Gelatin silver print
30 x 39 in. (76.2 x 99.1 cm.)
Collection of the Amateur Athletic
Foundation of Los Angeles

160. BONNIE DONOHUE
American, born 1946
Mary Decker, Women's 3,000 Meter Race,
1984 Olympic Games, Los Angeles, 1984
Four ektacolor prints
Overall 31 1/2 x 40 1/2 in.
(80 x 102.9 cm.)
Collection of the Amateur Athletic
Foundation of Los Angeles

* **161. SKEET McAULEY**
American, born 1951
Navajo Tribal School Near
Goulding, Utah, 1984
Cibachrome print
30 x 40 in. (76.2 x 101.6 cm.)
Courtesy of the artist and
Barry Whistler Gallery, Dallas

* **162. LARRY SULTAN**
American, born 1946
My Mother Posing for Me, Palm Springs,
California, from the series
"Pictures from Home," 1984
Ektacolor print
29 x 35 3/4 in. (73.7 x 90.8 cm.)
Courtesy Janet Borden, Inc., New York

* **163. NANCY HOLT**
American, born 1938
Untitled, from the series
"Time Outs," 1985
Gelatin silver print
15 3/4 x 23 1/4 in. (40 x 59 cm.)
Courtesy John Weber Gallery,
New York

* **164. NANCY HOLT**
American, born 1938
Untitled, from the series
"Time Outs," 1985
Gelatin silver print
15 3/4 x 23 1/4 in. (40 x 59 cm.)
Courtesy John Weber Gallery,
New York

* **165. JEFF KOONS**
American, born 1955
SILK, 1985
Photolithographic poster
36 1/4 x 22 1/8 in. (92.1 x 56.2 cm.)
Lehmann Collection, Geneva;
Courtesy Sonnabend Gallery,
New York

* **166. NIC NICOSIA**
American, born 1951
Drugs, from the series
"Life As We Know It," 1986
Cibachrome print
48 x 48 in. (121.9 x 121.9 cm.)
Courtesy Texas Gallery, Houston

* **167. LORIE NOVAK**
American, born 1954
False Starts, 1986
Ektacolor print, edition 9 of 15
22 x 18 in. (55.9 x 45.7 cm.)
Courtesy of the artist

* **168. ROBERT BECK**
American, born 1955
Swimmers, Ironman Triathlon, Hawaii, 1986
Ektacolor print
16 x 20 in. (40.6 x 50.8 cm.)
Courtesy of the artist

* **169. BALDWIN LEE**
American, born 1951
Untitled, Monroe, LA, 1986
Gelatin silver print
16 x 20 in. (40.6 x 50.8 cm.)
Courtesy of the artist

170. MARILYN BRIDGES
American, born 1948
The Equestrian, Mendon, New York, 1986
Gelatin silver print
20 x 24 in. (50.8 x 61 cm.)
Courtesy Etherton/Stern Gallery,
Tucson, Arizona, and Felicia Murray,
New York

* **171. FRANK MAJORE**
American, born 1948
Welcome to the Club, 1986
Cibachrome print
24 x 20 in. (61 x 50.8 cm.)
Collection of Jill and Richard Schloss,
New York; Courtesy Holly Solomon
Gallery, New York

* **172. JAN STALLER**
American, born 1952
*Batting Practice Facility in Jersey City,
New Jersey,* 1987
Dye transfer print
30 x 30 in. (76.2 x 76.2 cm.)
Courtesy of the artist and
Lieberman & Saul Gallery, New York

* **173. ANNIE LEIBOVITZ**
American, born 1949
Tom Seaver, Greenwich, Connecticut, 1987
Cibachrome print, edition 3 of 40
14 5/8 x 11 7/8 in. (37.1 x 30.3 cm.)
Courtesy James Danzinger Gallery,
New York

* **174. WALTER IOOSS, JR.**
American, born 1942
*Michael Jordan Practicing at Illinois
Benedictine College, Lisle, Illinois,* 1987,
printed later
Ektacolor print
20 x 30 in. (50.8 x 76.2 cm.)
Courtesy of the artist and *Sports
Illustrated*

* **175. MITCH EPSTEIN**
American, born 1952
*Sunday Cricket Match,
Gouyave, Grenada,* 1987
Ektacolor print
14 7/8 x 22 in. (37.8 x 55.9 cm.)
Courtesy of the artist

176. RICHARD MISRACH
American, born 1949
Swimmers, Pyramid Lake, 1987
Ektacolor print
40 x 50 in. (101.6 x 127 cm.)
Private Collection; Courtesy Fraenkel
Gallery, San Francisco

177. CATHRYN GRIFFIN
American, born 1955
Untitled, 1987
Gelatin silver print
16 x 20 in. (40.6 x 50.8 cm.)
Courtesy of the artist

* **178. JOHN BALDESSARI**
American, born 1931
Box (Blind Fate and Culture), 1987
Gelatin silver prints and
acrylic on board
48 1/4 x 64 1/4 in. (122.6 x 163.2 cm.)
Collection of the Fondation Asher
Edelman, Musée d'Art Contemporain,
Pully/Lausanne

179. RON GEIBERT
American, born 1952
*Little League Tournament Sponsored by
McDonald's, Okayama, Japan,* 1987
Ektacolor print
8 1/2 x 13 in. (21.6 x 33 cm.)
Courtesy of the artist

180. RICHARD MISRACH
American, born 1949
Desert Croquet #3 (Balls/Plane/Car), 1987
Ektacolor print
30 x 40 in. (76.2 x 101.6 cm.)
Courtesy Fraenkel Gallery,
San Francisco

* **181. JACK CARNELL**
American, born 1952
Mike Schmidt, Camera Night, Philadelphia,
1987
Ektacolor print
12 1/4 x 18 1/8 in. (31.1 x 46 cm.)
Courtesy of the artist

182. MARK STEINMETZ
American, born 1961
Jacksonville, Illinois, from
"Little League Series," 1988
Gelatin silver print
9 1/2 x 14 1/4 in. (24.1 x 36.2 cm.)
Courtesy of the artist

* **183. DAVID GRAHAM**
American, born 1952
*The Post Bulletins Practicing at Graham
Park, Rochester, Minnesota,* 1988
Ektacolor print
20 x 24 in. (50.8 x 61 cm.)
Courtesy Laurence Miller Gallery,
New York

* **184. JOEL MEYEROWITZ**
American, born 1938
Atlanta, 1988
Ektacolor print
18 1/2 x 23 1/2 in. (46.9 x 59.6 cm.)
Courtesy James Danzinger Gallery,
New York

185. RICHARD MISRACH
American, born 1949
Tennis Court and Pyramids, 1989
Ektacolor print
20 x 24 in. (50.8 x 61 cm.)
Courtesy Fraenkel Gallery,
San Francisco

186. VERNON MILLER
American, born 1948
Boxing Gloves, July 1989
Platinum print
9 1/2 x 7 3/4 in. (24.1 x 19.7 cm.)
Collection of Patricia Stevens
Lowinsky

* **187. FRANK MAJORE**
American, born 1948
Ultra, 1989
Cibachrome print
39 1/2 x 29 1/2 in. (100 x 75 cm.)
Collection of the Butler Institute of
American Art, Youngstown, Ohio

188. JACK CARNELL
American, born 1952
Wheelchair Athlete, Fort Washington, PA,
1989
Ektacolor print
18 1/16 x 12 1/4 in. (45.8 x 31.1 cm.)
Courtesy of the artist

* **189. LARRY FINK**
American, born 1941
Philly Boxing, January 1990
Gelatin silver print
16 x 20 in. (40.6 x 50.8 cm.)
Courtesy of the artist

* **190. NEIL WINOKUR**
American, born 1945
Football, from the series
"Self-Portrait: An Installation," 1990
Cibachrome print
11 x 14 in. (27.9 x 35.6 cm.)
Courtesy Janet Borden, Inc., New York

191. SKEET McAULEY
American, born 1951
*4th Green, La Paloma Resort,
Hill Course, Tucson, AZ,* 1990
Cibachrome print
14 x 40 in. (35.6 x 101.6 cm.)
Courtesy of the artist and
Barry Whistler Gallery, Dallas

* **192. RICHARD MISRACH**
American, born 1949
*Water Skiing, Pyramid Lake
Indian Reservation, Nevada,* 1991
Ektacolor print
20 x 24 in. (50.8 x 61 cm.)
Courtesy Fraenkel Gallery,
San Francisco

* **193. TINA BARNEY**
American, born 1945
Untitled from the album "Swimming,"
with text by Tina Howe. From the
series "Artists and Writers: American
Journals" published by the Library
Fellows of the Whitney Museum
of American Art, 1991
Ektacolor print
Plate size: 11 x 14 in. (27.9 x 35.6 cm.)
Book size: 13 x 16 1/2 in. (33 x 41.9 cm.)
Courtesy Janet Borden, Inc., New York

194. CHRIS HAMILTON
American, born 1957
*Championship Motion (Tom Glavine,
Atlanta Braves),* 1991
Cibachrome print
23 1/2 x 15 1/2 in. (59.6 x 39.3 cm.)
Courtesy of the artist

* **195. CHRIS HAMILTON**
American, born 1957
*The Winning Move (Dominique Wilkins,
Atlanta Hawks),* 1991
Cibachrome print
15 1/2 x 23 1/2 in. (39.3 x 59.6 cm.)
Courtesy of the artist

196. KENDA NORTH
American, born 1951
Untitled, from the series
"A Sport of Spectators," 1991
Two prints: Gelatin silver print
and ektacolor print
Each 20 x 24 in. (50.8 x 61 cm.)
Courtesy Etherton/Stern Gallery,
Tucson, Arizona

Photo Credits

Ben Blackwell: cat. 127

Georgia Department of Archives
and History, Atlanta: fig. 2 (page 20),
cat. 20

Rolf Jeck: cat. 38

Michael McKelvey: cats. 25, 26, 31,
45, 61, 95, 116, 117, 121, 128, 133,
150, 154, 158, 173, 181, 184

Lee Stalsworth: cat. 46

Ed Watkins: cats. 29, 32, 39-41, 46,
48-50, 57, 59, 62, 69, 70, 73, 90, 99,
122, 124, 130, 139, 141, 163, 164,
190, 193

George S. Whiteley IV: cat. 42

Harvey Green is Associate Professor of History and Coordinator for Public History Programs at Northeastern University, Boston, and author of *Fit for America: Health, Fitness, Sport, and American Society, 1830-1940.*

John M. Hoberman is Associate Professor of Germanic Languages at the University of Texas at Austin and author of *Sport and Political Ideology.*

Peter Schjeldahl, a poet, art critic, and contributing editor of *Art in America*, is the author of *The Hydrogen Juke Box: Selected Writings 1978-1990.*

Catalogue Credits

Designed by TIMES 3, Atlanta

Printed by Litho Specialties, Inc., St. Paul

Edited by Kelly Morris, Margaret Miller, Amanda Woods

The catalogue is set in Weiss and Futura Bold

Copyright 1992
High Museum of Art
All rights reserved

Published by the
High Museum of Art
Atlanta, Georgia

Distributed by the
University of Washington Press
Seattle and London

Library of Congress No. 92-70754
ISBN 0-939802-73-2